PRESERVED BR DIESEL ANI LOCOMOTIVES

PRESERVED BR DIESEL AND ELECTRIC LOCOMOTIVES

The complete illustrated stock-book

Howard Johnston

Silver Link Publishing Ltd

First published in March 1992

British Library Cataloguing in Publication Data

Johnston, Howard, *1952–*
Preserved BR diesel and electric locomotives
I. Title
625.2630941

ISBN 0 947971 74 2

Silver Link Publishing Ltd
The Trundle
Ringstead Road
Great Addington
Kettering
Northamptonshire NN14 4BW

Typeset by G&M, Raunds, Northamptonshire
Printed in Great Britain by Woolnough
Bookbinding Limited, Irthlingborough,
Northamptonshire

CONTENTS

INTRODUCTION

Where will it end? Interest in saving modern motive power continues to reach new heights, so much so that the withdrawal of each BR locomotive class is followed by purchases often into double figures.

The first edition of this book, published in 1987, listed 116 internal combustion or electrically-powered locomotives that had either been used by BR or operated in the immediate post-war pre-nationalisation years. Five years later, this total has more than doubled, and there is no shortage of buyers for anything that comes along.

There are some amazing stories to tell: who could have predicted that preserved Class 03 shunters would exceed three dozen with the prospect of others being re-imported from Europe; that preserved Sulzer Class 25s would number 21, and that over 20 English Electric Class 20s and 50s would be bought over the space of only a few weeks at the end of 1991?

If most recent types are well represented, the opposite is the case for less-successful and non-standard types that were eliminated during the first BR purge of the late 1960s and early 1970s. Most notable for their absence are the LMS-designed prototype diesels and North British diesel-hydraulics. BR's technical and research departments and private industrial concerns can be thanked for retaining locomotives long enough to be noticed.

A whole page with an illustration is devoted to each locomotive, although technical detail is deliberately kept to a minimum to avoid obvious repetition and because it is well covered elsewhere. Inevitably, main-line locomotives lend themselves to more lengthy histories by virtue of their high-profile careers compared with shunters which, until preservation, have generally made little impact.

Pictorially I have again tried where practicable to reflect the varying paint and number styles carried by the locos in BR service or preservation. Practically all the photographs are different from those in the first edition.

Thanks go to the many loco owners and preserved railways who have supplied historical information on their machines, but I accept that the biographies are not necessarily complete. Further information and anecdotes on the past and present status of the locomotives in this book would be most welcome for a possible updated further edition. Special thanks are due to: Adrian Booth, Murray Brown, David Clough, Roger Harris, Kevin Lane, Harry Needle, Norman Preedy, Angela Reynolds, David Strickland, and again not least, Margaret Johnston.

HOWARD JOHNSTON
Huntingdon
March 1992

HOW TO USE THIS BOOK

Since 1948 BR diesel and electric locomotives have been numbered and renumbered in four highly individual series, and their new owners have variously restored them in all these series. The number schemes can be outlined thus:

Pre-1948: Pre-Nationalisation number schemes
Pre-1957: Diesels 10000-15236, Gas Turbine 18000, Electrics 26000-27006
Pre-1973: Diesels D1-D9555, Electrics E3001-E6110
Post-1973: Diesels 01001-60100, Electrics 71001-91031

(Prototype and departmental locomotives were mostly in other series.)

For clarity, the 1957-73 number series has been used wherever possible for the chronological order of this book, essentially because it embraces the vast majority of the locomotives in preservation. The number at the top of each page, however, represents the number last known to be carried on the side of the locomotive. For example, Class 20 No 20001 (the former D8001) follows on from No D8000.

Numbers carried: The full sequence of renumberings, with industrial legend if applied after sale from BR.

Allocations: London Midland Region main-line locomotives had no specific allocations between 1965 and 1973, but were used in area pools. The central depot for this pool (eg Toton for the Midland Lines fleet) has therefore been used.

Preservation site: Specific locations are listed where the locomotive is known to be based. This is not the case in respect of some preserved lines, where a locomotive can be located anywhere along its length.

It is an increasingly common feature of 1990s preservation for locomotives to move bases, either permanently or on short-term loan. The locations listed in this book are accurate at the time of going to press.

Class 44 1Co-Co1 No D4 *Great Gable*

Built: BR Derby, July 1959
Numbers carried: (1) D4,
  (2) 44004
First allocation: Camden
Last allocation: Toton
Withdrawn: 30 November 1980
Preserved: Midland Railway
  Centre, Butterley

No D4 at Bewdley, Severn Valley
Railway, 21 September 1986.
M. Kerry

When first conceived, No D4's 2,300hp Sulzer diesel-electric power unit was the largest in Western Europe, noted for reliability, high tractive effort and good braking power. The first 10 BR locomotives were the first production series from a nationalised workshop, and took the lowest numbers of the 13 main-line prototype designs.

The order was placed with BR Derby Works in November 1955, and No D1 *Scafell Pike* took to the rails in April 1959. The body shape closely followed Derby's other famous product, No 10000 of 1947, and the Swiss-built Sulzer 12LDA28 power unit was selected instead of an English Electric engine on the basis of successful running in France and Romania. Like some of its sisters, No D4 *Great Gable* was named after an English mountain peak, and supplanted steam on Manchester Central to St Pancras expresses. Its Stone Vapor oil-fired steam generator was removed after a motive power switch-round in 1962 that saw Nos D1-D10 relegated to freight duties at Toton, mainly coal traffic to power stations, and Washwood Heath and Whitemoor goods.

Though the class was slated for withdrawal in 1969 as a non-standard type, it survived another decade until the lack of air brake equipment posed a handicap on unit coal trains. No D4, ironically the first of the class to acquire blue livery with small yellow panels in January 1967, was granted a final works overhaul in August 1975. Repainted green for its final months in traffic, it also regained its nameplates lost in 1976. Adopted as the Toton flagship, it worked a number of farewell railtours, and was handed over to preservation on 23 June 1982.

A thorough restoration job has taken place at Butterley, including re-equipment during 1987 with an original steam-heat boiler. No D4 featured at open days at Coalville and Cardiff, and was then withdrawn from traffic at the start of 1988 for majoroverhaul of the bogies, which involved lifting the body and removal of all eight wheelsets for re-tyring at a cost of £10,000. It ran again for the first time on 13 October 1991.

Class 44 1Co-Co1 No D8 *Penyghent*

Built: BR Derby, December 1959
Numbers carried: (1) D8
  (2) 44008
Names carried: (1) *Penyghent*,
  (2) *Schiehallion*,
  (3) *Penyghent*
First allocation: Camden
Final allocation: Toton
Withdrawn: 30 November 1980
Preserved: Peak Railway,
  Matlock

Two months after arrival and before rebuilding, No D8 stands at Matlock, 18 April 1987.
Brian Cuttell

No D8, new from Derby Works to Camden at the end of 1959, would have been a regular sight on London-Manchester expresses and Heysham boat trains until displacement by more powerful locomotives, including the Class 45. The decision to hand the first ten 'Peaks' over to heavy freight work was doubtless influenced by their lower-geared traction motors which provided greater starting power. No D8 was transferred to Crewe North in May 1960. Its Stone Vapor OK4625 oil-fired steam-heating boiler and water tanks were removed, and it was sent to Toton to work coal trains. The original livery was all-over Brunswick green, later with a small yellow nose-end warning panel, and eventually standard blue in July 1971. It was renumbered 44008 in March 1974.

Although slated for withdrawal in 1970, the 44s were reliable enough to survive until their lack of air brakes became an operational handicap. One of the last three in service, No 44008 gained a reconditioned power unit only three months before withdrawal, and was involved in farewell railtours through the Woodhead tunnel on 1 October 1977, and Chester and Shrewsbury on 21 January 1980.

After storage at Derby Works, No 44008 was displayed at the 7 July 1982 Glasgow Works Open Day before moving to the Strathspey Railway at Boat of Garten. It never turned a wheel there, and was secured by the North Notts Locomotive Group on 28 September 1986 for the Peak Railway. Despatched from Aviemore the following January, it was routed via Perth, Mossend and the Cumbrian Coast Line to Toton, arriving at Matlock behind Class 20 Nos 20100 and 20045 on 16 February.

The new owners of No D8 Penyghent have been forced to undertake an almost total rebuild to eliminate the extensive corrosion encouraged by 21 years of BR service and then a decade out of use. Virtually two-thirds of the body has been repanelled, and nose-end doors fitted from scrapped Class 44 No D7 *Ingleborough*. The cabs have been renovated, electrical cubicle reassembled, power unit attended to, and auxiliary equipment either replaced or refitted. A major problem facing the group in 1990 was locating replacement cylinder liners, especially as a quote for new ones was £8,600, way beyond the means of the owners!

Class 44 1Co-Co1 No 45132

Built: BR Derby, April 1961
Numbers carried: (1) D22,
  (2) 45132
First allocation: Derby
Final allocation: Tinsley
Withdrawn: 11 May 1987
Preserved: Mid-Hants Railway,
  Ropley

Part of the March depot line-up,
No 45132 carries a wreath on
6 January 1990 with sisters Nos
45127/37 nearby. *Terry Gurd*

Almost five years of open storage at March depot for rows of Class 45 'Peaks' made redundant from Trans-Pennine duties ended at the beginning of 1992 when they were removed to scrapyards in the North for dismantling. No 45132 was an exception, however, having been sold several months previously to a member of the Mid-Hants Railway, although the Winchester-Alton line could certainly not be regarded as one of its regular haunts during its BR career!

Built at BR Derby Works with steam heat boiler and split headcodes, No D22 was allocated new to the nearby Derby depot for Midland Main Line passenger work. It was unusual for a Class 45, however, in spending long periods on loan to Eastern Region depots. It spent the summer of 1961 at Tinsley for crew familiarisation, and in September of that year went to Gateshead, possibly as a prelude to the arrival of Crompton-Parkinson Class 46 versions of the same design. No D22 moved on the Neville Hill depot, Leeds, in June 1962, and nearby Holbeck the same December. It was

a further six years before the loco returned to the Midland, in August 1968, although it was back at Holbeck again in October 1971.

No D22 was dual braked upon overhaul at Derby in 1971. It lost its train heating boiler for electric train heat equipment in July 1974, when it was renumbered No 45132 and shorn of its headcode boxes in favour of a flush front end with integral marker lights. Reallocated to Toton, it was a top link loco again for a further 12 years until November 1986, when the full introduction of High Speed Trains on the St Pancras-Sheffield route saw it sent to Tinsley for a final spell on Scarborough/Newcastle/York-Liverpool Trans-Pennine duties. The loco had been given a heavy general overhaul at Derby as late as June 1981, but no other work existed for it, so in common with many others of the same type it was withdrawn at the start of the 1987 summer timetable and towed to March, Cambridgeshire, for secure storage. The Mid-Hants Railway bought the locomotive in mid-1991, but it was many months before transfer took place.

Class 44 1Co-Co1 No 45133

Built: BR Derby, July 1961
Numbers carried: (1) D40,
  (2) 45133
First allocation: Derby
Last allocation: Tinsley
Withdrawn: 11 May 1987
Preserved: Midland Railway
  Trust, Butterley

No 45133 arrives at Butterley
during the MRC's Diesel and
Steam Weekend, 16 June 1991.
Phil Crumpton

The success of the Class 44 'Peaks' prompted further large orders of the design, although the next 137 examples featured many improvements including a uprated, inter-cooled British-built 2,500hp Sulzer 12LDA-28B power unit. Externally, the bodyshell was cleaned up by dispensing with nose-end doors. A number of headcode variations were displayed before late-1970s overhauls saw them removed completely in favour of a flush front end.

No D40, one of the two-section centre-headcode variety, was delivered from Derby Works to the nearby depot in July 1961 for primary use on the Midland Main Line between St Pancras and Sheffield, a role which occupied most of its career prior to the introduction of High Speed Train sets.

From 1973, a three-year programme was instituted to equip 50 Class 45s with electric train heating equipment in place of the steam-heat boiler to enable them to work with more modern coaching stock. Locomotives were chosen at random, and it was No D40's turn for attention in July 1974. It emerged from Derby renumbered as No 45133 in the Class 45/1 series.

Outshopped from a final general overhaul at Derby Works in September 1981, No 45133 spent its final years regularly rostered for Trans-Pennine duties, which included regular visits over the North Wales line, but was withdrawn on 11 May 1987, to coincide with the start of the new timetable and Sprinter DMU introduction. Indeed, 12 Class 45/1s were withdrawn at a stroke, Nos 45105/11/2/8/9/25/7/30/2/3/6/43. BR seemed reluctant to consign them for scrap because of the outside chance of future work, and the isolated yard at March in Cambridgeshire was chosen as a secure haven for large numbers of the class for over four years. No 45133, an arrival on 21 May 1987 with Nos 45118/32, was kept in full running order throughout the 2$^1/_2$ years it took for a sale to be completed in January 1990 to the Class 45/1 Preservation Society, and was fully repainted in blue before it left March on 22 May that year. It made its debut at the Midland Railway Trust line three days later, worked on the Nene Valley Railway in October 1990, and was exhibited at the final Coalville Open Day on 26 May 1991.

Class 45 1Co-Co1 No 45112 *Royal Army Ordnance Corps*

Built: BR Crewe, March 1962
Numbers carried: (1) D61,
  (2) 45112
First allocation: Derby
Final allocation: Tinsley
Withdrawn: 7 May 1987
Preserved: East Lancashire
  Railway, Bury

No 45112, a new arrival at Bury Bolton Street, on 1 September 1991. *Paul Senior*

Only 26 of the Class 45 locomotives were honoured with names, and a latecomer to preservation in the summer of 1991 was one of this exclusive band. With one exception they honoured regiments, and mostly perpetuated or updated names carried by LMS 'Patriot' or 'Royal Scot' 4-6-0s.

One of the last 'Peaks' produced at Crewe before attention was turned to the construction of Brush/Sulzer Class 47s, D61 was first allocated to Derby, and as a common-user loco on the Midland Main Line was variously allocated at Cricklewood and Leicester before becoming the responsibility of Toton from mid-1965 onwards. The nameplates *Royal Army Ordnance Corps* and crests were fitted at Derby Works without ceremony on 14 September 1965.

No D61 was originally fitted with split-centre-type headcodes, later removed when flush ends became standard and marker lights were fitted in the same position. A heavy general overhaul was completed in 1980, and a halogen headlight was also added in the loco's final days.

In common with other late survivors, No 45112, as it had become in August 1973, was transferred to Tinsley at the end of 1986 for a final season on Trans-Pennine passenger workings before the arrival of the decidedly inferior Class 150 Sprinter DMUs, which formed the initial stage of Regional Railways' five-year strategy to withdraw from loco-hauled travel completely.

Casualties were severe from the end of 1986 despite their relatively recent heavy works overhaul, and No 45112 was withdrawn with many others on 7 May 1987 and towed to March on 27 June for storage. If no use was found, the scheme was at least to retrieve some of the best sets of bogies from the 'Peaks' there for conversion to snowploughs, although four years later this had still not been achieved. When tenders for the locos' disposal for scrap were issued in early 1991, there were a number of preservationists interested, not least because of the plentiful supply of spares and common parts with other Sulzer types still in operation on the BR system.

Class 45 1Co-Co1 No 45118 *The Royal Artilleryman*

Built: BR Crewe, May 1962
Numbers carried: (1) D67,
  (2) 45118
First allocation: Derby
Final allocation: Tinsley
Withdrawn: 9 May 1987
Preserved: Northampton &
  Lamport Railway, Pitsford

Stored at March on 2 August 1990, No 45118 awaits movement to Pitsford.
Philip Sutton

The very last 'Peak' repaired at Derby Works at the beginning of 1987 has survived into preservation, but only after for three years on the scrap line. The repair was hardly cost-effective, because the replacement bogies from sister No 45116 (D47), withdrawn on 17 December 1986, only kept it going for another four months.

One of 88 members of the class built at Crewe, *The Royal Artilleryman* was ex-works in May 1962. The switching of production batches from Derby because of a shortage of capacity meant that the 'Peaks' were not built in numerical sequence, and those from Crewe appeared as Nos D68-D137, D58-D67, and D50-57. Although selected for naming, No 45118 was not adorned and crested until September 1965, and then without ceremony at Derby Works.

No 45118 was always intended to be a passenger loco, and its use on the Midland Main Line is demonstrated by its allocation at variously Derby, Cricklewood and Nottingham, although it was uniquely allocated to Saltley, Birmingham, from March to May 1965 for crew familiarisation. The overhaul cycle for 'Peaks'

involved a visit to works for major attention every five to seven years, and *The Royal Artilleryman* was equipped with dual air/vacuum brakes and electric train heating equipment during a visit in December 1973, when it was also renumbered into the Class 45/1 series. It was outshopped from its final general overhaul at Derby in October 1980, although it did get another 'intermediate' in January 1986, again at Derby.

No 45118 was unexpectedly withdrawn on 9 May 1987 after suffering minor fire damage to its electrical systems, during a four-week spell that saw 17 'Peaks' condemned at the start of the summer timetable, marking the full-scale introduction of Sprinter DMUs on Trans-Pennine routes. No 45118 was towed to March for open storage on 21 May 1987, alongside many other redundant members of the same class.

No 45118 has been on public exhibition at least once, at the 23 April 1982 Laira Depot Open Day. It arrived at Pitsford from March by road on 16 September 1990, and is stored on a short length of track.

Class 45 1Co-Co1 No 45135 *3rd Carabinier*

Built: BR Derby, May 1961
Numbers carried: (1) D99,
  (2) 45135
First allocation: Derby
Final allocation: Tinsley
Withdrawn: 9 March 1987
Preserved: Peak Railway,
  Matlock

Minus nameplates, No 45135
was displayed at Cambridge Open
Day, 14 September 1991.
Howard Johnston

The London Midland Region perpetuated the policy of naming main-line locomotives after regiments, and a total of 26 of the 137 Class 45s were honoured in the period 1961-66. Even so, they were still known as 'Peaks', from the names carried by the initial ten Class 44s.

The desire to rid the London Midland Region's main lines of steam at the earliest opportunity saw the delivery of the entire second batch of 'Peaks' compressed into the short period of just 26 months. Derby was first off the mark with No D11 on 1 October 1960, but Crewe was only a week behind with its first example, D68. The D11-31 and D68-D107 series were provided with split box-type indicators on each corner of the nose-end. No D99 was christened without major ceremony at Derby Works in December 1965. It lost its Stone Vapor steam-heat boiler in favour of a Brush auxiliary alternator and rectifier at Derby in mid-1974, when renumbering to No 45135 also took place.

The arrival of High Speed Trains in the early 1980s saw No 45135 transferred to new duties, based on the Trans-Pennine corridor between Liverpool/Holyhead and Newcastle/ Scarborough. Although major overhauls were instituted, the electric-heat Class 45/1s were all withdrawn over the period 1986-88.

Having lost both its nameplates, No 45135's final days in traffic were spent on Liverpool-Scarborough passenger duties, but it was withdrawn at Tinsley on 9 March 1987 with a relatively minor turbocharger defect. It was removed intact to Derby Etches Park, and offered for sale in July 1988.

Sold for preservation at Peak Rail's southern base at Matlock, it joined sister No D100 *Sherwood Forester* (qv) there on 23 March 1989. The intention is to retain the later blue livery and computer TOPS number configuration. Little mechanical attention has been necessary during the restoration programme, but extensive bodywork restoration has been undertaken. It has visited a number of open days, including Tinsley and Cambridge.

Class 45 1Co-Co1 No D100 *Sherwood Forester*

Built: BR Derby, May 1961
Numbers carried: (1) D100,
    (2) 45060
First allocation: Derby
Final allocation: Toton
Withdrawn: 9 December 1985
Preserved: Peak Railway,
    Matlock

No D100 *Sherwood Forester* at
Basingstoke Rail Exhibition, 26
September 1987. *Norman Preedy*

Apart from being the 100th 'Peak' constructed, No D100 is also well remembered for its celebrated name, even though it spent much of its later years relegated to freight traffic. Unlike other preserved Class 45s, it retained its Stones oil-fired train heating boiler to the end, although latterly isolated.

One of the original split-headcode versions, No D100 was completed at Derby during the early summer of 1961, and was named inside the works prior to a ceremony at the Midland station five days later. Allocated to local depots for its entire BR career, apart from a spell at Cricklewood from November 1974 to July 1976, it acquired dual brakes in January 1975, and was renumbered No 45060 at the same time. Although always a celebrity, its working career was generally without incident.

Of lesser value to BR than their ETH-fitted sisters, the 77 steam-heat Class 45/0s were withdrawn from 1980 onwards, but it was fitting that some were amongst the very last survivors laid aside in 1988. *Sherwood Forester* was granted a major overhaul in 1980, and BR actually agreed to repaint it in its original colours if it was included amongst the final overhauls of the sub-class in 1985. In the event, it was not selected for the repair programme; one of five declared surplus at Toton that December, it was consigned to the long line of scrap locomotives then accumulating at the south of the depot.

Strenuous efforts were made to secure No 45060's preservation, and success was achieved in December 1986. Toton depot staff had gone to great lengths to make sure that the locomotive was not robbed for spares or vandalised during this time. Restoration has been to the original all-green livery, and replica split headcode boxes have been restored to the nose-ends. A later addition has been a small yellow warning panel. No D100, which is in full working order, has been exhibited at a large number of open days and displays, including an excursion over the Severn Valley Railway. When not is use, it spends most of its time amongst the 'Peaks' at the Matlock base of Peak Rail.

Class 45 1Co-Co1 No D120

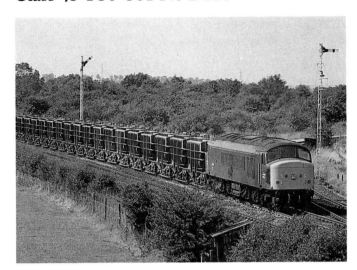

Built: BR Crewe, September
  1961
Numbers carried: (1) D120,
  (2) 45108
First allocation: Derby
Final allocation: Tinsley
Withdrawn: 4 August 1987
Preserved: Crewe Heritage
  Centre

No 45108 passes Melton
Junction with a Radcliffe-Fletton
flyash train, 16 August 1986.
Don Gatehouse

The fourth preserved Class 45 is another former Midland Main Line stalwart, which had the benefit of being in full working order at the time of withdrawal, and maintained in good condition during its two-year spell of storage at March depot prior to preservation.

New 'Peaks' emerged from Derby at the rate of more than one a week during most of 1961, and from No D120 at the end of September, it only took another 12 weeks for the series to be completed at No D137. No D120 sported central two-digit headcode boxes when new.

The main career of No D120 was devoted to the Midland Main Line, and it was based at Derby and Toton apart from a brief spell at Cricklewood at the end of 1964. ETH conversion and renumbering to 45108 took place in June 1973. It was outshopped after major refurbishment in November 1979, underwent unscheduled main generator repairs there in August 1982, and made its last visit in March 1985 for an intermediate overhaul. The loco made headlines on 5 May 1987 when it caused considerable disruption to North Wales services, becoming derailed at Llandudno while running round its York train.

No 45108 was withdrawn on 4 August 1987 and towed to March depot for storage, but unlike most of the locomotives there it was not allowed to drift into dereliction. When offered for sale by tender in January 1990, it was secured by a Crewe businessman for preservation at the nearby Heritage Centre.

The move from March, the loco's home for two years, started on 18 April 1990. Moved first to Toton yard, it was then tripped to Crewe Basford Hall yard behind a pair of Class 20s, and arrived at the Heritage Centre on the 21st behind shunter No 08784. A major step was a successful restarting of the engine on 2 July, and after some bodywork replating the loco was restored to green livery during 1991, with the central headcode panels restored in place of the headlight, a final BR modification fitted from the mid-1980s onwards. It has since visited several BR open days, including the Hereford Rail Festival on 5 May 1991.

Class 45 1Co-Co1 No D123

Built: BR Crewe, November
  1961
Numbers carried: (1) D123,
  (2) 45125
First allocation: Derby
Final allocation: Tinsley
Withdrawn: 7 May 1987
Preserved: Humberside
  Locomotive Group, Hull

No 45125 leaves Cheltenham
with the 09.22 Liverpool-
Penzance, 10 December 1983.
Norman Preedy

The Class 45 preservation story was enhanced at the end of 1991 when No 45125 was moved from the dump of dead load locomotives at Egginton Junction to North Humberside. The group of enthusiasts behind its purchase believes that it has the expertise to restore the 'Peak' to running order quickly despite its apparent poor condition after 4^1/$_2$ years of open storage. First, a locomotive is needed as an ETH source for the main-line coaching stock that is maintained at the former Dairycoaes depot. It will also be made available for exhibition at BR open days, and there is also the hope that it can run on BR if the ban on all preserved diesel operation is lifted. Restoration will be to the original green livery, which includes reinstatement of the split nose-end indicator panels removed wholesale during overhauls at Derby and Crewe Works during the mid-1970s.

No D123 was built at Crewe as part of the intended last series there, Nos D108-37. Its first allocation was Derby, and it spent the next 25 years attached to the Midland Main Line before a final transfer to Tinsley in November 1986.

Its initial livery was green, but an overhaul at Derby in 1967 resulted in the loss of the lower white bodyside stripe; it was noted in standard blue during February 1968. Electric train heating equipment was fitted during a heavy works overhaul at Derby during 1971, and No D123 duly became part of the 45/1 passenger classification emphasised by renumbering to No 45125 in April 1974.

The completion of the conversion of Sheffield-St Pancras services to High Speed Train working in 1986 left BR with the decision of what to do with locomotives which were still in relatively good condition but still prone to failure. Thus a heavy general overhaul programme was instituted to enable them to revitalise Newcastle/Scarborough-Liverpool services. There was, however, no prospect of further work when Sprinter DMUs arrived from 1987 onwards, and the 'Peaks' were quickly retired. No 45125 was towed to March with its sisters Nos 45111 *Grenadier Guardsman* and 45136 on 20 May 1987, theoretically awaiting further work which clearly never materialised.

Class 45 1Co-Co1 No D200

Built: English Electric, March
  1958
Numbers carried: (1) D200,
  (2) 40122
First allocation: Stratford
Final allocation: Crewe
Withdrawn: (1) 23 August 1981,
  (2) 16 April 1988
Preserved: National Railway
  Museum, York

On the last day of its 30-year BR
career, No D200 runs round at
Norwich, 16 April 1988.
Howard Johnston

The English Electric Company and its successors of Newton-le-Willows have made a vast contribution to British modern traction policy for 75 years, and even diesel designs being delivered to BR today can be traced directly back to the first LMS-built main-line locomotive No 10000, which was ignored for preservation in 1968. The survival of the first EE main-line diesel built for BR, Class 40 No D200, is itself miraculous as it was at one stage only a few hours from movement to Swindon Works for breaking up.

No D200 ran on BR for 30 years, but was only in the headlines at the very beginning and end. One of its first duties after delivery was to haul the inaugural diesel-hauled passenger train from London Liverpool Street to Norwich on 18 April 1958, a feat it mirrored on its very last run on 16 April 1988, prior to working under its own power into the NRM building. In between, D200 repaid its investment many times over. Starting life at Stratford depot, it was one of ten initially allocated to the Eastern Region's Great Eastern and Great Northern London depots, but all transferred to the LMR in August 1967 upon arrival of more powerful Class 47s. No D200 was dual-braked and

repainted blue at Crewe Works in April 1970.

What could have been the end of its career followed a serious main generator failure on 8 August 1981, but enthusiasts' pressure for reinstatement paid off and a full overhaul and repaint in green livery was undertaken during early 1983 at Toton depot, after which it returned to full revenue service on both passenger and freight workings. Special duties nationwide included the very first visit of a Class 40 to Penzance on 9 December 1986, and on 9 March 1987 it became the sole survivor of the class on BR. The last major repairs on No D200 were the fitting of replacement wheelsets from withdrawn sister No 40013 *Andania* at Crewe in January 1988. Stratford DRS undertook the final repainting, but did not complete it in time for a rostered railtour on 12 March. Enthusiasts were therefore treated to the sight of No D200 running out of Euston in pale green undercoat! The final working from London to Norwich provided a 105 min 40 sec non-stop run, reputedly a record for diesel traction. No D200 had an outing from York to Stratford on 26 March 1991 for display to mark the closure of the major repair shop.

Class 40 1Co-Co1 No 212 *Aureol*

Built: English Electric, May 1959
Numbers carried: (1) D212,
  (2) 40012, (3) 97407
First allocation: Willesden
Final allocation: Crewe
Withdrawn: (1) 8 February
  1985, (2) 4 April 1986
Preserved: Midland Railway
  Centre, Butterley

No 40012 *Aureol* stabled at
Toton depot fuelling point on
4 June 1983. *Howard Johnston*

The preservation of Class 40 No 212 was achieved by the Class 40 Appeal the hard way – five years of fund-raising stands at open days, and the collecting of single coins. The group wanted a split-headcode version of the class, and although in the event it had to settle for a different version, at least it was one of the best-known, one of only 25 to be honoured with nameplates.

As No D212, *Aureol* was named after the flagship of the Elder Dempster Line at Liverpool Riverside station on 20 September 1960. Allocated new to Willesden, it also worked from Crewe North (June 1959), Carlisle Upperby (September 1959), Camden (December 1960), Bescot (December 1965), LM Western Lines (April 1966), Longsight (August 1967), LM Manchester Division (June 1968), D10 Preston Division (June 1972), Carlisle Kingmoor (May 1973), Longsight (August 1973), and Carlisle Kingmoor again (December 1978). It gained blue livery during general overhaul and dual-braking at Crewe Works in June 1971, and made a final visit in June 1980 for an 'intermediate'. In its later years, *Aureol* received hand-painted names on its bodysides to replace the missing originals. In

August 1982 it visited Stratford DRS to swap bogies with No 40148. Withdrawn in February 1985 after derailment at Northwich, and moved to Crewe for disposal, it was resurrected with three others to assist the Crewe track remodelling scheme, a role it performed for another 14 months until cracked bogies forced its retirement.

No 40012 was parked out of use at Carlisle for over two years as a source of spare parts to keep BR's own preservation candidate, No D200, running. The locomotive was purchased in early 1988, together with two replacement bogies with traction motors from BREL Crewe. No 40012 arrived at Butterley in March 1989, via asbestos removal at Vic Berry's Leicester yard, in a woebegone condition. It has, however, benefited from weekly working parties, and members have rebuilt the cabs and electrical cubicles, and part-replated the bodysides. The most serious problem is a 2-foot frost damage fracture in the engine block because it was not drained while in open store at Carlisle – a replacement block is being sought. A ballot of members has chosen a repaint in BR blue as No 212.

Class 40 1Co-Co1 No 40013 *Andania*

Built: English Electric, June
  1959
Numbers carried: (1) D213,
  (2) 40013
First allocation: Willesden
Final allocation: Longsight
Withdrawn: 13 January 1985
Preserved: South Yorkshire
  Railway, Meadowhall, Sheffield

Awaiting asbestos inspection, No
40013 stands at Vic Berry's
scrapyard, Leicester.
Howard Johnston

No 40013, the second preserved Class 40 to have carried a name, applied without ceremony at Crewe Works in June 1962, was new from Vulcan Foundry in June 1959 for West Coast Main Line passenger duties. Commissioned at Willesden, it was then sent to Carlisle Upperby, the first Class 40 to be based there. It also worked out of Camden, Crewe, Longsight, and Wigan Springs Branch.

Andania's final intermediate overhaul was at Crewe in July 1980. It was, however, reprieved from withdrawal with a fresh set of bogies at Stratford DRS in September 1982, taken from withdrawn No 40094, and the unclassified repair at Crewe in May 1984 was the very last conducted on a member of the class. No 40013's final passenger fling was on the 'Cumbrian Whistler' railtour with No 40012 *Aureol* (qv) and No 40028 *Samaria* on 6 October 1984, and it was condemned at Wigan depot 12 days later. Reinstated after further repairs, it spent the New Year at March in Cambridgeshire before working back to Crewe via a Birkenhead freight on 3 January and, failing a C exam, was finally withdrawn on the 13th.

The pulling power of Class 40s at railway events had prompted the London Midland Region to give a cosmetic repaint to No 40063 after its withdrawal in April 1984, after which it was displayed at several shows including Stourbridge and Worcester. The same was the case with No 40013, which was retained after withdrawal. After a repaint, it was exhibited at Redditch, Shrewsbury, Blackburn, Southport and Leamington Spa in 1985, and Kidderminster, Aberystwyth, Rugby, Wrexham, Shrewsbury and Basingstoke during 1987.

The run-down and disposal of BR's Class 40 fleet took a total of 13 years, but ended in early 1988 when a long line of derelict machines parked at Crewe Works was sold to private scrap merchants for speedy disposal, and the last two on BR metals, Nos 40013 and 40118, were speculatively offered for sale. They were moved to Vic Berry's yard at Leicester on 11 May for inspection for asbestos content.

A stumbling block in the long-term restoration project will be the poor condition of the wheelsets. Those currently under No D213 were formerly those of the National Railway Museum's No D200, exchanged at Crewe depot in January 1988. D213 was taken by rail to Sheffield Brightside freight depot in January 1989 for onward road transit to Meadowhall.

Class 40 1Co-Co1 No D306 *Atlantic Conveyor*

Built: Robert Stephenson &
    Hawthorn, October 1960
Numbers carried: (1) D306,
    (2) 40106
First allocation: Crewe
Final allocation: Longsight
Withdrawn: 21 April 1983
Preserved: Nene Valley Railway,
    Wansford

Still masquerading as 'Great
Train Robbery' loco No D326,
No D306 leaves Loughborough
for Rothley on 7 November
1987. *W.A. Sharman*

No D306 was a product of Robert Stephenson & Hawthorn of Darlington, which had merged with English Electric in 1944. An overload of work at Newton-le-Willows at the end of 1960 prompted the switch of assembly of 20 Class 40s to Darlington, and Nos D305-24 were completed in just nine months. All spent their careers on the LM Region.

The second of the RSH batch, D306 was delivered in October 1960, being noted passing through York in tandem with a K1 2-6-0 *en route* to Doncaster for commissioning. It was transferred many times during its career, but all in the North West – Liverpool Edge Hill (December 1960), Crewe (March 1964), Willesden (November 1964), Crewe (January 1966), Western Lines (LMW, June 1968), Liverpool Division (D08, July 1968), Stoke Division (D05, November 1968), Manchester Division (D09, February 1970), and Longsight (May 1973). It was renumbered No 40106 in March 1974.

The reason for No 40106's survival is actually based on what it did *not* do. As the last main-line locomotive to survive in original Brunswick green livery in 1977, it developed sufficient celebrity status to earn a repaint in the same colour during its final overhaul at Crewe Works. It then became a popular railtour

loco and open day exhibit.

Lack of air-brake equipment saw No 40106's withdrawal in April 1983 in favour of the restoration of the more useful first-built No D200, but it was maintained in working order for resale. After an appearance at a Wrexham General station exhibition on 27 September, it was sold to Gerald Boden for movement to the Great Central Railway at Loughborough, where it arrived on 16 April 1984. No 40106 was named *Atlantic Conveyor* on 9 August that year in honour of the container ship of the same name lost in the Falklands War with the loss of nine lives. In November 1987 it was fitted with false split headcode boxes to appear in the motion picture *Buster*, masquerading as sister Great Train Robbery Class 40 No D326, the real locomotive involved in the Great Train Robbery at Sears Crossing, Buckinghamshire, on 8 August 1963, and which was scrapped at Doncaster in March 1984. D306 is now back in its original livery.

The transfer of No D306 from the landlocked Great Central to the Nene Valley Railway on 20 February 1990 allowed the locomotive to embark on a series of visits to BR open days and exhibitions for the first time in seven years.

Class 40 1Co-Co1 No 40118

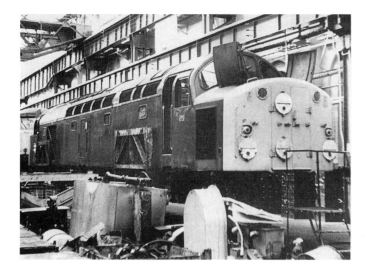

Built: Robert Stephenson &
   Hawthorn, February 1961
Numbers carried: (1) D318,
   (2) 40118, (3) 97408
First allocation: Crewe
Final allocation: Crewe
Withdrawn: (1) 12 February
   1985, (2) 4 September 1985,
   (3) 26 February 1986
Preserved: Birmingham Railway
   Museum, Tyseley

No 40118 undergoing
rectification at Crewe Works,
6 June 1981. *Howard Johnston*

The restoration to working order of Class 40 No 40118 will be a slow but thorough job by a small group of Birmingham enthusiasts. The loco was in a poor state when they bought it, having been out of use for over two years, and robbed for spares. It had led a precarious existence in its final eight years in BR ownership, surviving a major mechanical failure to be granted a works overhaul while others were being scrapped, and being condemned no less than three times in its last 12 months. No 40118 became an enthusiasts' favourite for all these reasons, together with its brief appearance in the opening sequence of the 1966 film *Robbery* (see also D306, which played the same role in *Buster*).

The 20 Class 40s assembled at RSH were decimated by early withdrawals, but No 40118 was to be a notable exception. New to Crewe in February 1961, it worked variously from Camden, Bletchley and Longsight, displaced by extensions of the West Coast electrification. It retained its train heating boiler during its final major works overhaul at Crewe in February 1978, but suffered a total main generator failure at Rockliffe on the 16.52 Bangor-Manchester on 2 November 1981. The repairs proved troublesome, and it took two years and several

trips back to the works, plus a new set of bogies, before BR accepted it back into traffic in March 1983.

One of No 40118's final passenger workings was on 15 December 1984, when it was selected to haul the Class 40 Preservation Society's 'Christmas Cracker' railtour from Manchester to Swindon. It was withdrawn at Tyseley on 12 February 1985 with worn tyres, but was resurrected as departmental No 97408 on 20 May to assist with the remodelling of the Crewe station area, and on 14 June it towed failed electric locomotive 85015 on the 1V43 22.17 Manchester-Penzance from Longport to Stoke. Withdrawn again on 4 September, it came back one more time on 6 November before a camshaft defect finally killed it off. It was towed to Carlisle for spares, then Crewe in January 1988, and finally Vic Berry's yard at Leicester with No 40013 (qv D213). It moved to Tyseley on 28 September 1988.

Up to 1992, work has been devoted to renovating the No 2 bogie, including wheelsets obtained from scrapped No 40087, and the No 2 cab. The power unit is next, followed by the No 1 cab, and the body given a cosmetic repaint in BR blue.

Class 40 1Co-Co1 No D335

Built: English Electric, March
  1961
Numbers carried: (1) D335,
  (2) 40135, (3) 97406
First allocation: Crewe
Final allocation: Longsight
Withdrawn: (1) 22 January
  1985, (2) 16 December 1986
Preserved: East Lancashire
  Railway, Bury

Memories of its days in blue
livery – No 40135 at Carlisle
Kingmoor. *Peter Walton*

Split headcode Class 40 No D335 was to survive the scrap man at the eleventh hour twice in five years. Rescued from the Doncaster Works cutting-up road in 1985 for departmental use, it narrowly escaped the torch again early in 1987 when it was redundant again and sent to Swindon for scrap.

It took until late 1960 for new Class 40 construction to incorporate nose-end four-character headcode blinds in two sections on either side of the nose-end doors, and only Nos D325-44 were built like this before inter-loco communication links were dispensed with. No D335 was new from Vulcan Foundry to Crewe diesel depot in March 1961, and stayed there until being moved to Longsight in May 1969. Moves followed to Wigan (January 1972), Carlisle (August 1973), and Longsight again (May 1975), from where it was withdrawn during the last week of Class 40 operation in January 1985. Its last works visit had been to Crewe for a light overhaul in September 1979.

After the completion of its departmental role, for which it was renumbered No 97406, No D335 was retained as a useful ballast locomotive on low-speed duties in the North West area. Its final working was due to be the

10 December 1986 7Z33 Eaglescliffe-Fazakerley PW train from Healey Mills, but was low on power and needed assistance from two Class 31s to reach its destination. It was towed to Wigan Springs Branch depot, and after inspection condemned there on the 16th. It was towed away that evening to Bescot destined for Swindon for component recovery, and actually reached Gloucester before the decision was reversed.

After repaint and restoration to green livery at Tyseley depot during September 1987, D335 was employed on specials between Kidderminster and Bridgnorth at the Severn Valley Railway's diesel festival. There followed brisk competition from preservationists, and successful bidders were the Class 40 Preservation Society, already owners of Class 40 No 40145 (qv). No D335 was sent to Vic Berry's yard at Leicester for asbestos inspection, and left for Bury on 13 January 1989, arriving on 5 February. It was successfully trialed to Ramsbottom on 27 May, and made its public debut on 6 October. The 1990/91 winter saw the loco fitted with new water tanks in readiness for refitting the train heating boiler, and repaint in all-over green followed.

Class 40 1Co-Co1 No 40145

Built: English Electric, May 1961
Numbers carried: (1) D345,
(2) 40145
First allocation: Neville Hill
Final allocation: Longsight
Withdrawn: 12 June 1982
Preserved: East Lancashire
Railway, Bury

No 40145 at Eastfield shed, Glasgow, on 21 June 1981. *Norman Preedy*

The 2,000hp locomotive which introduced diesel traction to the prestige 'Queen of Scots' Pullman between King's Cross, Leeds and Edinburgh was chosen after years of fundraising by the Class 40 Preservation Society, one of the most active groups of enthusiasts in the early 1980s.

No D345, distinctive as the first off the production line with a central integral one-piece headcode panel in place of nose-end door gangways, had a hectic first year in traffic after allocation to Neville Hill depot, Leeds, on 17 May 1961. Together with sisters Nos D346-8, it supplanted Gresley A3 Pacifics 60038/74/81/4/6 on top link work. But the glory was short-lived as the more powerful 3,300hp Class 55 'Deltics' from the same Vulcan Foundry works took over.

Having by now acquired a small yellow warning panel, No D345 was transferred to York in January 1963, followed by successive spells at Healey Mills (January 1967) and Gateshead (October 1969, after dual-braking), before re-organisation of the Class 40 fleet saw No 40145, now in blue livery, sent to the Scottish Region in October 1976. Its final spell of duty from May 1978 was across the Pennines

from Neville Hill with a mixed diet of freight and passenger turns from Manchester's Longsight shed, and its last light overhaul and engine change was at Crewe in November 1980. Its only distinguishing feature during all this time was the retention of its front-end headboard brackets.

Analysis of the best locomotives available for preservation demonstrated that No 40145, whose career ended with a minor derailment in Stourton yard, Leeds, was worth bidding for. Minus its air brake gear, it was moved from Crewe to the East Lancashire Railway in February 1984. Restoration to operational condition took four years to complete, and No 40145 made its debut run with four round trips between Bury and Summerseat on 4 April 1987. It has been a regular performer since then, and completed its 100th round trip to Ramsbottom in May 1988.

The first trip to Rawtenstall took place on 9 September 1990, reviving memories of the final BR freight hauled by a Class 40 in December 1990. It is intended to repaint the locomotive in blue livery, and a defective axle requires replacement.

Class 50 Co-Co No 50002 *Superb*

Built: English Electric, December
   1967
Numbers carried: (1) D402,
   (2) 50002
First allocation: Crewe
Final allocation: Plymouth Laira
Withdrawn: 23 August 1991
Preserved: Paignton &
   Dartmouth Railway

A recent arrival on the Western
Region, No 402 on the Old Oak
Common turntable, 16 March
1974. *Norman Preedy*

It is perhaps too early to discuss whether the English Electric Class 50 proved a worthwhile design for BR, but what is certain is that like any British passenger locomotive they have scarcely been out of the limelight during their careers. They covered an unremarkable two million miles each, and in the end it was disproportionate maintenance costs for a relatively small fleet and the move away from loco-hauled passenger trains by all three sectors, InterCity, Regional Railways and Network SouthEast, that hastened their withdrawal.

However, the following that the Class 50s had gained by the end of their BR careers was demonstrated by the amazing number purchased for preservation at the end of 1991. The supply of serviceable locomotives matched the demand, and No 50002 *Superb*, one of the last in operation on the Waterloo-Exeter route, was a popular choice for a group wanting to return it to Paignton, which it would have visited regularly over a ten-year period from the mid-1970s.

No 50002, in 1991 the oldest in private hands, although the pioneer No D400 was expected to survive, was new to the London Midland Region's Western Lines fleet a week before the end of 1967, and was selected as the driver-training loco at Polmadie depot, Glasgow, which provided and serviced the diesel power for main-line services. No D400 was transferred to the Western Region in mid-1972, prior to squadron release, and No D402 went to Bristol Bath Road in November 1973. It was based at Old Oak Common from May 1974 until April 1976, when it moved to Laira, its home for the next 15 years.

An exhibit at the 1975 Crewe Works Open Day, No 50002 received its *Superb* nameplates on 21 March 1978, and two years later was further honoured with the addition of bodyside crests. Refurbished and repainted in 'large logo' livery at Doncaster between April and October 1983, it received its final intermediate overhaul at the end of 1986, when it was also outshopped in Network SouthEast livery. Its final workings were part of the hard-slog 100mph Waterloo-Exeter pool.

The end came for No 50002 on 22 August 1991 when it suffered a loss of power and was removed to Laira for inspection. It was found to be passing oil, a sign of worn pistons and liners, and the cash restrictions on repairs dictated its withdrawal the following day. It was, however, kept intact for preservation.

Class 50 Co-Co No 50017 *Royal Oak*

Built: English Electric, April
  1968
Numbers carried: (1) D417,
  (2) 50017
First allocation: Crewe
Final allocation: Plymouth Laira
Withdrawn: (1) 22 July 1991,
  (2) 9 September 1991
Preserved: Crewe Heritage
  Centre

No 50017 *Royal Oak* was an
unusual visitor to Manchester
Piccadilly after working north on
an overnight ballast train to
Castleton on 17 November 1989.
Philip Crumpton

Perhaps the last true BR passenger diesel locomotive design, the 100 mph English Electric Class 50s generated a substantial enthusiast following from the late 1980s onwards, when it was realised that their days were numbered. They lost favour with all sectors of BR because of their high maintenance costs, and the last survivors were confined to just the Waterloo-Exeter route sponsored by Network SouthEast.

No D417 was new in April 1968, and became part of the London Midland Western Lines fleet at a time when specific allocations were out of favour (it was, however, based and maintained at Crewe). Steam was still then operational in the North West, and the arrival of the Class 50s was seen as vital for the completion of its replacement by cascaded Class 25s and 40s.

D417 was exhibited at Tyseley Depot Open Day on 29 September 1968, and from 1970 until the electrification of the WCML north of Weaver Junction in May 1974, it would have been seen regularly double-heading Anglo-Scottish expresses.

Thirty-one Class 50s moved to Bristol Bath Road to replace Class 52 diesel-hydraulics on the top West of England services; No 50017 paid a brief visit to the WR before recall to Crewe, but took up its permanent place in the fleet in January 1976. Named *Royal Oak* on 24 April 1978, No 50017 visited Doncaster Works for a six-month refurbishment programme in June of the following year, and was one of the last to be painted in all-over blue livery. The large logo style was applied after its next, intermediate, overhaul at Doncaster in December 1983. It adopted NSE livery in June 1986.

No 50017 was 'in the wars' three times. It was derailed in Norwood Junction yard on 21 January 1978 while working an inter-regional freight from Acton, again at Tiverton Junction on 13 November 1981 while on engineers duty, and sustained cab damage at the end of 1983. It was the last to get an F exam at Laira in February 1988.

Withdrawn on 22 July 1991 with main generator trouble, *Royal Oak* was reinstated the next day when sister No 50027 *Lion* succumbed with a more serious fault. No 50017 failed again at Eastleigh on 9 September with traction motor trouble, and this time the repairs were not authorised.

Class 50 Co-Co No 50019 *Ramillies*

Built: English Electric, April
    1968
Numbers carried: (1) D419,
    (2) 50019
First allocation: Crewe
Final allocation: Plymouth Laira
Withdrawn: 19 September 1990
Preserved: Groombridge

No 50019 *Ramillies* parked at
March en route to Doncaster,
27 January 1987. *Howard
Johnston*

The success of trials with English Electric prototype Co-Co No DP2 between 1962 and 1967 prompted BR to lease 50 modernised versions for West Coast Main Line services over the non-electrified section north of Crewe. Intended for 100 mph work, they reflected the then feeling of disillusionment with Sulzer-engined Class 47s, and incorporated the latest electronic control systems inside a new design of square body. Displaced by electrification, they were progressively cascaded to the Western Region from 1972 onwards to complete the eradication of the Class 52 'Western' diesel-hydraulics, and were purchased outright from the leasing company.

No D419 was transferred from Crewe to Bristol Bath Road in May 1974, and to Laira in July 1975. It is recorded as suffering a serious derailment at Reading on 24 May 1976 with a defective tyre while working a midday Penzance-Paddington service.

Named after the warship Ramillies on 18 April 1978, No 50019 was refurbished between September 1979 and March 1980. It spent part of 1981 as the Saltley depot crew-trainer, and received its final heavy general overhaul at Doncaster in April 1984. Its trip to the works

on 5 January 1987 for a power unit swap marked the end of maintenance there before work was transferred to Old Oak Common. A defect on the towing Class 47 meant that the loco was left in March yard until the 26th. It returned to the WR on 28 March in charge of the 16.00 Newcastle-Bristol parcels.

The Class 50s' reliability was always questionable, and their refurbishment at Doncaster Works was followed in the late 1980s by progressive displacement from the WR main line in favour of the Waterloo-Exeter route. Withdrawals had reached an advanced stage by the end of 1991.

Ramillies has carried several liveries. New in all-over blue, it wore 'large logo' blue until a repaint in Network SouthEast colours in November 1986. By February 1989 it had run up high engine hours and was pensioned off to the Bristol-based civil engineer's pool in exchange for healthier No 50049 *Defiance*. *Ramillies* was repainted back into blue to reflect its new role, but a main generator flashover on 28 August 1990 sealed its fate, and it was towed to Exeter for storage pending movement to the Tunbridge Wells-Eridge preserved line.

Class 50 Co-Co No 50027 *Lion*

Built: English Electric, June
   1968
Numbers carried: (1) D427,
   (2) 50027
First allocation: Crewe
Final allocation: Plymouth Laira
Withdrawn: 23 July 1991
Preserved: Mid-Hants Railway

No 50027 *Lion* at Birmingham
New Street on 24 March 1984.
John Tuffs

Although Class 50s were certainly not a regular sight on the Mid-Hants Railway in BR days, they were no strangers to the area, having spent many years on Waterloo-Southampton and Portsmouth passenger workings. No 50027 *Lion* was one of the last survivors of Network SouthEast's Waterloo-Exeter (NWXA) pool, succumbing to a main generator flashover in July 1991 which resulted in its withdrawal on the 23rd of that month. Sister loco No 50018 *Resolution* had been switched off the previous day with multiple faults.

New from English Electric's Vulcan Foundry as No D427 in June 1968, the loco was London Midland Region (Crewe) based for the first six years of its life, and was displayed at Crewe Electric Depot Open Day on 19 April 1970. It moved to the Western Region's Bristol Bath Road depot in March 1974 ready for the timetable change that would see West of England services upgraded with 100 mph diesel-electric power in the place of the Class 52 'Western' diesel-hydraulics. It went immediately on to Laira. No 50027, as it had

become by January 1974, is credited with being the first Class 50 to reach Penzance on 19 March 1974. It was the 15th of the class to be named, receiving *Lion* plates on 14 April 1978.

Lion was loaned to Saltley for crew training in January 1981, and became part of the London-based fleet at Old Oak Common in April 1982. It was long considered one of the most reliable of the class, and survived in its original condition until the summer of 1983, when it was called to Doncaster Works for refurbishment, one of the last four to get the treatment. It received the 'large logo' blue livery at this time. Network SouthEast red, white and blue was applied during an F exam at Laira in December 1987.

Although Class 50s were always relatively uncommon in South Wales, *Lion* made two notable visits there, being exhibited at Cardiff Canton Depot Open Day with No 50043 *Eagle* (qv) on 1 October 1977, and turning up at the same shed on 9 July 1991 for its wheels to be reprofiled, a surprise move as it was in fact to be withdrawn only two weeks later.

Class 50 Co-Co No 50031 *Hood*

Built: English Electric, July 1968
Numbers carried: (1) D431,
    (2) 50031
First allocation: Crewe
Final allocation: Plymouth Laira
Withdrawn: 5 August 1991
Preserved: St Leonards

Departmental No 50031 *Hood* at
Norton Junction with the Bristol-
Worcester parcels empties,
31 August 1990. *P.A. Waterman*

With such an evocative name – HMS *Hood* was sunk in May 1941 with heavy loss of life – No 50031 was thereafter regarded as a special locomotive. A further ceremony held at Old Oak Common depot on 22 April 1983 saw the additional application of plaques to the bodysides, unveiled by a survivor from the stricken vessel.

All the Class 50s ran from new in BR corporate blue livery. No D431, allocated to the Crewe diesel pool in July 1968, stayed on the London Midland Region until the very end of West Coast Main Line Class 50 operation in May 1976, moving south to take up residence at Plymouth Laira depot. It was at Doncaster for refurbishment from May to November 1981, and underwent its final intermediate overhaul in October 1985. It spent a brief time working from Old Oak Common from May 1980.

When sectorisation of BR saw the locomotive fleet carved up, No 50031 was sponsored by the civil engineer, and thus saw little passenger use. It received its last power unit change at Old Oak in September 1988, courtesy of No 50045 *Achilles*. When the Class

50 departmental fleet was disbanded on 25 January 1991, *Hood* was reprieved from withdrawal and transferred to the Network SouthEast reserve fleet, to be used on passenger work in desperate situations. It was, however, repainted in 'large logo' livery at Laira in May to mark the 50th anniversary of the *Hood* tragedy.

No 50031 was stopped at Laira on 21 July with two badly worn wheelsets, and repairs were not authorised, not least because the power unit had by then run up almost 10,000 hours since a works overhaul. In view of *Hood*'s obvious popularity, however, it was decided to keep the locomotive intact instead of dismantling it for spare parts.

Official condemnation came on 5 August, after which it was parked to await being put on the tender list for preservation. It was cleaned up for the autumn 1991 Laira Open Day, and when bought in November 1991, No 50031 became the third of the class to move to the preservation centre established within the former DEMU maintenance depot at St Leonards, Hastings.

Class 50 Co-Co No 50035 *Ark Royal*

Built: English Electric, August
  1968
Numbers carried: (1) D435,
  (2) 50035
First allocation: Crewe
Final allocation: Plymouth Laira
Withdrawn: 3 August 1990
Preserved: St Leonards

Still a West Coast Main Line
loco, No 435 stands at Polmadie
depot, Glasgow, on 7 September
1971. *Norman Preedy*

The first Class 50 to pass into preservation was formally handed over to the Class Fifty Fund at the 16 August 1991 Old Oak Common Depot Open Day by the then Network SouthEast director, Chris Green. As this book demonstrates, many more were sold in the months ahead.

Initially on hire from English Electric, *Ark Royal* was new to the Crewe Division on 3 August 1968, coincidentally the last day of steam operation on BR. It became the formal responsibility of Crewe diesel depot in May 1973. Further transfers were to Bristol Bath Road (January 1976), Laira (December 1976), Old Oak Common (June 1980), and finally Laira (July 1990).

Ark Royal has enjoyed an enthusiastic following since it became the first of the class to receive nameplates in a ceremony at Plymouth on 10 January 1978, followed nine days later by the fixing of crests of the aircraft carrier's heraldic badge. It was further visually distinctive at the time because of trials with sealed-beam lamps in its plated-over headcode boxes.

While early overhauls were carried out at Crewe Works, complete refurbishment took place at Doncaster from November 1980 to March 1981, during which its all-over blue livery was replaced a new style of wrap-round yellow ends and full length BR symbol. No 50035's final intermediate repair was completed in July 1986, and it was unusually sent back to the WR in grey primer ready for an application of the new red, white and blue NSE livery at Old Oak Common.

In its later years as an Old Oak-based loco, *Ark Royal* would have been a regular sight on Paddington-Oxford diagrams, together with trips to Cheltenham, Worcester, Hereford and Birmingham. It did, however, also haul the final Paddington-Newquay loco-hauled service on 4 October 1987, and the final Class 50 07.18 Paddington-Wolverhampton on 30 June 1990.

London-based survivors were sent to Laira to ease the motive power crisis on the Waterloo-Exeter route, but No 50035 only survived for another fortnight. Its owners plan to replace its worn wheelsets.

Class 50 Co-Co No 50042 *Triumph*

Built: English Electric, October
  1968
Numbers carried: (1) D442,
  (2) 50042
First allocation: Crewe
Final allocation: Plymouth Laira
Withdrawn: 15 October 1990
Preserved: Bodmin Steam
  Railway

No 50042 *Triumph* on the 08.00
Hereford-Paddington at Malvern
Common, 11 April 1987. *John
Chalcraft*

No 50042 is destined to be the southernmost preserved Class 50 following its purchase in December 1991 by a group based in Cornwall; and unless there is a relaxation of the ban on privately-owned diesels working on BR, it is unlikely to show much of its potential on this short Cornish branch.

Part of the WCML pool from October 1968 to May 1974, D442 became a replacement for Class 52 'Western' diesel-hydraulics on Paddington-West of England services, then was itself later replaced by High Speed Trains. When the lease-hire agreement with English Electric ended, Doncaster Works was chosen to undertake heavy overhauls, and No 50042 was there in the autumn of 1978 for attention. It was on a test run to Peterborough on 14 September when it was commandeered for one of its most spectacular outings, being used to double-head failed Class 55 'Deltic' No 55017 *Durham Light Infantry* on the 06.50 ex-King's Cross through to Hull.

D442 was christened *Triumph* on 4 October 1978, and was refurbished at Doncaster from January to May 1982, and given a final intermediate overhaul there in May 1985. At the start of sectorisation it was sponsored by Parcels in 1987-88, and therefore retained its 'large logo' blue and yellow livery to the end of its BR service days. No 50042 was next transferred to a special Departmental fleet (DCWA) for high-mileage locomotives considered unsuitable for express passenger operation on the Waterloo-Exeter route.

The Class 50s' demise was hastened by the availability at the end of 1990 of Cardiff-based Class 37s brought in from other sectors, themselves displaced by new Brush-built Class 60s. *Triumph* was one of three Class 50s simply switched off during October 1990 (the others were Nos 50023 *Howe* and 50032 *Courageous*) as surplus.

By the time of preservation, the loco had been out of service for over a year, but despite some minor vandalism while parked at Plymouth Tavistock Junction it was chosen in preference to several other Class 50s which had been taken out of service much more recently.

Class 50 Co-Co No 50043 *Eagle*

Built: English Electric, October
  1968
Numbers carried: (1) D443,
  (2) 50043
First allocation: Crewe
Final allocation: Plymouth Laira
Withdrawn: 31 January 1991
Preserved: Tyseley

No 50043 *Eagle* at Exeter St
Davids, 7 July 1984. *Norman
Preedy*

Preservation of Class 50s seemed destined to move well into double figures during 1992 following a series of purchases from those laid up at Plymouth's Laira depot when Network SouthEast withdrew sponsorship of the class on the Waterloo-Exeter route in favour of push-pull-fitted Class 47/7s, themselves ousted by Class 158 DMUs on Glasgow-Edinburgh/Aberdeen InterCity shuttles.

Renumbered No 50043 in February 1974, three months before transfer to the Western Region, this locomotive acquired its *Eagle* nameplates on 28 June 1978. Its first major public recognition came when it was chosen to attend Cardiff Canton Open Day on 1 October 1977; members of the class were only normally seen there for tyre-turning.

No 50043 was one of the last Class 50s to remain in its original condition, not being called to Doncaster Works for rebuilding until December 1982, and being outshopped from there the following May in the new 'large logo' paint style. It made a class debut to Scarborough on 12 May 1984 with a special excursion from Leamington Spa.

At first allocated to the Provincial Railways sector, No 50043 joined NSE's Solent & Sarum pool in the autumn of 1988, acquiring red, white and blue livery, but proved a less than reliable performer in its latter years. It was out of use for most of the summer of 1989, and in little over a year had four main generator changes at Laira. It developed further serious main generator problems on 30 January 1991 while partnering sister loco No 50029 *Renown* on the 07.12 Newton Abbot-Exeter local service, and was condemned the next day.

This was regarded as a rather surprising decision considering that its power unit had only worked 5,500 hours since its previous F exam at Laira, not to mention the amount of time and money that had been spent on it. It was nevertheless towed with several other Class 50s to Plymouth's Ocean Sidings to await disposal.

No 50043's new owners are the D318 Preservation Group, and it should provide much less of a renovation headache than the English Electric Class 40 No 40118 (qv) described on an earlier page of this book.

Class 50 Co-Co No 50044 *Exeter*

Built: English Electric, October
  1968
Numbers carried: (1) D444,
  (2) 50044
First allocation: Crewe
Final allocation: Plymouth Laira
Withdrawn: 11 January 1991
Preserved: St Leonards

No 50044 *Exeter* on test from
Doncaster Works, 29 April
1982. *Neville Stead.*

Although certainly upstaged by sister Class 50 No 50041 *Bulwark*, which required a total rebuild after a high-speed derailment at Paddington, No 50044 *Exeter* was perhaps the next worst damaged in a high-speed collision in Bristol's Malago carriage sidings on 9 August 1982. It was under repair at Doncaster Works for several months, requiring partial replacement of one nose end. No major mechanical attention was required as it had only left works the previous April after total refurbishment. Although by now missing the slow-speed equipment fitted from new to work merry-go-round coal trains, the ex-works loco made one its most celebrated workings. Before working back to Plymouth via the traditional North East-South West corridor, the passenger loco was loaned to Railfreight for a Frodingham (Scunthorpe)-Wath coal duty.

No D444 was new to Crewe in October 1968, and after 5½ years' work on the West Coast Main Line was transferred to the Western ready for the start of the May 1974 timetable, in place of Class 52s. The loco was

named after the warship HMS *Exeter* at the city's St Davids station on 26 April 1978, and the same location witnessed the fitting of additional crests above the plates on 20 August 1981 to mark a closer liaison with the Royal Navy vessel.

Its final overhaul was an intermediate at Doncaster at the end of 1986, and it was soon duly repainted in NSE livery by its adopted owners. Less than eight months later it was painted again, this time in the revised scheme with blue front cab surrounds in place of white.

At the end of 1990 the decision to reduce the size of the NWXA Waterloo-Exeter fleet to 18 meant the end of No 50044. Several Class 50s were shipped from Old Oak Common to Stratford Major Repair Depot for stripping of spares prior to breaking up, and Nos 50021 *Rodney* and 50044 were moved together at the end of May. In the event, very little was removed, and preservationists looking for a further suitable locomotive for the St Leonards centre were attracted to *Exeter*'s generally good condition apart from some body damage.

Class 50 Co-Co No 50149 *Defiance*

Built: English Electric, November 1968
Numbers carried: (1) D449, (2) 50049, (3) 50149, (4) 50049
First allocation: Crewe
Final allocation: Plymouth Laira
Withdrawn: 16 August 1991
Preserved: Plymouth Laira

In Railfreight livery, No 50149 *Defiance* climbs from Westbury at Upton Scudamore on a test run on 18 October 1987. *John Chalcraft*

Towards the end of its career, the final production Class 50 was subjected to an abortive experiment in an attempt to find a use for the large numbers of Class 50s likely to be surplus from InterCity and Network SouthEast passenger duties. Railfreight financed the equipping of No 50149 with Class 37 CP7-type bogies to enable it to be better tried on heavy stone and ballast trains. Ironically, it was the removal of vital but then irrelevant wheelslip protection equipment at refurbishment in the early 1980s which made the experiment a virtual non-starter.

No D449 was accepted by BR at the end of 1968, and assumed a familiar role on Anglo-Scottish expresses until transfer from Crewe to Bristol Bath Road in May 1974, migrating to its final Laira base in April 1977. It was named on 2 May 1978, and entered Doncaster Works for rebuilding in the spring of 1983.

Laira undertook the conversion during an F exam in September 1987, at the same time applying the unique three-tone grey Railfreight Construction livery with bodyside decals, yellow backing to the nameplate, and the amended number 50149 to differentiate it from

passenger Class 50s. Load trials were conducted on Warminster bank, south of Westbury, on 18 October 1987, and although *Defiance* had little difficulty restarting a 1,380-tonne train, too much wheelslip was involved and rail burning took place. Railfreight declined to finance the reinstallation of anti-wheelslip equipment, and No 50149 was consigned to departmental duties until a collision involving two Class 37s at Plymouth found a place for the loco on china clay workings in Cornwall.

Network SouthEast recognised the loco's generally good condition, and in February 1989 agreed to sponsor it in exchange for the inferior No 50019 *Ramillies*. It was refitted with standard bogies to enable its top speed to be raised from 80 mph to 100 mph, and after a repaint into NSE colours and renumbering back to No 50049, the loco took up Waterloo-Exeter diagrams. It developed engine problems in the summer of 1991, and was laid up at Laira on 16 August when repair finance was not forthcoming. The Class 50 Society, the longest-established Class 50 support group, were successful in their tender, and intend to keep the loco in the West Country.

Class 42 B-B No D821 *Greyhound*

Built: BR Swindon, May 1960
Number carried: D821
First allocation: Plymouth Laira
Final allocation: Plymouth Laira
Withdrawn: 3 December 1972
Preserved: Severn Valley Railway

The first BR-built main-line diesel locomotive to be preserved – Class 42 'Warship' No D821 *Greyhound* passes Darnholm on the North Yorkshire Moors Railway, 23 November 1988. *Gavin Morrison*

No D821 was the first ex-BR main line diesel locomotive to be sold for preservation. The first generation of diesel-hydraulics for the Western Region owed a great deal both internally and externally to West German designs. The twin 1,100hp high-speed Maybach MD650V power units and Mekydro transmission were encased in a hand-built bodyshell that was a scaled-down version of the German Federal Railway (DB) Class V200.

No D821, named after a Royal Navy vessel, entered traffic at Plymouth Laira depot in May 1960 as part of the scheme to oust steam from all West of England passenger workings, duly completed within four years. Originally painted Brunswick green, No D821 acquired maroon livery in 1965, and standard blue at the end of 1967. After transfer to Newton Abbot in March 1967, it returned to Laira in March 1970, going again to Newton Abbot in October 1971 for just two months before returning to Laira for the last time.

Greyhound was a familiar sight on the Exeter-Waterloo line at that time, and as late as 5 October 1970 was chosen for a Royal duty, to convey the Emperor of Japan from Gatwick to Victoria. Plymouth Railway Circle had hoped to take the locomotive into West Sussex on a Bluebell Railway excursion on 16 April 1971, but it ran short of fuel at Salisbury.

The end finally came on 3 December 1972 after the loco had run up a grand total of 1,088,000 miles. It worked under its own power from Laira to Didcot on 24 May 1973, and under Diesel Traction Group ownership had successive homes at Reading (from 9 February 1974) and Swindon Works (February 1977 to Easter 1981). Fully restored to maroon livery, it left the Western Region for good on 4 April 1981, towed with Class 35 cousin No D7029 (qv) to its present home on the NYMR.

In deference to its German origins, No D821 was humorously painted in DB colours during 1989 with fictitious number V200 821, and even a German version of the *Greyhound* name, *Vindhund!* The loco was returned to 1968-style BR blue livery in April 1991, with small yellow panel, early-style numbers behind the cab doors, and red circular weight restriction marks. It was on display at the August 1991 Old Oak Common Depot Open Day, moved on to Laira the following month, and most recently to the Severn Valley Railway.

Class 42 B-B No D832 *Onslaught*

Built: BR Swindon, February
  1961
Number carried: D832
First allocation: Plymouth Laira
Final allocation: Plymouth Laira
Withdrawn: 16 December 1972
Preserved: East Lancashire
  Railway, Bury

No D832 *Onslaught* at
Ramsbottom on 26 July 1987.
Howard Johnston

'Warship' No D832 *Onslaught* is such a reliable performer on the East Lancashire Railway nowadays that it is difficult to imagine the condition in which it reached preservation back in 1979 from Derby Technical Centre. Officially it had been a test locomotive for seven years before purchase, but in reality the last three years had seen it exposed to the elements and vandalism at Eggington Junction.

No D832 was officially the last 'Warship' in service with BR, lasting 13 days longer than the rest of the class, although it had been in store since the previous month. Built at Swindon Works and delivered to Laira on 8 February 1961, it spent its entire life allocated to the West Country, being transferred to Newton Abbot in July 1961, back to Laira (June 1965), Newton Abbot (September 1965), Laira (August 1967), Newton Abbot (October 1971), and finally Laira again (January 1972). In the process it covered 1,132,000 miles, one of the highest of the class. No D832's first livery was green, later maroon, and finally blue.

While the rest of the class were towed to Swindon for scrap, No D832 went north to Derby in January 1973, being used for special dead load tests. The locomotive was rescued for preservation in time to make it a surprise highlight at the 1 September 1979 Derby Works Open Day, and it travelled to Horwich Works the following June for storage prior to a move with No D1041 *Western Prince* (qv) to Bury Transport Museum.

During restoration, standard and electrical components shared by the WR diesel-hydraulics have proved particularly useful. A spare power unit for No D832 has been obtained, and there was no small celebration on 1 September 1984 when one Maybach engine was reassembled and the loco moved under its own power for the first time in 12 years. Repainted in Brunswick green with small yellow warning panels, its made its inaugural run to Ramsbottom on 17 January 1987. A regular performer on the railway since then, it was used as the crew-training locomotive in the build-up to the re-opening of the ELR's 4-mile northern extension to Rawtenstall in April 1991.

Class 52 C-C No D1013 *Western Ranger*

Built: BR Swindon, December
  1962
Number carried: D1013
First allocation: Cardiff Canton
Final allocation: Plymouth Laira
Withdrawn: 28 February 1977
Preserved: Severn Valley
  Railway, Bridgnorth

No D1013 *Western Ranger*
leaves Foley Park tunnel,
Kidderminster, on 14 October
1989. *Gavin Morrison*

The large 2,700hp six-axle diesel-hydraulics of the WR captured the attention of enthusiasts in their latter days because they represented the last vestige of Great Western individuality. Seventy-four Class 52s were built at Swindon and Crewe between 1961 and 1964, but they lasted little over 15 years because of high maintenance costs compared to diesel-electrics.

Based at Old Oak Common and Laira, their initial duties were to replace steam and reduce the Paddington-Birmingham-Wolverhampton service to a less than 2-hour run. They were seen at Shrewsbury and Chester, and in South Wales by the end of 1962, and Penzance and West Wales the following year.

Ever-distinctive by their GW-style cast name and numberplates, the 'Westerns' also broke the mould with a wide variety of liveries. No D1013 was turned out from Swindon in maroon, and went to Cardiff Canton in December 1962. It was successively allocated to Old Oak Common (March 1963), Cardiff (April 1963), Landore (February 1965), Cardiff (February 1966), Laira (April 1966), Landore (April 1968), and finally Laira again from October 1971. Dual brake equipment was added at overhaul in January 1972.

In its final year *Western Ranger* was notable for its superior external condition and red-backed nameplates, and waited until its last weeks in service for its most remarkable working – the 07.30 Swansea-Leeds service throughout, after a replacement loco was not available *en route*. No D1013 was one of a pair used on the final 'Western Tribute' railtour from Paddington to Plymouth and back on 26 February 1977 to complete 1,320,000 miles in traffic.

Privately purchased from store at Newton Abbot, it had a short spell on the Torbay Steam Railway from June of that year before tyre-turning at Cardiff and arrival on the Severn Valley Railway on 29 September 1978. The blue livery was replaced for a short time by desert sand, as first carried by pioneer No D1000 *Western Enterprise*, but it is now back in blue. No D1013 made its first appearance at a BR Open Day at Gloucester Horton Road on 17 September 1989. It visited Cambridge on 30 September 1990, the following week the Nene Valley Railway, and Laira on 17 September 1991.

Class 52 C-C No D1015 *Western Champion*

Built: BR Swindon, January
    1963
Number carried: D1015
First allocation: Cardiff Canton
Final allocation: Plymouth Laira
Withdrawn: 13 December 1976
Preserved: Old Oak Common

D1015 *Western Champion* at
Laira Open Day, 15 September
1991. *Howard Johnston*

No D1015 has proved by far the most daunting Class 52 'Western' restoration project because it was withdrawn for scrap and partly stripped at BREL Swindon for spares before preservation was even considered. Thus the Diesel Traction Group took on a locomotive that not only had slight collision damage, but also part-missing electrical wiring, and well-worn Maybach power units. However, the early 1990s should see it back in operational service on a preserved line.

No D1015 was put on the books of Cardiff Canton depot on 21 January 1963 after it had been used in the livery experiments that were occupying WR design teams at the time. *Western Champion* was uniquely outshopped in golden ochre livery, based on William Stroudley's 'Improved Engine Green' and copied directly from LB&SCR 'Terrier' 0-6-0T No 82 *Boxhill* (then preserved at the Museum of British Transport, Clapham), red buffer beams and apron, and black-backed nameplates. Publicity pictures show one nose-end carrying a peculiar T-shaped wrap-round yellow warning apron that was never carried in revenue service. The colours obviously did not please, and it was soon changed to maroon; it finished its days in standard blue.

No D1015 was moved on to Old Oak in March 1963, to Cardiff again in June and back to Old Oak in the September. Laira took responsibility in February 1964, a link that ended with transfer to Landore, Swansea, in November 1968, but was re-established with final allocation at Plymouth in October 1971. The locomotive's most famous working was with the empty stock of Sir Winston Churchill's funeral train from Handborough to London in January 1965.

Withdrawal came after a minor derailment at Castle Cary, after which it was towed to Swindon for disposal. After purchase, restoration started in the summer of 1977, and the loco was repainted in golden ochre for exhibition at Old Oak Common Depot Open Day on 15 September 1985. Laid up at Swindon since then with a cracked axle, heavy lifting gear was brought in on 31 March 1990 for the Territorial Army to replace the troublesome bogie with a spare loaned by the National Railway Museum. *Western Champion* then moved from Swindon to Old Oak on 30 November 1990 for the installation of two overhauled power units.

Class 52 C-C No D1023 *Western Fusilier*

Built: BR Swindon, September
 1963
Number carried: D1023
First allocation: Cardiff Canton
Final allocation: Plymouth Laira
Withdrawn: 28 February 1977
Preserved: Buckfast Steam
 Railway, Devon

After a repaint, nameless No
D1023 stands at Swindon Works
on 5 December 1980. *Howard
Johnston*

The National Railway Museum's own preserved 'Western' is particularly noteworthy in having been the last main-line locomotive to be given a major overhaul at Swindon Works; the most widely used in farewell excursions; and jointly the final diesel-hydraulic to be retired, ending the long Great Western tradition of motive power independence. Numerically the 47th 'Western' delivered to traffic from Swindon on 27 September 1963, its first paint style was maroon with half yellow warning panels. Its first allocation was Cardiff Canton, and it was a familiar sight on South Wales-Paddington expresses. Transferred to Landore in February 1965, it returned to Cardiff the following March, but within a month had migrated to Laira where it stayed for the rest of its career. It was in blue livery by the end of 1967, and hauled a Royal Train conveying the Duke of Edinburgh to Plymouth on 8 March 1968.

Despite the impending withdrawal of the class, No D1023 became prominent at the end of 1972 when it was allowed a final visit to Swindon for dual braking, a task which took a year to complete. It re-entered service on train 1A19, the 10.50 Penzance-Paddington, on

29 September 1973, and had a narrow escape from withdrawal after being derailed at Oxford on 29 January 1975 while in charge of the 14.05 Paddington-Birmingham.

By then a favoured locomotive, it found itself on many special duties. In its last year in traffic it was uniquely fitted with front-end marker lights in place of headcodes, and worked railtours to such far-flung outposts as York (20 November 1976), and Crewe and Chester (29 January 1977) prior to double-heading with No D1013 *Western Ranger* (qv) on the 'Western Tribute' railtour (Paddington-Swansea-Plymouth-Paddington) on the very last day of operation, 26 February. Its recorded mileage was 1,256,000.

After preservation and restoration to maroon livery, No D1023 was put on exhibition at the NRM, York, on 20 December 1977. It went back to Swindon Works for attention during 1982, has been on display at several depot open days, and was once a working exhibit on the Torbay & Dartmouth line. It left Devon on 10 May 1990 for display at the Swindon 'NRM on Tour' exhibition and paid a visit to Laira the following year.

Class 52 C-C No D1035 *Western Yeoman*

Built: BR Swindon, October
   1962
Numbers carried: (1) D1010
   Western Campaigner,
   (2) D1035 *Western Yeoman*
First allocation: Old Oak
   Common
Final allocation: Plymouth Laira
Withdrawn: 28 February 1977
Preserved: West Somerset
   Railway

A recent arrival at Merehead,
No D1010 (later No D1035) in
ex-BR condition. *Kevin Lane*

Foster Yeoman, the owner of this Class 52 'Western', chose to switch the identity of No D1010 *Western Campaigner* to masquerade as No D1035 *Western Yeoman*, which had been scrapped at Swindon a year before interest was generated. BR presented the loco to mark the type's association with stone traffic during its declining years.

As No D1010, one of the Swindon batch, the locomotive was new to Old Oak Common. It made few moves compared with the rest of the class: to Laira in January 1964, Landore in January 1968, and back to Laira from November 1968 after overhaul dual braking. In 24 years' service, covering some 1,300,000 miles, No D1010 recorded several 100 mph runs; on a 27 May 1974 railtour it covered Paddington-Penzance in 5 hours 25 minutes net with 15 coaches (560 tons gross).

No D1010 was the last 'Western' on a stone train out of Westbury, the 12.45 to Severn Tunnel Junction and 16.25 return empties, in February 1977. It worked a railtour from Paddington to Cardiff and Valleys branches to Aberdare, Treherbert and Merthyr Tydfil, and was standby loco to Nos D1013 and D1023 for the final 'Western' working, before being moved to safe store at Newton Abbot. It became a static exhibit at Merehead on 7 July 1977, when it acquired its new identity and a green livery which it also never carried in BR service.

Handed over to the Diesel & Electric Group on 17 May 1986, No D1035 was towed to Didcot by General Motors loco No 59001. It has required heavy repairs, but made its first run for over ten years, on one power unit, at Didcot on 27 May 1989.

On 5 May 1990 the locomotive was unveiled in desert sand livery as carried by the pioneer No D1000 *Western Enterprise* when new in 1961. It was by that time running on one overhauled power unit, but a spare, from No D1058 *Western Nobleman*, was acquired from a scrapyard near Wallingford. *Western Yeoman* was towed to Cardiff Canton depot by No 59001 on 15 December for tyre-turning prior to Christmas storage at Merehead and transfer in the New Year to the West Somerset Railway.

* For the record, the original No D1035 Western Yeoman was the first of the batch built at Crewe Works in July 1962, was withdrawn from Laira on 1 January 1975 with fire damage, and scrapped at Swindon in September 1976.

Class 52 C-C No D1041 *Western Prince*

Built: BR Crewe, October 1962
Number carried: D1041
First allocation: Old Oak
 Common
Final allocation: Plymouth Laira
Withdrawn: 22 February 1977
Preserved: East Lancashire
 Railway, Bury

No D1041 on a visit to the
Keighley & Worth Valley
Railway, at Oxenhope on
6 November 1988. *Gavin
Morrison*

After ten years in the shadows, No D1041 *Western Prince* has gained perhaps the highest profile of the seven preserved Class 52s in recent times. The last to remain in ex-BR condition, it was completely renovated at Crewe Works in 1988, and returned to its original all-over maroon livery with yellow front-end buffer-beam skirts. No D1041's survival at all is remarkable in itself, as it managed to see the end of diesel-hydraulic operation on the Western Region in 1977 despite seven years without a works overhaul (as its appalling external condition showed!). Its mileage of 1,384,000 was the second highest run up by a 'Western', only 8,000 less than the record set by now-scrapped No D1005 *Western Venturer*.

No D1041 was one of 44 Class 52s constructed at Crewe because of an overload of work at Swindon, and was outshopped in October 1962 for use out of Old Oak Common. It was dual braked in October 1969. Other allocations were Cardiff Canton (March 1963), Old Oak again (September 1963), Bristol Bath Road (January 1964), Landore (April 1968), and Laira from December 1968 until withdrawal. It was the last 'Western' on china clay traffic out of St Blazey on 15 February

1977, and its last recorded BR working was the 17.45 Plymouth-Penzance seven days later, when it failed with a defective dynostarter; it needed a tow back by Class 50 No 50026, and was promptly condemned.

Sold from store at Newton Abbot, D1041 was towed on 26 June 1978 by Class 31s Nos 31135+31165 with sister No D1048 (qv) to Swindon for repair. In June 1980 the locomotive was towed via Derby (to pick up Class 42 Warship No D832 *Onslaught*, qv) and on to Horwich Works behind No 31315 for the 16 August 1980 Open Day. After winter storage, No 40115 towed the hydraulics down the branch and into Bury Bolton Street station the following February. Exhibited at the BREL Crewe Open Day on 4 July 1987, and the subsequent Heritage Festival, D1041 was rolled out in maroon on 8 February the following year, when HM The Queen walked past it at Crewe on 4 July 1988.

No D1041's debut passenger run in preservation was at the Midland Railway Centre, Butterley, on 26 June 1988, after which it returned to Bury. It was displayed at Winchfield on the Southern Region on 24-25 September 1988.

Class 52 C-C No D1048 *Western Lady*

Built: BR Crewe, December
    1962
Number carried: D1048
First allocation: Cardiff Canton
Final allocation: Plymouth Laira
Withdrawn: 27 February 1977
Preserved: Bodmin & Wenford
    Railway, Cornwall

Minus cast plates, No D1048
Western Lady was at St Blazey
en route to Bodmin on 4 August
1988. *Ian Blackburn*

A ten-year exile in Yorkshire and Lancashire ended for No D1048 *Western Lady* on 13 July 1988 when it arrived back in the West Country for restoration to working order on the Bodmin Steam Railway. *En route*, its first resting place was Laira depot, from where it was withdrawn, work-weary, in the very last days of 'Western' operation on BR.

Another Crewe product, No D1048 was delivered in maroon livery, with small yellow warning panels, to Cardiff Canton in December 1962, but was loaned immediately to Bristol Bath Road for a couple of weeks. It was back in Cardiff in January 1963, to Newton Abbot in September 1964, and Laira in June 1965. It was dual braked in July 1970, and ran up a mileage of 1,368,000.

After use on some final railtours, when it became a favourite if only because of its exceedingly scruffy external condition, *Western Lady* was withdrawn and retired to store at Newton Abbot with the last Class 52 survivors in February 1977; after sale it was towed to Swindon on 26 June 1978 for attention. Moved to the North Yorkshire Moors Railway on 6 October 1978, D1048 was restored in the green livery, not previously carried by the locomotive, but worn by seven others of the class when new (Nos D1002-4/35-8). It hauled its inaugural train between Pickering and Goathland on 19 March 1979. However, financial difficulties involving the owner saw it sequestrated and moved to Horwich from 21 May 1980. It stayed there until 27 July 1983 when it was reported earmarked for the Plym Valley Railway; it was towed to Steamport, Southport, for safe-keeping.

The long spell in the North West ended in 1988. Towed to the West Country and to Laira by Class 37 No 37263, *Western Lady* moved on to St Blazey on 21 July for minor attention prior to a final transfer to the Bodmin & Wenford Railway base on 7 August. It moved under its own power for the first time in 12 years on 19 November 1989 after overhaul of the B engine. During 1991, work on returning the second power unit to operational condition was making good progress. The bodywork has been subjected to substantial effort, and a ballot of shareholders was to be staged to decide on the livery.

Class 52 C-C No D1062 *Western Courier*

Built: BR Crewe, May 1963
Number carried: D1062
First allocation: Old Oak
    Common
Final allocation: Plymouth Laira
Withdrawn: 23 August 1974
Preserved: Severn Valley
    Railway, Bridgnorth

No D1062 *Western Courier* (far right) with fellow Class 52s Nos D1015 and D1023 at Laira Open Day, 15 September 1991. *Howard Johnston*

Survival is rare for one of the first of a class to be withdrawn, but No D1062's demise in August 1974 was its good fortune. Although earmarked for major overhaul at Swindon Works, it became the centre of a major industrial dispute when the work was not authorised, and the newly formed Western Locomotive Association immediately declared its interest. The loco was reprieved from being cut up, and stored on the outside turntable where external restoration to maroon livery was carried out with WLA labour during 1976-77.

No D1062 covered 1,096,000 miles in BR service, arriving new from Crewe Works at Old Oak Common in May 1963. Other allocations were Cardiff Canton (June 1963), Landore (March 1964), Laira (April 1966), Landore (November 1968), and finally Laira (October 1971). It was dual braked in October 1968.

Western Courier left Swindon for the Torbay & Dartmouth Railway on 27 May 1977, arriving at Kingswear three days later. It made its working debut on 31 July on the 'Western Reunion' special over that line. It was moved to the Severn Valley Railway the following year and, after tyre-turning at Cardiff Canton depot, arrived on 29 September 1978. No D1062

broke the BR diesel ban in May 1980 to run in the cavalcade at the Liverpool & Manchester Railway 150th anniversary celebrations at Rainhill.

The locomotive is currently running with engines which previously saw service in locos Nos D1005 *Western Venturer* (withdrawn November 1976), and D1018 *Western Buccaneer* (withdrawn June 1973), the latter located recently powering a car-crushing plant in Jersey. Although built with one Voith-built and one North British-built transmission, it now has two sets of German-built Voith equipment. 1991 saw the society pondering a livery alteration by the addition of full yellow ends.

The 'Westerns' achieved high mileages in their careers, but suffered from a number of basic design faults which contributed to their eventual downfall. The Voith transmissions and steam-heat boilers were troublesome, while the poor positioning of electrical control gear increased the amount of time spent on maintenance. However, as more than one driver was heard to remark, if one engine failed, at least you could get home on the other!

Class 47 Co-Co No D1842

Built: BR Crewe, May 1965
Numbers carried: (1) D1842,
   (2) 47192
First allocation: Crewe
Final allocation: Crewe
Withdrawn: 18 May 1988
Preserved: Crewe Heritage
   Centre

A magnificent restoration job has been done on No D1842, seen here ex-Works at Crewe Open Day on 21 July 1990. Robin Stewart-Smith

At full fleet strength, the Class 47s, a development of the Sulzer-engined Class 45 and 46 'Peaks', with many similar components, totalled 510 (two more were scrapped early on with collision damage), although more modern construction concepts involved dispensing with the cumbersome bogies. Although Brush-designed, the sheer volume of construction dictated that assembly work was shared by Falcon Works, Loughborough, (310) and BR Crewe (202). Today considerably reduced in numbers, the Class 47s will be the backbone of InterCity and Railfreight services on non-electrified routes for perhaps the next ten years, and replacements are not yet even on the drawing-board.

No D1842, the first Class 47 to be preserved, was a second choice after Crewe Heritage Centre discovered that its first choice, a gift from the nearby BREL Works, would be too expensive a proposition to restore to running order. Restoration work had in fact started on this other Class 47, Brush-built No 47001 (D1521), when it was realised that power unit repairs would be too complex to achieve. The availability of recently withdrawn No 47192

was therefore seized upon, and this latter locomotive was in running order literally within a few months.

As it transpired, No D1842 was historically significant as the first of the second series of Class 47s constructed at Crewe from May 1965 onwards. In addition, the locomotive had the rare distinction within the class of being attached to Crewe diesel depot for its entire BR working life. The last general overhaul on No D1842 was completed at Crewe in January 1980, and withdrawal came on 18 May 1988 when it was decided to withdraw three surplus locomotives, 47159/89/92, rather than pay for repairs.

No D1842 made its preservation debut on the East Lancashire Railway on 28 September 1989, working the re-opening special for Irwell Vale station, north of Ramsbottom. It also attended the Keighley & Worth Valley Railway's diesel weekend in November 1989, worked trains on the Severn Valley Railway during 1990, and has visited a number of BR open days. When not on loan, No D1842 is normally be to be seen stabled at Crewe Heritage Centre.

Class 03 0-6-0 No D2022

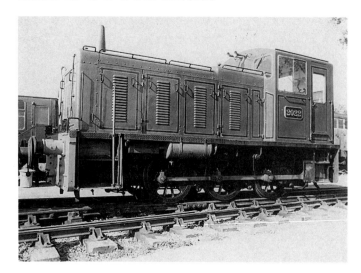

Built: BR Swindon, May 1958
Numbers carried: (1) D2022,
  (2) 03022
First allocation: Immingham
Final allocation: Gateshead
Withdrawn: 7 November 1982
Preserved: Swindon

Lined out in GWR livery with cast numberplates, No D2022 at Blunsdon in 1987. *Susan Sharman*

It is difficult to imagine now that BR's modernisation scheme for secondary freight yards included the construction of over 470 diesel-mechanical 0-6-0 shunters with 204hp Gardner engines. BR workshops at Swindon and Doncaster collaborated to build a total of 230 small shunters between 1957 and 1962, later designated Class 03, but it was quickly apparent that a substantial over-capacity existed as lines and yards closed under Beeching, or went over to containers and bulk traffic.

Although longer lived than most, even the favoured standard Class 03s began to fall by the wayside from 1968, and the earliest built were inevitably amongst the casualties. No D2022 is the oldest of around three dozen preserved examples, emerging from Swindon Works in May 1958. It was also the last to be allocated a steam-series number, 11209, but this was never carried.

Immingham took delivery, and No D2022 spent the next 23 years working in Lincolnshire, and as a Lincoln loco from May 1969, it was a common sight working traffic out of Boston Docks. Lack of work there saw No D2022 transferred to Darlington in September 1980, and as a Gateshead loco from April 1981 it was regularly seen as Newcastle station pilot.

No D2022 was given its first general overhaul at Doncaster Works from 4 April to 10 May 1963, followed by further generals at Doncaster from 5-29 May 1970, and 15 January to 28 March 1979. Despite its generally good condition, its lack of train air brakes restricted its versatility, and withdrawal was inevitable at the end of 1982. It departed south to Swindon on 7 January 1983 for breaking up, but happily this was not carried out before intervention by the nearby Swindon & Cricklade Railway, and the locomotive was moved to Blunsdon on 18 November of that year.

External restoration has been to lined BR Brunswick green, and false '2022' cast brass cabside plates have been fitted in the local Great Western tradition. Since 1988 it has been shunting the sidings of a Swindon industrial concern.

Class 03 0-6-0 No D2023

Built: BR Swindon, August 1958
Numbers carried: (1) D2023,
   (2) T & HA No 5, (3) KESR
   No 46
First allocation: Lincoln
Final allocation: Lincoln
Withdrawn: 4 July 1971
Preserved: Kent & East Sussex
   Railway, Tenterden

No D2023 at Grangetown,
3 August 1983. *A.J. Booth*

Although numerically following on from No D2022 mentioned on the previous page, the next two Class 03s off the production line were for the Civil Engineer's department at Cambridge (see No D2371), as Nos 91 and 92. Then came No D2023, which marked the first of a small batch sent to Lincolnshire to replace steam over that rural county's yards and dock branches. Apart from occasional visits to Doncaster Works for overhaul or major repair, the locomotive did not stray too far during its career, moving to Boston in October 1958, Colwick in January 1964, Immingham in December 1965, and back to Lincoln in May 1969.

No D2023 was declared surplus to requirements in July 1971, and sold in full working order to the Tees & Hartlepool Port Authority for use at Middlesbrough Docks. It became No 5 in the docks fleet, and also acquired a curious home-made stovepipe exhaust stack in place of the original inverted conical variety. No D2023 worked in the North East area until being rendered redundant for a second and final time in September 1980, when it was moved to nearby Grangetown for storage and disposal.

Brought to the attention of the Kent & East Sussex Railway, No D2023 was purchased along with another member of the class (see next page), and arrived with two other T & HA shunters to the security of the preserved line on 14 August 1983.

Restoration was expected to be complete during 1991 after a major overhaul which included extensive gearbox repairs. Originally given the number 46 in the KESR fleet, the later intention was to return it to BR green livery with its original number of No D2023.

Class 03 0-6-0 No D2024

Built: BR Swindon, August 1958
Numbers carried: (1) D2024,
    (2) T & HA No 4
First allocation: Lincoln
Final allocation: Lincoln
Withdrawn: 4 July 1971
Preserved: Kent & East Sussex
    Railway, Tenterden

Awaiting restoration, No D2024
stands at Rolvenden on 14
August 1991. *Philip Sutton*

Deliveries of Class 03s from the former GWR Swindon Works began with No D2000 in December 1957 and they then appeared at the rate of about four per month until the middle of the next year.

Wherever its sister No D2023 went, No D2024 seemed to follow, from the production line right through to preservation on the Kent & East Sussex Railway. Like No D2023, No D2024 was taken into stock at Lincoln, seven days later, but did not move from Lincoln until March 1959, going on to Colwick's books in June 1961, Immingham in December 1965, and Lincoln in May 1969. The rest of the story is familiar, and it is now stock number 47 on the Kent & East Sussex Railway, having arrived there by road on 4 September 1983.

No D2024 is basically in the same condition despite 22 years' use, vouching for the success of the original concept, which was victim only of the decline in the rail business it was intended to handle. The design was only a slight modification of the Drewry design which dated back to London & North Eastern Railway days, but with larger wheels, modified cab design, and a greater 300-gallon fuel capacity. The first handful, of which No D2023 was one, was built with the distinctive conical exhaust chimney at the front of the bonnet.

Restoration has always been regarded as a long-term renovation project, although considerable progress was being made by 1991, when extensive replating of the cab area had been undertaken to arrest corrosion.

Class 03 0-6-0 No 03027

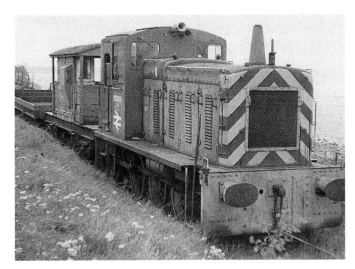

Built: BR Swindon, September
1958
Numbers carried: (1) D2027,
(2) 03027
First allocation: Lincoln
Final allocation: Colchester
Withdrawn: 30 January 1976
Preserved: South Yorkshire
Railway, Meadowhall, Sheffield

No 03027 at Queenborough
wharf, Kent, on 4 June 1979.
Brian Cuttell

By 1991 it seemed that every Class 03 shunter in industrial service was earmarked for preservation as soon as its owners declared their intention to cease use, and three of the five Class 03s delivered new from Swindon to Lincoln are now in safe hands (see also Nos D2023/4).

No 03027 is yet another shunting loco with an interesting history. Despite having been out of use for some time, it was not broken up like some other ex-BR 204hp shunters, but survived 15 years in the hands of a North Kent scrap metal merchant and locomotive dealer, who was also responsible for the export of many Class 03s to the parent company in Italy during the 1970s.

Following delivery No D2027 worked in the Lincoln area at Boston, Colwick and Immingham before a decline in traffic dictated transfer away from Lincoln to Stratford in December 1970 and on to Colchester the same month. Withdrawn in January 1976 along with ex-Lincoln sister No 03135, the pair were moved from store at Stratford six months later

to Hither Green for sale to P.Wood Shipbreakers of Queenborough, near Sheerness. Other acquisitions, Nos 03010 and 03153 from Thornaby, 03098 from Darlington, 03156 from Gateshead, and 03157 from Botanic Gardens, were exported to Italy for industrial use in the Trieste area. No 03135 was scrapped for spares, but No 03027 was retained as Queenborough yard pilot. It represented the last unpreserved Class 03 with the early style chimney resembling an inverted ice-cream cone.

Although in working order, No 03027 has seen little use in recent years. Its industrial owners had applied a new livery of lighter blue without number markings, and its new owners intend to restore it to post-1973 BR condition with TOPS number and 'barbed wire' BR logo. It became the third Class 03 to be moved to Meadowhall, but more were to follow, as revealed elsewhere in this book. The aim is to run them on the $3^1/_2$ miles of the old Great Central route between Meadowhall and Chapeltown, which survived as a freight branch until 1986.

Class 03 0-6-0 No D2041

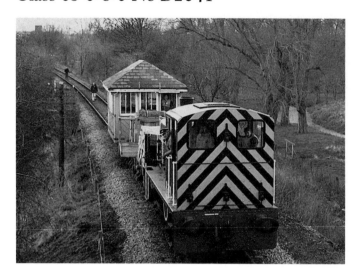

Built: BR Swindon, April 1959
Number carried: D2041
First allocation: Ipswich
Final allocation: Selhurst
Withdrawn: 1 February 1970
Preserved: Colne Valley Railway,
   Castle Hedingham

No D2041 hauling Wrabness
signal box into position, Colne
Valley Railway, 10 January
1987. *Paul Lemon*

Although inter-regional transfers of locomotives are now an everyday occurrence, they were relatively rare until the mid-1960s. Over-capacity on the Eastern and a proportionate shortfall south of the Thames saw several Class 03s moved away from May 1966 onwards, swapped with a smaller number of older Drewry Class 04s. Included in this deal were Ipswich's Nos D2040-3, which had been there since new from Swindon Works in 1959.

No D2041 found itself at Norwood Junction, was moved on to Guildford in September 1966, Eastleigh in July 1967, and to Selhurst in September 1968. It was withdrawn on 1 February 1970, and sold to the Central Electricity Generating Board for use at Richborough power station in Kent. That duty did not last long, as the CEGB moved it to Rye House power station next to the Liverpool Street-Cambridge main line near Hoddesden, Hertfordshire, in March 1971. It was also loaned to Barking between May 1971 and August 1974.

On its return to Rye House, No D2041 saw little use, and was sold to the Colne Valley Railway in January 1981. It was put into service within a few days of arrival, and has proved thoroughly reliable ever since, having now performed virtually all the railway's shunting operations for almost a decade. A full service was carried out over the winter of 1989/90.

No D2041 was readily identifiable from a distance from the CVR's other two Class 03s, Nos 03063 and D2184, by its white tyres, and the fact that it faced in the opposite direction!

Class 03 0-6-0 No D2059

Built: BR Doncaster, May 1959
Numbers carried: (1) D2059,
    (2) 03059
First allocation: Gateshead
Final allocation: Norwich
Withdrawn: 5 July 1987
Preserved: Isle of Wight Steam
    Railway, Havenstreet

D2059 in the Havenstreet depot
yard, 31 August 1989. *Howard
Johnston*

East Anglia's links with the small type of BR diesel-mechanical shunter date back to the early 1950s, when immediate advantages were seen in yards where venerable and inefficient Great Eastern steam tank locomotives held sway. But by the late 1980s, Ipswich and Norwich were the last outposts of 204hp Class 03s in South East England.

No D2059 started life at Gateshead depot in May 1959, and worked in the Newcastle area uneventfully for 25 years. It was dual braked during overhaul at Doncaster in the summer of 1968. Transferred to East Anglia, the 03s were employed on the tight curves and slender bridges leading to Ipswich Docks, a system which resisted total standardisation with the larger 350hp Class 08 0-6-0s until April 1978, when No 08661 was transferred from Swansea, and the trials were declared a success. The closure of Ipswich depot in 1968 saw maintenance responsibility for No D2059 transferred to Colchester, which in turn was downgraded from January 1987 in favour of Norwich, where 03s were popular for pilot, yard and trip workings around Thorpe station and the motive power depot; they were also outstationed at Yarmouth and Lowestoft.

Heavy overhauls on No D2059 were carried out between April-June 1975 and finally May 1983, prior to despatch to Colchester as replacement for a life-expired vacuum-brake-only Class 03. Delivery took place in April 1984, and it was not long before it received the unofficial name *Edward* on its nose-end, courtesy of local enthusiast Mark (Edward) Pyke who was a regular visitor to Ipswich maintenance point. The plate was retained beyond the end of its working life to 5 February 1988, and the nickname has stuck.

No D2059 rose to public recognition because it survived to the end of Class 03 operation in the area in 1987, and was even repainted in all-over green livery for the May 1988 Colchester Depot Open Day. The locomotive was purchased by the Isle of Wight Steam Railway in preparation for the eastwards extension of the line from Havenstreet to meet up with the BR Ryde-Shanklin line at Smallbrook Junction, and departed from Colchester depot by road on 13 October 1988. It became the third of the type on the island, as BR maintains No 03079 and No D2059's former Colchester stablemate No 03179 on the island for departmental duties.

Class 03 0-6-0 No 03062

Built: BR Doncaster, July 1959
Numbers carried: (1) D2062,
  (2) 03062
First allocation: Selby
Final allocation: Norwich
Withdrawn: (1) 15 June 1976,
  (2) December 1980
Preserved: Dean Forest Railway,
  Norchard

No 03062 at Lowestoft Central
on 29 September 1979. *Norman
Preedy*

The run-down of the Class 03 shunter fleet went through several phases, and the survival of No 03062 beyond the summer of 1976 is due to a shortage of serviceable stock at Norwich depot, a reprieve from condemnation, and a further working life of four years.

No 03062's 21-year career was spent entirely on the North Eastern and Eastern Regions, which relied on 204hp locomotives as main station and yard pilots longer than anywhere else on the system. Although nominally delivered new to Selby from Doncaster Works in 1959, No D2062 was in fact a member of the then large York stable of 204hp shunters, drifting off to Hull Botanic Gardens in February 1969, and Barrow Hill the same December.

Norwich became its new home in October 1970 as a superior replacement for some of the depot's less reliable 0-6-0s, and it soldiered on until 15 June 1976 when its vacuum-brake-only status made it an obvious condemnation candidate. It was, however, reprieved until October 1980 when, after two months in store, it was written off the books and towed to Swindon in February 1981 for breaking up.

The Dean Forest Railway recognised it as a bargain, and secured its purchase in May 1982. It arrived at Norchard on 30 September of that year, but has received little attention since then. Still in blue livery, it has been stored out of use south of Norchard station, attention having been devoted to the restoration of sister No D2119 (qv) instead.

Class 03 0-6-0 No 03063

Built: BR Doncaster, July 1959
Numbers carried: (1) D2063,
  (2) 03063
First allocation: York
Final allocation: Gateshead
Withdrawn: 26 November 1987
Preserved: Swanage Railway

No 03063, as Newcastle station
pilot, on 27 October 1984. *Philip
Sutton*

The arrival of ex-Tweedmouth yard pilot No 03063 on the Colne Valley Railway on 11 November 1988 took the line's Class 03 total to three, the highest working complement of any operational preservation centre until inevitably eclipsed by the efforts of South Yorkshire Railway members a year later.

Built at Doncaster Works in 1959 to the standard design, No D2063 spent its entire 28-year career working from depots associated with the former North Eastern Railway. It was a York station pilot and local yard shunter until June 1968, when it was moved to Bradford Hammerton Street. A visit to Doncaster Works for overhaul took place in April 1968, which also included the fitting of dual air and vacuum brake equipment and a repaint from green to corporate blue livery. It was sent back to York in April 1969, and given a further general overhaul in September-October 1974. The next move was to Hull Botanic Gardens in January 1976, but after another overhaul between July 1981 and January 1982, the locomotive was declared redundant again, moving with two others to Gateshead in August 1982 to replace the depot's vacuum-braked examples.

It is reported that No 03063 was often chosen for Berwick and Tweedmouth pilot duty, a 70-mile trek each way from Newcastle that involved complex diagramming to weave in and out of the paths of InterCity 125 High Speed Trains. No 03063 was, however, laid up during April 1987, and used as a source of spares to keep other 03s in traffic. Official withdrawal did not take place until the very last day of Class 03 operation at Gateshead.

With No 03371 (qv D2371) one of the last pair of Class 03s to be sold from Gateshead, No 03063 arrived at Castle Hedingham station yard by low-loader, and was successfully started within a few days. Some components were missing, mainly from the air system, but these were obtained and replaced to allow the loco to be commissioned on Colne Valley services on 8 April 1989. In contrast to Nos D2041 and D2184 (both qv), it retains blue livery, the five-figure TOPS numbering and the modern BR 'barbed wire' emblem for the present.

Class 03 0-6-0 No 03066

Built: BR Doncaster, August
   1959
Numbers carried: (1) D2066,
   (2) 03066
First allocation: York
Final allocation: Gateshead
Withdrawn: 8 January 1988
Preserved: South Yorkshire
   Railway, Meadowhall, Sheffield

No 03066 in Tyne Yard,
Newcastle, on 12 March 1978.
Norman Preedy

The change of circumstances at the former Lancashire & Yorkshire Railway Works at Horwich, Lancashire, gave the South Yorkshire Railway the opportunity to increase its Class 03 locomotive fleet even further early in 1991, the new arrival at Meadowhall on 6 April being Class 03 No 03066, demonstrating the final BR development of the design with dual air and vacuum brake equipment. It was one of the last handful in service on the Eastern Region, surviving as a pilot at Gateshead depot and Newcastle Central station until the beginning of 1988, and was only outlived by a couple of days by fellow preserved No 03078 (qv).

No 03066's BR career, although longer than most of the class, was relatively simple. The last of a quartet allocated from new to York, it was ex-works from Doncaster in August 1959. The only reallocation it experienced was that to Gateshead in July 1968 after fitting with dual brake equipment during general overhaul at Doncaster Works. It was renumbered from No D2066 to 03066 in February 1974. The loco's final general overhaul was completed at Doncaster in June 1982.

The sale of the former BREL Works foundry at Horwich to a private company in 1987 saw the firm looking for its own motive power, and two short-wheelbase dual braked Class 03 diesel-mechanicals were obvious choices, not least because of their excellent condition. With sister No 03094 (qv), No 03066 was delivered to its new owners over the weekend of 9-10 July 1988, allowing the hired BR Class 08 shunter No 08925 to be returned to Wigan Springs Branch depot.

Before long the new company in charge at Horwich, Parkfield Castings, had no further use for No 03066, and it was released for sale early in 1991.

Class 03 0-6-0 No 03069

Built: BR Doncaster, September
 1959
Numbers carried: (1) D2069,
 (2) 03069
First allocation: West Hartlepool
Final allocation: Gateshead
Withdrawn: 18 December 1983
Preserved at: Gloucestershire
 Warwickshire Railway,
 Toddington

Gateshead depot was home for
No 03069 on 30 November
1977. *Norman Preedy*

The locomotive which shunted countless others to their doom during its seven years as yard shunter at Vic Berry's scrapyard at Leicester was purchased for preservation on 1 August 1991, the Gloucestershire Warwickshire Railway being the successful bidders. The assets of the Berry company went under the auctioneer's hammer after the firm got into financial difficulty, and this included the Class 03 shunter, three industrial diesel locos, a number of other vehicles, many yards of track, and even an iron footbridge!

The Leicester site was very much the centre of attention from 1984 onwards when BR decided to halt all dismantling of withdrawn locomotives using its own manpower, and sell them instead to private contractors. The threat of the presence of poisonous asbestos meant only specialist contractors were allowed to tender for the work, and in the event Vic Berry landed almost all the work until 1990, when much of it was taken over by M.C.Metals operating from the site of the former St Rollox

Works at Glasgow. The need for a serviceable loco to shunt the stock which arrived at Leicester saw redundant dual braked Class 03 shunter No 03069 sent down from Gateshead depot during the first week of January 1984, it having been out of use at the Tyneside depot for some five weeks previously.

Until then, No 03069's career had been relatively unexciting. New from Doncaster Works in September 1959, it saw service at Thornaby (June 1960), Darlington (March 1965), Gateshead (January 1976), Darlington (October 1980), and finally back to Gateshead in April 1981. It had been renumbered from No D2069 in October 1973.

No 03069 is recorded as having had three general overhauls during its career, all at Doncaster Works. The dates were December 1967 to February 1968 (when it was repainted blue), August to October 1973, and June to October 1980. Its final visit there was between February and April 1982 for minor attention.

Class 03 0-6-0 No D2070

Built: BR Doncaster, October
    1959
Number carried: D2070
First allocation: West Hartlepool
Final allocation: Thornaby
Withdrawn: 28 November 1971
Preserved: South Yorkshire
    Railway, Meadowhall, Sheffield

No D2070 at Shipbreakers yard,
Queenborough, 23 September
1978. *Brian Cuttell*

Newly preserved Class 03 shunter No D2070 became the 16th ex-BR locomotive to arrive at Meadowhall, Sheffield, on 5 October 1990, also making it the 24th of the class to find security at a preservation centre. Its purchase reflected the continued interest in this type of locomotive, although the virtual non-existence of examples in the main-line fleet means that would-be purchasers have to resort to scouring the yards of generous industrial concerns.

P.Wood Shipbreakers of Queenborough, near Sheerness, Kent, maintained an interest in shunters with 204hp Gardner engines, and in the period 1972-77 exported no fewer than 12, Nos D2010/9/32/3/6/98, D2153/6/7/64, D2216 and D2432 for new careers at Italian steelworks. A number of others were retained for spares or domestic duties, of which Nos D2027 (qv) and

D2070 survived into 1990.

No D2070 was withdrawn in blue livery with 'double arrow' symbols, but too early to gain its rightful TOPS number 03070. It had led a quiet life on BR and only worked from two depots in the North East, West Hartlepool and Thornaby, before withdrawal in November 1971.

It was sold into industrial use the following year, and was in working order until the late 1980s when it was laid up and used as a source of spares. The loco lost its identity at an early stage, being given a repaint in a non-standard mid-blue scheme without cabside markings. The black and yellow chevrons were retained. Restoration plans include a repaint to BR livery as No D2070.

Class 03 0-6-0 No 03072

Built: BR Doncaster, October
  1959
Numbers carried: (1) D2072,
  (2) 03072
First allocation: Bradford
  Hammerton Street
Final allocation: Darlington
Withdrawn: 8 March 1981
Preserved: Lakeside &
  Haverthwaite Railway,
  Cumbria

Repainted in BR colours, No
03072 is seen at work on the
Lakeside Railway during 1990.
Nigel Harris

The Lakeside & Haverthwaite Railway has gone against the trend of modern traction preservation by not restoring its second 204hp Class 03 0-6-0 shunter back to its original BR green – it chose a fresh coat of BR blue instead.

No 03072 is also one of the least travelled members of the class — apart from visits to Doncaster Works for repair, it never strayed from the boundaries of the former North Eastern Region during its 22-year BR career.

Five 03s, Nos D2071-5, were delivered new to Bradford Hammerton Street depot at the end of 1959, and No D2072 moved on to Darlington in July 1968. As one of the later series, it was built with a cast-iron plant-pot-style exhaust stack on the bonnet, which is also reported to have had some value as extra ballast

weight; it was also part of the unconscious desire of early diesel designers to perpetuate the steam shape in their shunting machines.

No D2072 was renumbered No 03072 in February 1974, and received a full overhaul at Doncaster during the same September, involving an application of blue livery with yellow buffer-beams and connecting-rods. Although Darlington experienced a sizeable drop in locally generated freight traffic, No 03072 soldiered on there until withdrawal from BR operating stock in March 1981.

The locomotive was held in store for a further five months before being sold to the Cumbrian preservation centre as a partner for the already tried and successful sister loco No D2117 (qv).

Class 03 0-6-0 No 03073

**Built: BR Doncaster, November
1959**
**Numbers carried: (1) D2073,
(2) 03073**
**First allocation: Bradford
Hammerton Street**
**Final allocation: Birkenhead
North**
Withdrawn: 23 May 1989
**Preserved: Crewe Heritage
Centre**

No 03073 as Hull Paragon
station pilot on 29 June 1978.
Kevin Lane

After 42 years, Class 03 operation by BR on the mainland ended at the beginning of 1989 with the loss of regular work over the lightly laid Birkenhead Docks lines. The trio of surviving locos were withdrawn, including the spare loco, No 03073, which by then was sponsored by the Provincial Sector and normally stabled at Birkenhead North depot.

No 03073, in all ways a standard dual braked machine, was new to Bradford Hammerton Street depot in November 1959. It also saw service at Healey Mills (from July 1967), York (December 1968), Hull Botanic Gardens (May 1973), Gateshead (August 1982), and York (August 1982), before lack of work in the North East and a new set of duties on Merseyside saw it transferred across to Birkenhead Mollington Street in October 1985. Class 03s were required to minimise the wear on the Duke Street swing-bridge which provided access to the Spillers and Rank Hovis McDougall flour mills, across which passed a thriving traffic of grain in Polybulk wagons.

Mollington Street depot's closure on 24 November 1985 saw No 03073 nominally become the responsibility of Chester, but it was reallocated again in March 1986, this time to Birkenhead North electric depot.

The locomotive is recorded as having had two major overhauls at Doncaster Works. It was outshopped on 11 November 1968 after a four-week stay that also included dual braking and repainting from original green to blue livery. Its final general overhaul took place between October and December 1975. The loco had gained its five-figure TOPS number in March 1974.

For preservationists, the disposal of No 03073 after withdrawal followed the frustratingly slow pattern developed by BR from the mid-1980s. It was taken to Chester depot on 30 March 1990 for safekeeping, and was parked opposite the station for ten months before being acquired by Crewe Heritage Centre. The loco was duly towed to Basford Hall yard during January 1991, and it is now in the safe custody of Crewe's expanding railway museum.

Class 03 0-6-0 No D2078

Built: BR Doncaster, December
    1959
Numbers carried: (1) D2078,
    (2) 03078
First allocation: Thornaby
Final allocation: Gateshead
Withdrawn: 8 January 1988
Preserved: Tyne & Wear
    Museum, North Tyneside

No 03078 under repair at
Gateshead shed, 10 May 1986.
Philip Sutton

The locomotive credited with performing the final Class 03 station pilot duties at Newcastle Central station on 11 January 1988 has been preserved just a few miles away at the North East's latest museum of motive power. This last duty was undertaken three days after official withdrawal, following which the locomotive was moved under its own power to Gateshead depot and switched off without any apparent mechanical defects.

The last Class 03 built in the 1950s – it was new to Thornaby's allocation on Christmas Eve 1959 – No D2078 enjoyed a low-key existence. Its only allocations over the next 29 years were Darlington (March 1965), West Hartlepool (March 1966), back to Thornaby in September 1967, and finally to Gateshead from September 1968. It was dual braked at Doncaster Works in 1968, and received its last overhaul there in December 1983. It had been renumbered under the TOPS scheme in February 1974. Like many Class 03s used in main-line areas, No 03078 was often coupled to a match wagon to provide a longer wheelbase for operating track circuits when running light.

After acquisition by the Tyne & Wear Museum, No 03078 was moved from Gateshead depot to the expanding preservation centre and demonstration line at Middle Engine Lane, near Percy Main, on 11 May 1988.

Class 03 0-6-0 No 03084

Built: BR Doncaster, March
  1959
Numbers carried: (1) D2084,
  (2) 03084
First allocation: Ashford
Final allocation: Norwich
Withdrawn: 5 July 1987
Preserved: Not yet decided

No 03084 at Yarmouth Vauxhall
on 25 July 1971. *Norman Preedy*

As if to prove that anything is preservable, a virtually derelict Class 03 shunter that had been standing exposed to the elements for over four years was sold for restoration at the very end of 1991. The state of No 03084 after so long dumped in the old steam shed area at March, Cambridgeshire, left the new owners under no illusion of the task ahead of them. It did, however, beg the question why BR had allowed the loco, and sister No 03158, to stand so long when there was no shortage of potential buyers. Most removable parts will now need to be located and replaced.

As No D2084, the shunter was the second of a batch of three assembled numerically out of sequence at Doncaster for the Southern Region. Ashford was the first allocation for the 204 hp shunter in March 1959, and the loco moved to and fro between Ashford and Hither Green until May 1969 when it visited the works for overhaul and fitting with dual brakes, noticeable by the air cylinders installed on the front of the cab and the large box on the right-hand side of the footplate.

The loco was then transferred to Bournemouth to form a new fleet there for docks and Weymouth tramway duties. It moved back to Selhurst in South London, however, in December 1969, then Bournemouth again in September 1971. The disbanding of the shunter fleet there in October 1975 saw it transferred away with most of the others to East Anglia, and Norwich depot was the recipient in April 1984 for station pilot duties and work at the outstations of Yarmouth and Lowestoft. Previously given a general overhaul at Doncaster Works in March 1976, No 03084 was given a further general in October 1985, so many important components such as wheelsets should still be in generally good condition.

As will be noted elsewhere in this book, No 03084 was a victim of progress again in July 1984 when the entire Norwich Class 03 allocation was withdrawn. Interestingly, all but one has survived. When restored, it is the intention of the owners to repaint No 03084 into its final BR blue livery, although at the beginning of 1992 they were undecided as to where to take their new acquisition.

Class 03 0-6-0 No 03089

Built: BR Doncaster, May 1960
Numbers carried: (1) D2089,
    (2) 03089
First allocation: Bradford
    Hammerton Street
Final allocation: Norwich
Withdrawn: 26 November 1987
Preserved: Mangapps Farm,
    Burnham-on-Crouch

No 03089 during its final months
at York, on 19 March 1986.
Howard Johnston

The Class 03 stronghold at Norwich depot was broken in the spring of 1988 when eight of the nine locomotives allocated to Crown Point were withdrawn en masse. Their replacements were dual braked 350hp Class 08s, by then in plentiful enough supply to be transferred from other depots or from works overhauls. Curiously, however, while Nos 03059/84, 03112/58/79/97 and 03397/9 were parked up, a solitary Class 03, No 03089, was allowed to continue for another six months while the full 08 complement was made up. No 03089 was then in turn laid aside, and moved to March yard with the rest for storage.

New from Doncaster as No D2089 in May 1960, it worked from Bradford Hammerton Street continuously until May 1979, when York took control. In its later years, it was well known as Scarborough pilot, and is even credited with a late-night journey out towards Malton to rescue a failed passenger train because there was no other local motive power available; its 28 mph maximum speed must

have contributed considerably to the passengers' late arrival on the Yorkshire coast! No D2089's longevity was aided its dual brakes, fitted during its first general overhaul at Doncaster Works between June and August 1968. It later made further visits between May and August 1975, and January to April 1980. The final rebuild in August 1983 hardly seems justified considering the amount of work it was to do subsequently.

The closure of York motive power depot to main-line locomotives took place at the end of 1981, and to shunters in May 1983, and No 03089 went to nearby Clifton rolling-stock depot instead. This allocation also ended when the last two 03s were sent south to Norwich.

From storage in March No 03089 was moved to the Nene Valley Railway at Peterborough with sister Class 03 No 03112 (qv) on 2 September 1988, but was stabled within the British Sugar Corporation factory sidings close to the city centre. It moved to Essex at the end of 1991.

Class 03 0-6-0 No 03090

Built: BR Doncaster, May 1960
Numbers carried: (1) D2090,
    (2) 03090
First allocation: Bradford
    Hammerton Street
Final allocation: York
Withdrawn: 18 July 1976
Preserved: National Railway
    Museum, York

No 2090 at Bradford Hammerton
Street depot on 20 June 1970.
Norman Preedy

It was a very short trip indeed into preservation for this Class 03 shunter, which was actually allocated to York depot at the time of its withdrawal, and solved the National Railway Museum's domestic problem of needing a suitable loco to move its larger exhibits to and from the then newly opened roundhouse museum. If it was chosen on account of its mechanical condition and redundancy through inability to handle air-braked rolling-stock, No D2090 is one of the least notable Class 03s saved. The choice of a York example was probably based on convenience – the NRM can claim exhibits free from BR under the terms of the 1968 Transport Act, but it is obliged to pay transport costs to the museum.

New to Bradford Hammerton Street depot in May 1960, No D2090 was surrounded by DMUs until it moved to York in November 1972 for the second and most fortunate stage of its career. It was renumbered No 03090 in February 1974.

The loco is in full working order, and can normally be seen amongst the exhibits on the north side of the NRM. The intention is to keep it in final BR blue livery with yellow and black stripes.

Class 03 0-6-0 No 03094

Built: BR Doncaster, June 1960
Numbers carried: (1) D2094,
     (2) 03094
First allocation: York
Final allocation: Gateshead
Withdrawn: 8 January 1988
Preserved: South Yorkshire
     Railway, Meadowhall, Sheffield

No 03094 at Gateshead depot, 15
July 1979. *Norman Preedy*

This, the second of a pair of Class 03s maintained at Horwich Works foundry in Lancashire, swelled the lines of ex-BR shunting locos at the South Yorkshire Railway preservation site at Meadowhall on 6 April 1991. Like its older sister No 03066 (qv), No 03094 started life at York depot, and completed its career with BR at Gateshead.

The sheer size of York's responsibility is reflected in the decision to commit Doncaster's entire Class 03 production for five months — 14 locomotives – to boost the already sizeable fleet allocated to the depot; the first of this series, No D2094, arrived in June 1960, and a further 20 were to be required over the next two years. This particular loco moved on to Bradford Hammerton Street the following month, and to Gateshead, its final base, in July 1968.

No 03094 is recorded as having made three return visits to Doncaster Works. It was overhauled, dual braked and repainted from green to blue livery during August-September 1968. It arrived for a further general overhaul on 19 June 1975, being outshopped precisely eight weeks later on 19 August. A host of mechanical troubles saw the locomotive parked at the Works for six months from September 1978 to March 1979.

The progressive elimination of Class 03 power at Gateshead reached an advanced stage during 1987, and minor faults resulted in No 03094 being laid up towards the end of the year. These faults were, however, easily rectified in order for the loco to be re-sold to the owners of the former BREL Horwich Works with No 03066 (qv), and the pair were moved across the Pennines on 9 July 1988.

Class 03 0-6-0 No D2112

Built: BR Doncaster, December
  1960
Numbers carried: (1) D2112,
  (2) 03112
First allocation: York
Final allocation: Norwich
Withdrawn: 5 July 1987
Preserved: Nene Valley Railway,
  Peterborough

No 03112 as Berwick station
pilot, 24 August 1985. *Howard
Johnston*

Regular weekend travellers on the East Coast Main Line in the early 1980s will have seen No 03112 on many occasions parked at Berwick station, the northernmost outpost of the Gateshead 03 allocation. Its role was to shunt Tweedmouth yard, east of the line 1 mile south of the station. Other duties for dual braked 03s at the time were Newcastle station pilot, the Team Valley industrial estate off Low Fell Junction, Newcastle, and the Tyne & Wear freight depot on the east side of the Sunderland line.

A batch of four 03s, Nos D2110-3, were new to York at the end of 1960, but No D2112 left in August 1967 for Goole to replace a Hunslet-built Class 05. A general overhaul at Doncaster Works preceded its transfer to Leeds Neville Hill (November 1968), and Leeds Holbeck (October 1969). It moved on to Hull Botanic Gardens in February 1971. While undergoing a final general overhaul at Doncaster, the type was eliminated from South East Yorkshire, and its new base became York for a new role as Scarborough pilot.

Within days, however, D2112 was off to East Anglia. A belated transfer south to Norwich took place in March 1986, and the locomotive was amongst the Class 03 fleet withdrawn en masse there in 1987. Its last major works overhaul was at Doncaster in July 1982, and it made a late visit there at end of 1986 for attention to its gearbox.

Most of the Norwich fleet were towed to March depot for storage, where No 03112 was chosen for its sound condition by a private buyer from Lincolnshire who wanted to commemorate the class's work there over two decades. The loco arrived at Peterborough on 2 September 1988, but has had few outings on the Nene Valley line so far. Until the 1991 works closure, it was parked within the confines of the British Sugar Corporation site. It has been repainted back into green livery as a contrast to fellow preserved 03 No D2089 (qv 03089).

Class 03 0-6-0 No 03113

Built: BR Doncaster, December
    1960
Numbers carried: (1) D2113,
    (2) 03113
First allocation: York
Final allocation: York
Withdrawn: 3 August 1975
Preserved: Milford Haven
    Heritage & Maritime Museum

After restoration, No D2113
stands at Milford Haven in
October 1991. *Gulf Oil*

A Class 03 shunter which spent its entire 15-year BR career based at York shed has been preserved after a slightly longer spell of duty at the Gulf Oil refinery in the far south-western corner of Wales.

D2113 was the last of a batch of 20 204hp 0-6-0s assembled at Doncaster in the second half of 1960, all of which were commissioned at York before many were despatched to depots in the North East to complete the elimination of steam shunting locomotives. The next Doncaster loco was No D2395 in June 1961 for the London Midland Region, and further examples for the North Eastern were built at Swindon.

Gulf Oil acquired sister loco No D2046 (withdrawn from Thornaby in October 1971) second-hand from the Teesport refinery in May 1972, and purchased 03113 straight from BR four years later, surplus but in full working order. Based at Waterston refinery, it lost its BR identity for the Gulf Oil house colours of dark blue and orange with white bodyside lettering. Although No D2046 was still operational in

1991, No 03113 had been laid aside for a number of years as a source of engine spares, and was at one time considered for sale to a scrap merchant.

The emergence of the Milford Haven Heritage & Maritime Museum prompted the gift of No 03113 for display along with an oil tank wagon. A sizeable sum of money was allocated to allow a private contractor to undertake a comprehensive external restoration of the locomotive, although engine components were not replaced, and the side panels were secured to prevent danger to visitors while the loco is on static outside display on a specially laid short length of track at the museum.

The tank wagon was moved by BR free of charge via the refinery's spur to Johnston, and then down the main line into Milford Haven. The Class 03 was more a problem, requiring a road journey to the dockside site. A crane was then used to lift it into position. The official handing-over ceremony of No 03113 took place on 17 October 1991.

Class 03 0-6-0 No D2117

Built: BR Swindon, September
  1959
Numbers carried: (1) D2117,
  (2) L&HR No 8
First allocation: Swansea
  Danygraig
Final allocation: Wigan Springs
  Branch
Withdrawn: 9 October 1971
Preserved: Lakeside &
  Haverthwaite Railway,
  Cumbria

L&HR No 8, the former No
D2117, at Haverthwaite after a
repaint to crimson lake, 11 July
1990. *Nigel Harris*

Local industrial concerns expressed an interest in No D2117 when it was withdrawn from Wigan Springs Branch depot in October 1971 as merely surplus to operating requirements, but happily it was promised a more secure future on the southern edge of the Lake District.

Evidence of a shortage of worthwhile long-term work throughout its career is evidenced by a whole series of somewhat diverse transfers. Nos D2114-6 were allocated new to the Western Region, No D2117 to Swansea's Danygraig depot until closure in March 1964 saw it moved, on paper at least, to Landore. Nos D2117/8 were then towed across country to Barrow-in-Furness in April 1967 (the latter went into industrial service in Norfolk), followed by Workington (June 1967). No D2117 then moved on to Speke Junction,

Liverpool, in June 1968, Allerton in May 1969, and Birkenhead in January 1970.

No D2117 was out of use again at Wigan from May 1970, but was resurrected for a final five weeks' work from 1 September. Unlike many of its sisters, it was withdrawn too early to receive a TOPS number. After purchase, the L&HR arranged for it to be repainted in LMS-style maroon livery as the line's No 8 before being moved under its own power to Ulverston on 14 April 1972. Ten days later, a low-loader moved it to Haverthwaite, where it has seen regular passenger service deputising for steam, handling four coaches on the steeply graded line to Lakeside with comparative ease. As will be noted elsewhere, the railway was sufficiently pleased with its performance to acquire a second Class 03 loco, No 03072 (qv), in 1980.

Class 03 0-6-0 No D2119

Built: BR Swindon, September
  1959
Numbers carried: (1) D2119,
  (2) 03119
First allocation: Swansea
  Danygraig
Final allocation: Landore
Withdrawn: (1) 24 January
  1970, (2) 17 July 1985,
  (3) 21 February 1986
Preserved: Dean Forest Railway

The first step to preservation –
No 03119 at A.E.Knill's, Barry,
on 4 December 1986. *Mike Ware*

The severe height restriction on the Burry Port & Gwendraeth Valley Railway in South Wales has always necessitated exclusive use of specially modified locos, and until 1985 they were 204hp Class 03s with $4^1/2$ inches cut from the cab height. A total of 11 were converted over the years, but the value of maintaining a specialised fleet was always questionable because of the need to operate three in tandem on occasions. Eventually, withdrawal of the freight trip over the Central Wales Line to Llandovery and the opening of a new spur on the West Wales Line at Kidwelly direct from Coed Bach Washery contributed to the 03s' replacement by modified Class 08s.

Such was the anticipated level of traffic in the Swansea area in 1959 that 14 new Class 03s, Nos D2114-27, were despatched from Swindon Works. No D2119 moved on to Landore's books in March 1964, was loaned to Worcester in January 1966, Swindon in March 1966, Plymouth Laira in October 1967 and, after a spell in store from July 1969, was condemned in January of the following year.

Reinstated after a year-long overhaul and conversion to BP&GV loading gauge, it was sent back to Landore to work coal traffic. Granted another general overhaul at Swindon in September 1981, No 03119, as it had by then become, survived to the end of Class 03s in South Wales, being withdrawn at Landore on 17 July 1985. Although nominally restored to traffic in November, it did little if any work before being condemned for a third and final time on 21 February 1986.

It was then moved to A.E.Knill's scrapyard at Barry in November 1986 and sheeted over pending delivery to the Dean Forest Railway the following month. It was repainted green in early 1989.

Class 03 0-6-0 No 03120

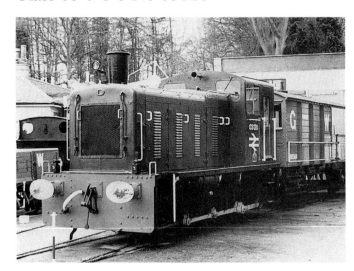

Built: BR Swindon, October
  1959
Numbers carried: (1) D2120,
  (2) 03120
First allocation: Swansea
  Danygraig
Final allocation: Landore
Withdrawn: (1) 17 July 1985,
  (2) 23 February 1986
Preserved: Fawley Hill, Henley-
  on-Thames

Restored to green livery,
No 03120 at Fawley Hill on
24 March 1990. *Nick Pigott*

The conversion of Class 08s to meet the restricted height of bridges on the former Burry Port & Gwendraeth Valley system in West Wales reduced Landore's Class 03 allocation to a mere three, Nos 03119/20/44, on strategic standby by the early part of 1986, and BR initially seemed reluctant to part with this final trio.

No D2120, new from Swindon towards the end of 1959, spent its entire working life in the Swansea area, broken only by trips to works for overhaul. It was one of these visits in 1972 that saw its cab reduced in height, and dual air/vacuum brake equipment installed. It was given its final general overhaul at Swindon in May 1983.

Duties were progressively reduced with the incessant closure of smaller South Wales mines throughout the 1980s, but even at the end of its career No 03120 could be seen hard at work, either alone or in tandem, in the yard on the east side of Pembury & Burry Port station, on trips over the Cwmmawr branch or to Carmarthen Bay power station, or up the Central Wales line from Llandeilo Junction to Llandovery. It was withdrawn in July 1985, but then reinstated for another six months' work.

When offered for sale, the successful bidder was *Flying Scotsman* owner Sir William 'Bill' McAlpine; the locomotive was destined for use at his private railway at Fawley Hill, near Henley-on-Thames. Since arrival in 1987, it has been repainted in all-over green livery.

Class 03 0-6-0 No D2134

Built: BR Swindon, February 1960
Numbers carried: (1) D2134, (2) 03134, (3) 6G2
First allocation: Newton Abbot
Final allocation: Bristol Bath Road
Withdrawn: 4 July 1976
To be preserved: South Yorkshire Railway, Meadowhall, Sheffield

Renumbered but still in green livery, No 03134 stands at Laira depot on 28 March 1975. *Norman Preedy*

One of the most unlikely Class 03s to be preserved at a British museum site, No D2134 is due to be repatriated from a museum in Belgium; it is also now a diesel-hydraulic. The sixth of the type to move to Meadowhall in mid-1991 and the 34th Class 03 to be preserved, No D2134 was acquired from the Maldegem Stoomcentrum near Bruges whence it had been moved with a sister Class 03 loco after their initial role as a Zeebrugge Harbour Board shunter ended with a decline in traffic.

Always a Western Region loco during its BR career, No D2134 started life allocated to Newton Abbot in February 1960, and was transferred to Bristol Barrow Road (December 1960), Bristol Bath Road (November 1964), Worcester (July 1965), Taunton (September 1966), Bristol Bath Road (June 1968), Laira (May 1969), and finally Bristol Bath Road again (June 1976). Its final workings would probably have been along the tight curves of the recently closed freight branch to Avonside Wharf until the restrictions were eased to allow the passage of BR Standard Class 08s.

Upon withdrawal in July 1976, it was stored at the depot for a few months before sale to Bird's of Long Marston, a scrap dealer who had discovered a small overseas market for workable locomotives. Along with fellow Bristol engine No 03128 (qv), it was exported the following year to Belgium. A peculiarity of both locomotives now is their possession of a replacement V&M power unit with hydraulic transmission, which has also involved some minor modifications to the external bodywork. Both locos subsequently moved to the steam museum at nearby Maldegem. No D2134 currently carries a livery of pale blue and white and Zeebrugge number 6G2, and the intention is for it to keep this paint style. Although the locomotive has suffered some minor vandalism and is not in working order, parts have been obtained to bring it back up to standard.

There is considerable interest in Class 03s working abroad, and we should therefore not rule out the return of further examples to Great Britain.

Class 03 0-6-0 No D2138

Built: BR Swindon, April 1960
Number carried: D2138
First allocation: Gloucester
    Horton Road
Final allocation: Swindon
Withdrawn: 18 May 1969
Preserved: Midland Railway
    Centre, Butterley

The rebuilding of No D2138 had
reached an advanced stage at
Butterley by September 1991.
Murray Brown

British Rail can hardly have got its money's worth from this particular Class 03 shunter, which ran for little more than nine years before withdrawal as surplus.

Built at Swindon as part of Lot No 441 (Nos D2131-42), No D2138 was turned out in the typical livery of the day with large cabside numbers. It was despatched to Gloucester, where it worked until August 1967 when Swindon depot took control. It was taken out of stock in serviceable condition, and was sold in May 1970 to the National Coal Board for use at Bestwood Colliery in the South Nottinghamshire area with No D2132, being moved to its new home via Birmingham the

following 23 October. Subsequently D2138 made occasional return trips to BR metals for attention at Toton depot.

No D2138 never lost its original BR green livery, cabside numbers or emblem, and a subsequent move to Pye Hill Colliery at Ironville made it an excellent preservation prospect for the nearby Midland Railway project, where it arrived in August 1985. The following seven years have been spent on a protracted overhaul of the Gardner 204hp power unit, which was removed for rebuilding, and at the end of 1991 was close to being refitted.

Class 03 0-6-0 No D2148

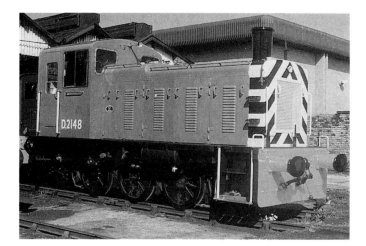

Built: BR Swindon, May 1960
Numbers carried: (1) D2148,
 (2) 03149
First allocation: York
Final allocation: Healey Mills
Withdrawn: 19 November 1972
Preserved: Steamport, Southport

Restored No D2148 at
Steamport, Southport, on 18
September 1988. M. *Hilbert*

The future of industrial locomotive No D2148 looked distinctly bleak in 1983 when it suffered severe cab collision damage in a shunting accident at Bowers Row coal disposal point during 1983. The solution was a complete replacement cab from Doncaster Works, where sister No 03149, coincidentally the next locomotive off the Swindon Works production line in 1960, was being broken up.

Delivered new with the York depot Class 03 complement in May 1960, No D2148 moved on to Percy Main, Newcastle, the following month, and Gateshead the month after. It moved on to Bradford Hammerton Street in February 1967, and finally Healey Mills

(Wakefield) in April 1967. Blue livery was applied after a works overhaul at Doncaster in January 1968.

The loco was declared surplus in November 1972, and travelled the short distance to the National Coal Board disposal point at Bowers Row, Astley, north-east of Wakefield, in August 1973. It was loaned to Gatewen disposal point near Wrexham from September to December of that year.

This hybrid machine is now a working exhibit at Steamport, Southport, where it arrived by road from Bowers Row on 14 March 1987. No D2148 has been repainted in its original colours.

Class 03 0-6-0 No D2152

Built: BR Swindon, June 1960
Numbers carried: (1) D2152,
  (2) 03152
First allocation: York
Final allocation: Landore
Withdrawn: 2 October 1983
Preserved: Swindon Heritage
  Museum

No 03152 at Gloucester Horton
Road depot, 20 May 1984.
Norman Preedy

The complex career of Class 03 shunter No D2152 went full circle early in 1988 when it arrived at Swindon Works, its birthplace 28 years earlier, to shunt exhibits around No 19 shop, the section of the old Great Western Railway complex earmarked for a new museum.

No D2152 was a curious choice for cut-down cab conversion for South Wales coal traffic in 1974, as it was an Eastern Region loco at the time! Along with fellow conversion candidate No D2151, it had started its working life in the environs of York. From there its working career took it to Bradford Hammerton Street within days of delivery, then Healey Mills in April 1967, Goole from April 1968, until that depot's closure in February 1973, then Hull, and finally to Swansea after a major overhaul in July 1974,

having been renumbered 03152 in May of that year. Reduction in coal traffic took its toll on the then least mechanically sound examples from 1983 onwards, No 03152 amongst them.

The locomotive has survived into preservation via storage on the Swindon Works scrapline, and provides an interesting comparison to unconverted Class 03 shunter No D2022 (qv), which is elsewhere in the town. Both were kept at the Swindon & Cricklade Railway at Blunsdon for a time, No 03152 having arrived there via Gloucester and Swindon on 6 March 1984.

An agreement with the Swindon Heritage Museum saw it transferred there in early 1989, since which time it has been repainted in all-over black livery.

Class 03 0-6-0 No 03158

Built: BR Swindon, August 1960
Numbers carried: (1) D2158,
    (2) 03158
First allocation: York
Final allocation: Norwich
Withdrawn: 5 July 1987
Preserved: Not yet decided

No 03158 during its final major
overhaul at Doncaster, 26 July
1981. *Norman Preedy*

The last BR-owned Class 03 shunter on the UK mainland was finally sold at the end of 1991 after four years in open store at Whitemoor yard, March. Even though it was in extremely poor condition after vandalism and removal of many parts, there was still no shortage of buyers. The successful bidders now have the task of a complex rebuild of a loco which was actually in full working order when Norwich disposed of its last 204 hp shunters in the summer of 1987.

No D2158, like several others in preservation, was assembled at Swindon Works, and dispatched to York depot in August 1960. It spent its entire career on the North Eastern and Eastern Regions, with transfers to Goole (August 1967), Bradford Hammerton Street (April 1968), Colchester (March 1970), Stratford (August 1970), Hull Botanic Gardens (February 1971), Colchester (July 1976), and finally Norwich (January 1984). It owed its long-term survival to a works overhaul in 1968

when it was one of 17 to be equipped with dual air/vacuum brakes.

The normal time between classified overhaul at works was approximately seven years, and No 03158, as it became under the TOPS renumbering scheme in March 1974, was last given major attention at Doncaster Works in September 1981, so was therefore nearing life expiry anyway when the decision was taken to replace the East Anglian Class 03s with Class 08 shunters transferred in from other areas.

No 03158 experienced considerable gearbox and final drive problems during its last couple of years, and made several lengthy trips to Doncaster for attention. When restored, its new owners intend to repaint the loco in BR blue livery, which it has carried since 1968. As yet they are undecided as to a home for their new acquisition, although there would be no shortage of takers for these now highly sought-after machines.

Class 03 0-6-0 No D2162

Built: BR Swindon, September
    1960
Numbers carried: (1) D2162,
    (2) 03162
First allocation: York
Final allocation: Birkenhead
    North
Withdrawn: 23 May 1989
Preserved: Llangollen Railway

No D2162 shunts Cavendish
sidings at Birkenhead Docks on
20 August 1987. *R.W.Cragg*

BR's long relationship with 204hp shunters ended on 9 March 1989 when the final three were laid up at Birkenhead North depot. They had experienced a loss of traffic over lightly laid docks lines, and there was no other worthwhile work available anywhere on the system.

The popular No D2162, which had re-acquired green livery and its pre-TOPS number of the time of withdrawal, was saved for preservation. Another, No 03170, was sold on to a Salford rail customer for continued use, albeit on private tracks.

No D2162's life of 28 years was exceptional for the class. New from Swindon Works to York in September 1960, it was employed in the North Eastern Region for a total of 17 years: it moved to Normanton (September 1960), then Percy Main (October 1960), Gateshead (October 1960), Leeds Holbeck (February 1967), and Bradford Hammerton Street (November 1972). General overhauls had been completed at Doncaster in December 1968 (when it was dual braked) and April 1975.

It was sent south to Colchester in January 1977 to increase the dual braked fleet there. The Eastern Region still had a widespread need for Class 03s, and No 03162, as it by then

become, was granted a third general overhaul at Doncaster Works before its next duties based at Lincoln from November 1982.

It moved on to Gateshead in February 1983, then the creation of a small fleet for Merseyside saw it selected for transfer to Birkenhead in March 1983. A nominal transfer later to Chester depot in November 1985 for three months was purely a paper transaction.

Although built with a 'flower-pot'-style exhaust stack, No D2162 acquired a non-standard stubby conical device some time during the mid-1980s. The green repaint was completed at Birkenhead North depot on 7 January 1987, together with the addition of the legend 'Birkenhead South 1879-1985' on its cabsides to commemorate the now closed Birkenhead Mollington Street (South) depot. All three 03 survivors were moved from Birkenhead to Chester on 30 March 1989 for safekeeping.

Now owned by Wirral Borough Council, No D2162 was moved to the Llangollen Railway in October 1989, and has seen frequent use on shunting work and the occasional passenger train to Berwyn, deputising for steam.

Class 03 0-6-0 No D2178

Built: BR Swindon, January
 1962
Number carried: D2178
First allocation: Ashford
Final allocation: Oxford
Withdrawn: 13 September 1969
Preserved: Caerphilly Railway
 Society

D2178 under wraps at
Caerphilly, 5 April 1991.
A.J. Booth

The Southern Region's allocation of small 0-6-0 diesel-mechanical shunters was completed with the delivery of the final six, Nos D2175-80, between December 1961 and February 1962, and a couple of them survived on the region as late as 1975. (One of them, No D2179, now No 03179, is one of the pair still in BR capital stock as shunters on the Isle of Wight.)

No D2178 only stayed a few days on the SR before being loaned to Plymouth Friary depot, and was transferred formally to nearby Laira depot in August 1962. It was eventually caught up in the massive Western Region fleet reductions of the late 1960s; stored from March 1969, it then led a precarious existence, based at Oxford and loaned to contractors for various line demolition projects until final condemnation the same September.

Newport firm A.R.Adams bought several locomotives from BR's stockpile, and acquired No D2178 in February 1970 for subsequent hire to various works, including Aberaman Colliery, a paper mill at Ely (Cardiff), and Powell Duffryn Fuels at Gwaun-cae-Gurwen.

No D2178 eventually passed permanently to National Smokeless Fuels for their plant at Coed Ely, Tonyrefail, Mid-Glamorgan, in mid-1974, and made one trip back to Swindon Works for overhaul in August 1979 to allow another five years' service before being donated to its present preservation home. It arrived at the Caerphilly Railway Society's headquarters on 12 November 1985, and little work was required to return it to operational service.

Class 03 0-6-0 No 03180

Built: BR Swindon, February
  1962
Numbers carried: (1) D2180,
  (2) 03180
First allocation: Hither Green
Final allocation: Norwich
Withdrawn: 31 March 1984
Preserved: South Yorkshire
  Railway, Meadowhall, Sheffield

No 03180 during its time as
Norwich station pilot, 25 July
1981. *Norman Preedy*

Although the Southern Region only ever had a relatively small number of 204 hp shunters on its books, a disproportionate number of them have been saved for preservation. The principal reason is their possession of dual air/vacuum brakes, which ensured their survival as replacements for other less versatile versions of the same design. No 03180 joined the South Yorkshire Railway collection at the beginning of 1992, and represented one of the most substantial renovation tasks because its previous owner, Mayer Parry of Snailwell, Newmarket, had largely dismantled it to obtain spares for its now sole operational Class 03 No 03020. No 03180 had given six years of good service at the Suffolk railway breaker's yard before mechanical failure forced its retirement.

No 03180's first allocation after construction at Swindon Works was Hither Green from 1 February 1962, and it moved to nearby Feltham marshalling yard in December of that year. The first substantial move was to Bournemouth in September 1974, and it was a regular sight on Weymouth tramway duties

before it was cleared for heavier locomotives. Its moved to Eastern territory (Stratford) took place in July 1975, and Colchester was its next port of call three months later, primarily to shunt at Ipswich docks. The run-down of the Colchester allocation in November 1982 saw it make one final move to Norwich.

BR has not surprisingly always had to be sympathetic to the requirements of its customers, and the need for more power at Mayer Parry (then Mayer Newman) saw No 03180, one of the most long-in-the-tooth 03s at Norwich, sold to the firm in January 1984. It took another two months for the paperwork authorising its condemnation to catch up!

No 03180 now incorporates some parts from sister No 03012, broken up for parts in about 1989-90. It had been hoped that this latter locomotive would be preserved as it was the oldest Class 03 then in existence in the UK, although No 03010 may still exist in Italy, whence it was exported in 1976. When renovated, it is intended to repaint No 03180 in final BR blue.

Class 03 0-6-0 No D2182

Built: BR Swindon, March 1962
Number carried: D2182
First allocation: Taunton
Final allocation: Worcester
Withdrawn: 11 May 1968
Preserved: Victoria Park,
     Leamington Spa

No D2182 at Victoria Park,
Leamington Spa, 4 October 1986.
Brian Cuttell

It seemed a pity at the time of its preservation that 18 years of rugged industrial use by No D2182 should be rewarded by a place in a children's playground where visitors often have little respect for industrial history. The locomotive was actually in full working order when it was taken to Leamington Spa's Victoria Park on 20 April 1986.

No D2182, outshopped from Swindon Works in 1962, was another example of waste of capital investment. It worked successively from Exeter, Swindon, Llanelli, Whitland and Landore depots before being laid up at Worcester in July 1967. Officially withdrawn the following May, it was offered for sale in working order to the then hungry industrial sector, keen to rid itself of steam traction.

Sold like No D2178 (qv) to A.R.Adams of Newport, No D2182 was loaned to Caerphilly Tar Works, then to the Sir Lindsay Parkinson plant at Glyn Neath in February 1969; it was later sold to that firm, then to the National Coal Board Opencast Executive's Gatewen disposal point near Wrexham.

Under NCB ownership, new homes beckoned at Shilo and Wentworth, South Yorkshire, in 1981-83, and finally Hugglescote, Leicestershire, at the end of 1983. Lack of any further work saw No D2182's acquisition by Leamington Council for display in Victoria Park. It was actually driven off the low-loader under its own power before being defuelled, stripped of cab fittings and window glass and made safe to be climbed upon. Wooden steps were provided on each side for easy access. The light green livery has recently been replaced by a darker shade, although still far from authentic, with crude numbering and a yellow BR symbol on the right-hand cabside only. No D2182 is standing up remarkably well to the elements and even after five years in the park was generally free of graffiti.

Class 03 0-6-0 No D2184

Built: BR Swindon, April 1962
Number carried: D2184
First allocation: Llanelli
Final allocation: Landore
Withdrawn: 28 December 1968
Preserved: Colne Valley Railway,
    Castle Hedingham

No D2184 at Southend coal
depot in June 1986. *Harry
Needle*

The 228th of 230 Class 03s off the BR production lines was No D2184, which emerged from Swindon Works in April 1962, two months before the very last. Part of Lot No 452, which also turned out to the last shunting locomotives assembled at Swindon for BR, Nos D2178-84 were inevitably the shortest-lived, as the WR found little use for them, and neither were they wanted by other regions. No D2184 itself operated from depots at Danygraig, Neath, Whitland, Landore, Worcester and Swindon.

Nos D2184-6 were sold off in 1968-69 to private industry (the other two have since been scrapped). No D2184 went to Southend coal concentration depot in August 1969, where it shunted in full view of Southend Victoria-London Liverpool Street commuters until it was declared redundant again in 1986.

This time there was considerable interest amongst preservationists in acquiring the loco, which ran without a single repaint during its working life. The successful purchaser was the Colne Valley Railway, who wanted a partner for sister Class 03 No D2041 (qv). The locomotive was moved to the Castle Hedingham site on 17 October, since when it has undergone renovation and reinstatement of the partly dismantled vacuum brake gear. It was available for use during the 1990 season, repainted in BR green livery, and often sees use on the line's popular weekend wine-and-dine trains, perhaps the only time you can regularly expect to see a Class 03 shunter in charge of Pullmans!

Class 03 0-6-0 No 03189

Built: BR Swindon, March 1961
Numbers carried: (1) D2189,
   (2) 03189
First allocation: Swindon
Final allocation: Chester
Withdrawn: 16 March 1986
Preserved: Steamport, Southport

In passenger use – No 03189 at
Barrow Hill Depot Open Day, 22
September 1974. *Norman Preedy*

Almost six years after it was withdrawn from traffic, Class 03 shunter No 03189 was rescued for preservation; the reason for its survival all this time was the slowness of the BR bureaucratic system. When condemned on 16 March 1986, it was the last vacuum-only shunter of its type still in use on the BR mainland.

No D2189 was completed at Swindon Works in March 1961 and first allocated to the steam depot nearby. Clearly surplus to the depot's requirements, it spent some time out of use before transfer to Derby in November of the same year for a month's work. Unusually for a Class 03, it was a works shunter at Crewe from December 1967 to August 1968 before being consigned to store for a second time at Crewe South steam shed. The surplus of small shunters at that time was demonstrated when the entire and relatively new D2181-95 series was withdrawn and either sold for scrap or for industrial use. No D2189 was the only exception, and after overhaul was sent on to Barrow Hill (Chesterfield) in December 1968, its home for the next 13 years.

It was renumbered 03189 in February 1974, and a further general overhaul was completed at Doncaster Works in July 1980. After a gap of

several years without 204 hp motive power, new traffic at Birkenhead Docks saw the transfer of a handful of redundant Eastern Region 03s to Mollington Street in October 1981. Responsibility was handed over in November 1985, but it made no difference to the loco's duties.

Withdrawn on 16 March 1986, it was at first reported as having been resold for industrial use, but it stayed on BR Merseyside metals for a further five months before being towed via Crewe, Bescot, Toton and March yards to Norwich, a journey that took nearly five weeks to complete. It arrived in East Anglia on 12 September as a possible deputy for other Class 03s there, either in the works or under repair, but in the event was not repaired or used.

The withdrawal of the entire Norwich dual-braked ensemble took place the following summer, and they were eventually towed away to Whitemoor yard, March, for storage prior to disposal. No 03189 went with them, and although some found new homes quickly, it was not until December 1991 that a buyer came forward to remove No 03189 – back the North West from whence it had come!

Class 03 0-6-0 No D2192

Built: BR Swindon, May 1961
Numbers carried: (1) D2192,
  (2) DVR No 2
First allocation: Swindon
Final allocation: Swindon
Withdrawn: 25 January 1969
Preserved: Dart Valley Railway,
  Buckfastleigh

No D2192 at Buckfastleigh,
21 June 1990. *Steve Worrall*

The fledgling Dart Valley Railway was the first preservation scheme to recognise the value of an ex-BR 204hp shunter as a useful alternative to historic steam traction: cheaper to use for domestic yard duties, capable of handling a 'main-line' service at a push, and more acceptable to enthusiasts than a machine with a purely industrial background.

Despite is high position in the Class 03 number series, No D2192 was not one of the final batch, but was delivered from Swindon Works in May 1961 to the nearby Swindon depot. Apart from a two-month spell at Danygraig, Swansea, from August to October of that year, it spent the rest of its career at Swindon. The locomotive's main claim to notoriety is its short BR career – just $7^{1}/_{2}$ years before the Western Region admitted it was overstocked and made drastic cuts in its small shunter fleet. It was stored for the whole of October 1968, returned to work in November, but was withdrawn the following January.

No D2192 spent a long period in store prior to being sold to the DVR, arriving at Buckfastleigh in August 1970. It currently works on the Torbay & Dartmouth Line, based at Paignton. At first painted black as the line's No 2, it was named *Ardent* by Thomas the Tank Engine children's book author the Rev Wilbert Awdry in July 1982. It has recently undergone major engine repairs, re-entering service at Paignton at Easter 1990.

Class 03 0-6-0 No 03196

Built: BR Swindon, June 1961
Numbers carried: (1) D2196,
    (2) 03196
First allocation: Swindon
Final allocation: Birkenhead
    Mollington Street
Withdrawn: 15 June 1983
Preserved: Steamtown, Carnforth

No 03196 shunts grain wagons at
Birkenhead Docks on 7 April
1982. *R.W.Cragg*

No 03196 can claim to have worked on no fewer than four regions during its 22-year BR career – Western, Southern, Eastern and Midland. Its withdrawal in June 1983 was somewhat of a surprise because dual braked Class 03s had hitherto been generally exempt from the continued run-down of the class, and were still being given major works overhauls. It was, however, for a reason – this particular example was offered to a Carnforth industrial operator, Boddy's, for shunting their yard next to the West Coast Main Line. It retained the final BR blue livery for its eight years in private ownership before moving to Steamtown early in 1991.

No D2196, new from Swindon Works in June 1961, represented still more shunting over-capacity for the Western Region. It worked from Gloucester Horton Road depot from November 1963 until consigned to store in August 1967. Its transfer to Selhurst on the Southern Region in December 1967 was a stroke of good fortune, because within another six months large numbers of contemporary surplus 03s were to be sold for scrap. A visit to works in 1968 saw it dual braked, and allocation to Bournemouth in June would see it used regularly on boat trains over the Weymouth tramway. The decision to use main-line locomotives over the tramway saw No 03196 redundant again in October 1975, and it was moved to Colchester along with other dual braked 03s to displace vacuum-only examples as Ipswich station and yard pilots, as well as working over the weight-restricted docks branch.

New requirements in Birkenhead Docks saw No 03196 reallocated to Birkenhead Mollington Street in November 1981. Along with sisters Nos 03170/89, it took over shunting operations, previously conducted by a privately-owned fleet of 0-4-0 and 0-6-0 diesels based at Bidston Ore Dock and Duke Street Wharf, after the firm ceased trading.

No 03196 was exhibited at the BR Northwich Depot Open Day on 7 March 1982, and was unusually given two names, *Joyce* on one bodyside and *Glynis* on the other, to honour two 8E Association members, Joyce Southworth and Glynis Coulter.

Boddy's were on the lookout for a replacement locomotive when their veteran 1951 Hudswell Clarke 0-6-0 diesel mechanical shunter (now at Keighley) suffered a serious failure, so No 03196 made a final BR journey to Carnforth under its own power on 13 June 1983 and was officially withdrawn two days later.

Class 03 0-6-0 No 03197

Built: BR Swindon, June 1961
Numbers carried: (1) D2197,
    (2) 03197
First allocation: Swindon
Final allocation: Norwich
Withdrawn: (1) 12 January
    1986, (2) 5 July 1987
Preserved: South Yorkshire
    Railway, Meadowhall, Sheffield

No 03197 at Norwich depot,
25 July 1981. *Norman Preedy*

This Swindon-built product stood idle on BR at the unlikely location of Leicester depot for three years before being secured for preservation in July 1991.

No D2197's career was distinctly varied. New to Western Region stock from Swindon Works on 15 June 1961, it was soon allocated to Laira, Plymouth, as a steam replacement, and moved to Taunton in May 1967. Although only six years old, a lack of work saw it consigned to store within three months, to be returned to use back at Laira in the November. It was back in store by January 1968 but the search for useful employment was successful and No D2197 was transferred to the Southern Region in January 1968 for a month's planned work at the once vast marshalling yard at Feltham in West London.

The next month it was off to Bournemouth, where it joined a small pool whose duties included passenger workings over the Weymouth tramway; it was equipped with a warning bell for this purpose. Eastleigh took responsibility for the 03s from October 1968, and Bournemouth again from March 1969, when No D2197 had just emerged from a general overhaul at Swindon Works, during which it received dual brakes and a repaint in corporate BR blue livery. A curious reported reallocation was to Slade Green in March 1974.

Class 03s were almost all concentrated on Eastern Region depots during the mid-1970s, and No 03197 became part of the Norwich fleet from October 1975. It was granted a final general overhaul at Doncaster Works in the summer of 1977, and was ex-works on 20 September. While in East Anglia, its duties would have included pilot duty at Norwich depot, Yarmouth and the yard at Lowestoft.

No 03197 was officially withdrawn on 6 December 1985, but continued to work for another five weeks. It was then reprieved, and was back in use in March 1986, surviving until the end of Class 03 operation from the depot in the following summer, displaced by a plentiful supply of dual-braked Class 08s after track improvements allowed the use of heavier locomotives. It was moved to BR Leicester depot as a source of spares, and moved to Sheffield in November 1991. It needs engine repairs, and will retain its 03197 number.

Class 03 0-6-0 No D2199

Built: BR Swindon, July 1961
Numbers carried: (1) D2199,
   (2) No 1
First allocation: Speke Junction
Final allocation: Barrow-in-
   Furness
Withdrawn: 8 June 1972
Preserved: South Yorkshire
   Railway, Meadowhall, Sheffield

Before preservation, No D2199
at the NCB's Houghton Main
Colliery, 10 August 1980. *Brian
Cuttell*

National Coal Board Class 03 shunter No D2199 was a victim of the 1985 miners' strike, losing its employment after the closure of Royston Drift Mine in South Yorkshire. Fortunately, interest from the preservation movement in Class 03s was reaching the level whereby sale for restoration as a working museum exhibit was little more than a formality.

Numerically the 200th Class 03, it was not the 200th built, as batches were built out of order. No D2199 was used briefly on the Western Region in July 1961 when new before finding a permanent base at Speke Junction, Liverpool. Reallocations took place to Birkenhead Mollington Street (December 1966), Wigan Springs Branch (March 1970), and Barrow-in-Furness (October 1971) for a final eight months before being declared surplus. It had at least one works visit, being noted at Derby in August 1967 undergoing repairs.

No D2199 was towed to Doncaster Works the following year for overhaul prior to sale to the National Coal Board for use at Rockingham Colliery, Birdwell, near Barnsley, from February 1974. It was painted black and given a simple No 1 on its cabsides. It moved on to North Gawber and Royston Drift Mine (August 1980), but further redundancy and an attack of minor vandalism saw it removed to Monckton Machinery Stores for safekeeping and eventual sale.

No D2199 subsequently joined the growing collection of ex-BR shunters at Attercliffe, Sheffield, arriving by road on 12 August 1987. It was successfully started three days later after several years of inactivity. External restoration will be to BR green livery, and the locomotive will see use again under the aegis of the South Yorkshire Railway Preservation Society, which has the aim of running services over $3^{1}/_{2}$ miles of former Great Central Railway route from Meadowhall in the Don Valley to Chapeltown Park, which was closed to passengers in 1953, but retained to serve Smithywood Colliery and coking plant until 1986.

Class 04 0-6-0 No D2203

Built: Vulcan Foundry, June
   1952
Number carried: (1) 11103,
   (2) D2203
First allocation: March
Final allocation: Crewe Works
Withdrawn: 16 December 1967
Preserved: Yorkshire Dales
   Railway, Embsay

Flashback to 23 May 1956 –
No 11103 in the cattle dock at
Yarmouth Vauxhall station.
Bill Ashcroft

The oldest 204hp Gardner-engined locomotive in preservation is No D2203, which is close to celebrating its 40th birthday. It is also the only surviving example of motive power from the long-closed Wisbech & Upwell Tramway, being officially allocated to nearby March for the purpose, and equipped with side valances for working through public streets.

Industry had just started to gear up to the benefits of the small diesel shunter when BR got in on the act from 1952, ordering large quantities from private contractors while it simultaneously developed capacity within its own workshops at Swindon and Doncaster. The first delivery was No 11100 from Robert Stephenson & Hawthorn, taken into stock at Ipswich on 1 May 1952. This loco later became No D2200 when the separate number scheme was developed away from the steam series; no Class 04 survived long enough to get an 04xxx TOPS five-digit number.

No D2203 had a moderately more interesting life than the rest of the early series. It only stayed at March for two months before heading off for Yarmouth Vauxhall in August 1952, moving to nearby South Town depot in January 1959, Norwich in February 1960, and then, remarkably, Hereford in August 1964. A general surplus there saw it transferred to the Crewe Works domestic fleet from 9 September 1966, until withdrawal in December of the following year.

No D2203 was bought by the Hemel Hempstead Concrete Co, who took delivery in March of the following year. It worked until rail operations at the firm ceased in 1979, and was then acquired by the Welland Valley Revival Group. Resold to the Yorkshire Dales Railway in the summer of 1982, it has been restored to full working order and is a valuable member of the line's motive power fleet.

Class 04 0-6-0 No 11106

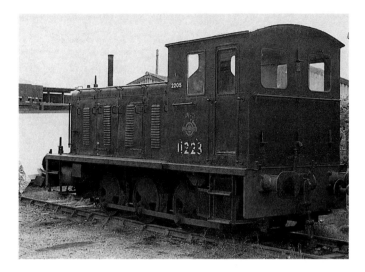

Built: Robert Stephenson &
  Hawthorn, March 1953
Numbers carried: (1) 11106,
  (2) D2205, (3) T & HA
  No 4, (4) T & HA No 6
First allocation: West Hartlepool
Final allocation: Thornaby
Withdrawn: 7 July 1969
Preserved: West Somerset
  Railway, Dunster

Soon after transfer from the
K&ESR, No 11106 is seen at
Williton on 13 June 1990, in the
guise of No 11223. *Steve Worrall*

Design-wise, the first 12 30-ton 25 mph Drewry Class 04s appeared rather crude by comparison with subsequent members of the class and the BR-built versions, which continued to feature minor refinements throughout the 11-year production period. Even by No 11106, the seventh of the class, the small square windows in the cab front had given way to much larger versions of a distinctive angular design. However, the buffer-beams were still relatively lightweight, and the exhaust was emitted through a simple stovepipe chimney on the nose-end.

No 11106 started life in all-over black livery at West Hartlepool in March 1953, the second Class 04 to be allocated to the North Eastern Region. It stayed in the locality for 14 years before its one and only move under BR ownership to Thornaby as No D2205 in September 1967. It lasted but another two years

before purchase by the Tees & Hartlepool Port Authority with sister No D2243 (written off in a collision in 1972) for shunting at Middlesbrough Docks. No D2205 ended its career in all-over yellow livery embossed with red.

Like the later-design Class 03s Nos D2023/4 (both qv), it became redundant when the docks closed down in September 1980, and was moved to Grangetown for storage before sale to the Kent & East Sussex Railway, where, after restoration in 1986, it was given the false number 11223 (later No D2253) to commemorate a sister loco which hauled the last KESR goods train on 10 June 1961. Since transferred to the West Somerset Railway, No 11106's new base is intended to be the renovated goods shed at Dunster, where a new permanent way depot is being established.

Class 04 0-6-0 No D2207

Built: Vulcan Foundry, February 1953
Numbers carried: (1) 11108, (2) D2207
First allocation: Parkeston
Final allocation: Crewe Works
Withdrawn: 16 December 1967
Preserved: North Yorkshire Moors Railway, Grosmont

No D2207 at New Bridge, Pickering, on 5 October 1991. *Colin Tyson*

Usually the resident shunter at the southern end of the North Yorkshire Moors Railway at Pickering, veteran 204hp Drewry Class 04 0-6-0 diesel-mechanical shunter No D2207 has been a vital part of the motive power fleet for over 15 years. It has even been known to venture down the line on the occasional light passenger train. The high standard of external restoration is also inspiration for other groups who may only just be starting down the road of renovating an ex-BR industrial.

Once the shine of newness had worn off, the unlined all-over black livery of No 11108 must have been a particularly drab sight at the embryonic Parkeston Quay yards back in 1953, when only the steam shunting locomotive appeared to be under threat from the internal combustion engine.

No 11108 transferred its allegiance from Great Eastern to Great Northern haunts in September 1954 with a new home at King's Cross Top Shed, but by November 1955 it was on the move again, this time to Immingham as

a start to the depot's long association with Gardner 204hp locos.

Renumbering to a more conventional No D2207 also took place there. Eight years were to elapse before it moved again, this time to Colwick in Nottinghamshire; by early 1967 it had moved to March. The writing was already on the wall by the time it was despatched to Newton Heath, Manchester, in September 1966, and the end came little over a year later after a spell as Crewe Works shunter.

No D2207's generally good condition attracted purchase in February 1968 by concrete firm CAEC Howard Limited of Hemel Hempstead, Hertfordshire, which employed it for five years of shunting before agreeing to its acquisition for preservation.

D2207's life on the North Yorkshire Moors Railway has been varied. It had a spell restored to its original unlined black livery as No 11108, but has more recently been in mid-1960s Brunswick green with nose and cab-end 'wasp' stripes. It often ventures out on diesel days.

Class 04 0-6-0 No D2229

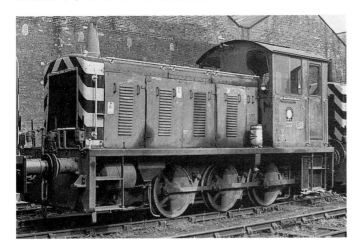

Built: BR Darlington, November
    1955
Numbers carried: (1) 11135,
    (2) D2229
First allocation: Stratford
Final allocation: Gateshead
Withdrawn: 7 December 1969
Preserved: South Yorkshire
    Railway, Meadowhall, Sheffield

No D2229 a few days after its
arrival at Meadowhall from
British Coal's Manton Colliery.
Brian Cuttell

No D2229 was the last ex-BR locomotive in service with British Coal, and the last in the South Yorkshire coalfield, when it was retired for preservation in May 1990. It was also the 14th ex-BR locomotive to be acquired for the South Yorkshire Railway. Over a 20-year period, British Coal purchased 89 diesel shunters from BR, a decision which did untold damage to home locomotive builders, but eventually provided much valuable and popular motive power for preservation.

No 11135 was ex-works in November 1955, the last of a batch of nine Class 04s delivered to Stratford depot in East London. They were soon widely redistributed, and No D2229 (it was renumbered thus in October 1960) was reallocated to three depots in the same month, September 1963 – Norwich, Ipswich and March.

A shift-round of East Anglian shunters in July 1968 saw several 04s despatched to the North East, including No D2229 to Gateshead depot. It was a short-lived move, however, as withdrawal followed little over a year later. No D2229 was surplus in December 1969, but was earmarked for resale to the National Coal Board for work at Brookhouse Colliery, Beighton, near Sheffield. It was consigned thence from store at Thornaby depot in August 1970.

Further moves over the years were to Orgreave Colliery the following year, Brookhouse Colliery in 1972, back to Orgreave in 1973, and then again to Brookhouse in 1974. The locomotive worked at Manton from March 1983 onwards, and had been eyed by enthusiasts for six years before it was finally made redundant by the commissioning of rapid-loading facilities at British Coal's Manton Colliery during August 1989.

The intention is to restore No D2229 to its original condition with black livery and five-figure number 11135.

Class 04 0-6-0 No D2245

Built: Robert Stephenson &
   Hawthorn, November 1956
Numbers carried: (1) 11215,
   (2) D2245, (3) DVR No 2
First allocation: Neville Hill
Final allocation: Goole
Withdrawn: 28 December 1968
Preserved: Battlefield Line,
   Shackerstone, Leics

No D2245 as Derwent Valley
Railway No 2 at Layerthorpe on
25 February 1970. *John
Meredith*

Dieselisation of North Eastern railway yards was gathering pace by the time No 11215 arrived at Neville Hill, Leeds, from Darlington's RSH works. It was a somewhat refined version of the Drewry Car Co 0-6-0 diesel-mechanical shunter with the familiar Gardner 8L3 engine and Wilson-Drewry five-speed mechanical gearbox and transmission. By this time the cabside windows had virtually doubled in size, much stouter buffer-beams had been provided, and the front-end modified with an inverted 'ice-cream cone' exhaust.

Renumbered No D2245 into the diesel-only series in February 1959, the loco was transferred to Selby that June, and came to York in July for a stint of eight years before 16 final months at Goole. Preservation came by way of the Derwent Valley Railway, a private freight line

east of York which had been hiring 204hp shunters from BR since 1961. In May 1969 it decided to buy its own, and No D2245 thus became No 2, and sister No D2298 (qv) No 1.

Although many energetic attempts were made to keep the DVR alive, falling traffic receipts caused by road competition meant that the 15-mile line to Selby had been trimmed back to 9 miles by 1965, and just 4 by February 1973. Even steam excursions failed to generate a profit, and the entire system was abandoned in 1978, when No D2245 was moved to Shackerstone, then a 3-mile section of LNW & Midland joint line with ambitions to extend to the Leicestershire site of the Battle of Bosworth Field. The locomotive has been repainted in all-over early BR black livery.

Class 04 0-6-0 No D2271

Built: Robert Stephenson &
    Hawthorn, March 1958
Number carried: D2271
First allocation: Stourton, Leeds
Final allocation: Bradford
    Hammerton Street
Withdrawn: 26 October 1969
Preserved: West Somerset
    Railway

Actively demonstrating its
Gardner allegiance, repainted No
D2271 at Minehead on 14 June
1990. *Steve Worrall*

This West Somerset Railway Class 04 shunter has carried Midland Railway crimson lake and LNER garter blue liveries before settling for an equally distinctive lined dark blue scheme in November 1987 after its spell out of traffic for power unit and gearbox repairs.

No D2271 represents the intermediate variation of the Class 04, where the wheel diameter of 3 ft 3 in of the first series had been increased to 3 ft 6 in for Nos D2215-73. It was delivered new to Stourton in March 1958, and did not stray from the Leeds/Bradford area during its entire 11-year BR career, taking in Holbeck, Royston and Bradford Hammerton Street before being put into store there in October 1969 as surplus to requirements, and ready for sale to a private concern.

The first ex-BR post-Modernisation Plan capital stock locomotive to be sold into preservation, No D2271 was acquired from scrapyard owner C.F.Booth of Rotherham, who used it to shunt condemned stock until May 1970. It was first based at the Midland Railway Centre at Butterley before transfer to Somerset on 15 May 1982, to share the base of the Diesel & Electric Preservation Group at Williton. It has often been used as Minehead station pilot, as well as enjoying the occasional outing on passenger trains organised for enthusiasts. Early 1991 saw the loco venture south as far as Norton Fitzwarren on the weedkilling train, and is noted for its outstanding reliability. It must also be one of the few locomotives whose maintenance schedule includes waxing of the external paintwork!

Class 04 0-6-0 No D2279

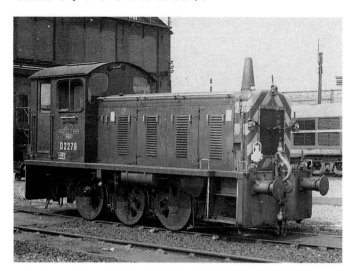

Built: Robert Stephenson &
    Hawthorn, February 1960
Number carried: D2279
First allocation: Norwood
    Junction
Final allocation: Colchester
Withdrawn: 23 May 1971
Preserved: East Anglian Railway
    Museum, Chappel & Wakes
    Colne

D2279 photographed at
Doncaster Works on 13 July
1969. *A.J. Booth*

One of the longest-lived Class 04s in BR service, No D2279 nevertheless only saw 11 years' use before withdrawal as surplus and non-standard. The final series of Class 04s, Nos D2274-D2339, were fitted with slightly larger 3 ft 7 in wheels.

No D2279 was first used at Norwood Junction but, in common with some of its sisters, was exchanged for a Class 03 from the Eastern in May 1966, heading for Parkeston depot on the Essex coast.

Colchester took over responsibility from January 1967, but No D2279 was then surprisingly moved up to Lincoln the same October before heading back to Colchester for its final turn of duty in March 1969. It visited Doncaster Works for minor attention in the summer of 1969. After storage in the London area for long periods, it was eventually sold to the Central Electricity Generating Board as a replacement for its steam loco at Rye House power station near Hoddesden, Hertfordshire (coincidentally another Robert, Stephenson & Hawthorn product, 0-6-0T No 7597 built in 1949).

Work existed for No D2279 from 1971 onwards, and it was a familiar sight from the Liverpool Street-Cambridge main line until made redundant again in February 1981. It was then moved to the home of the East Anglian Railway Museum on the Marks Tey-Sudbury line, where remarkably No 7597 was also stabled for a time. D2279 is in full working order, and external restoration has taken place.

Class 04 0-6-0 No D2284

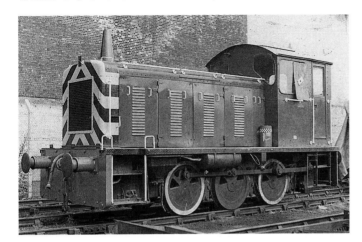

Built: Robert Stephenson &
    Hawthorn, March 1960
Number carried: D2284
First allocation: Hither Green
Final allocation: Colchester
Withdrawn: 11 April 1971
Preserved: South Yorkshire
    Railway, Meadowhall, Sheffield

No D2284 at the South
Yorkshire Railway, Meadowhall,
28 May 1990. *Brian Cuttell*

The National Coal Board was a good customer of BR in the late 1960s when it came to replacing its extensive but venerable South Yorkshire steam fleet with more modern motive power, picking up many bargain buys in the shape of small 0-6-0 shunters which were ideal for colliery use. It was, however, appalling news for the locomotive building industry, but the ex-BR machines served the coal industry well until the large-scale closures of smaller pits after 1985 saw them rendered redundant for a final time. One of the 1971 Class 04 withdrawals, No D2284 was sold into a further 14 years of industrial use.

One of the 1960 series with larger wheels and reduced tractive effort of 15,285 lb, No D2284 was allocated new to Hither Green depot on the Southern Region, but moved to Guildford in April 1962. Several of the type migrated north of the Thames in early 1966, No D2284 going to Ipswich in May. Its final depot was Colchester from May 1968.

The NCB took possession in July 1974, and No D2284 became the responsibility of the Barnsley area. It started work at North Gawber Colliery, but later moved on to Grimethorpe in 1976, and finally to Woolley Colliery in March 1978. It retained its BR identity throughout its industrial career.

Preserved first at Chapeltown, Sheffield, from August 1985, it was moved to the South Yorkshire Preservation Society's new home at Attercliffe late the following year. Its third home in preservation is at Meadowhall.

Class 04 0-6-0 No D2298

Built: Vulcan Foundry, October
  1960
Numbers carried: (1) D2298,
  (2) DVR No 1
First allocation: Lincoln
Final allocation: Gateshead
Withdrawn: 28 December 1968
Preserved: Buckinghamshire
  Railway Centre, Quainton
  Road

No D2298 in DVR livery at
Quainton Road on 14 May 1984.
John Robertson

The second Drewry 204hp Class 04 shunter to pass into the hands of the Derwent Valley Railway at York after withdrawal from BR service was No D2298 (see also D2245).

No D2298 started life as part of the six-strong Class 04 batch sent new to Lincoln at the end of 1960, but they were soon dispersed. No D2298 moved to Boston in July 1963, to Colwick in October 1963, back to Lincoln in November 1965, and up to Gateshead for the last five months of its BR career. The DVR renumbered it No 1 and, later repainted in North Eastern Railway livery by its new owners, it was named *Lord Wenlock* after the private line's first chairman from 1907-10.

Dieselisation of the DVR did not prevent the line's inevitable closure, although No D2298's safety was ensured when it was put up for sale in September 1981 and ended up at Quainton Railway Centre in October 1982. It retained its DVR livery for some time.

Class 04 0-6-0 No D2325

Built: Robert Stephenson &
   Hawthorn, April 1961
Number carried: D2325
First allocation: Gateshead
Final allocation: Goole
Withdrawn: 8 July 1968
Preserved: Mangapps Farm,
   Burnham-on-Crouch

Heading out into the country
with a demonstration freight at
Mangapps Farm is No D2325.
John Jolly

A whole new railway has grown up on a green field site on the Essex coast thanks to local farmer and lifelong enthusiast John Jolly, whose quarter-mile of track acquired its own Light Railway Order in May 1990 and now offers Class 04-hauled passenger trains.

Credit for the initial rescue of Drewry Class 04 shunter No D2325 from the jaws of a scrap merchant rests, however, with a former maintenance engineer linked to the National Coal Board's Norwich Victoria coal concentration depot, who secured it upon the yard's closure in September 1986. It was in fine condition, having been serviced on a regular basis since arrival in 1968, and having done little actual work.

New to Gateshead at the end of April 1961,

No D2325 went to Leeds Holbeck in February 1967, and finally Goole in October 1967. The following year saw a massive clear-out of redundant Class 04s from across the whole of the North Eastern Region, and No D2325 was duly condemned in July. It was stored until December, and bought by the Coal Board based on its generally good condition. It was repainted in GER blue, with decorative scrolled numbers on its cabsides, by North Norfolk Railway volunteers.

Its future was doubtful until secured for the Burnham-on-Crouch railway on 19 March 1987. It was restored to mid-1960s BR Brunswick green the following year, and is in regular use on demonstration trains.

Class 04 0-6-0 No D2334

Built: Robert Stephenson &
   Hawthorn, July 1961
Number carried: D2334
First allocation: Heaton
Final allocation: Darlington
Withdrawn: 8 July 1968
Preserved: South Yorkshire
   Railway, Meadowhall, Sheffield

Still in faded BR green livery, No
D2334 stands in the open at the
NCB's Thurcroft Colliery, South
Yorkshire, on 27 July 1980.
Brian Cuttell

By the time a South Yorkshire Railway member stepped in to save this Class 04 shunter, it was little more than an engineless shell dumped at the back of Maltby Main Colliery. The availability of a replacement Gardner 8L3 204hp engine made preservation a practical possibility.

A North Eastern machine throughout its life on BR, No D2334 was delivered new from RSH's Darlington works to Heaton depot, Newcastle, on 25 July 1961. It moved to nearby Percy Main in June 1963, Gateshead in January 1965, and finally Darlington in February 1968 for a final five months.

One of a large number of National Coal Board acquisitions, it went where the work was, first the coal preparation plant at Manvers Main Colliery, Wath, South Yorkshire, followed by spells at Thurcroft, Dinnington and finally Maltby. It was offered for sale during May 1985, and secured for preservation.

Class 04 0-6-0 No D2337

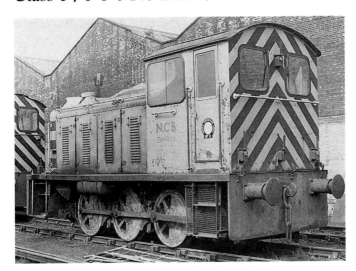

Built: Robert Stephenson &
    Hawthorn, August 1961
Number carried: D2337
First allocation: Darlington
Final allocation: Darlington
Withdrawn: 15 July 1968
Preserved: South Yorkshire
    Railway, Meadowhall, Sheffield

No D2337 still in NCB yellow
livery and named *Dorothy*, at
Meadowhall, 28 May 1990. *Brian
Cuttell*

The Class 04 production line was two months from producing its final example when No D2337 emerged from the RSH works at Darlington, and the complementary BR Class 03 was also near its completion total. Even so, No D2337 only survived in service 7 years and 11 months before being declared surplus at Darlington depot, its only allocation since construction.

It was held in store at Thornaby depot for almost a year before sale to the National Coal Board for work at Manvers Main coal preparation plant at Wath-upon-Dearne, near Barnsley. No D2337 also saw a period of service at Barnburgh Main Colliery in 1974-77 before returning to Manvers for its final years. It latterly carried the name *Dorothy*, and was sold from Manvers Main Colliery to the nearby preservation site in early 1988.

Class 03 0-6-0 No D2371

Built: BR Swindon, July 1958
Numbers carried: (1) No 92,
    (2) D2371, (3) 03371
First allocation: Cambridge
    Engineers Dept
Final allocation: Gateshead
Withdrawn: 26 November 1987
Preserved: Rowden Mill,
    Hereford & Worcester

In its final days as Newcastle
station pilot, No 03371 on duty
on 10 May 1986. *Philip Sutton*

Despite its high number for a Class 03 shunter, No D2371 is in fact one of the oldest preserved, and its out-of-sequence numbering explains its interesting history. Two Class 03s were ordered for the Eastern engineers' track maintenance depot at Chesterton Junction, Cambridge, in 1958, and were delivered from Swindon Works after No D2022 (qv, also preserved). Originally intended to carry the numbers 11210/1 in the steam locomotive series, they in fact appeared as departmental Nos 91/2, and performed their intended role until a change of domestic policy in July 1967 saw them both released to capital stock. The numbers D2370/1 were chosen as the two most convenient gaps below the then D2372-99 series.

No D2370, by then No 03370, was condemned at Norwich at the end of 1982, but No 03371 survived because it had by then been dual braked during overhaul at Doncaster Works in 1968. It had been transferred north to work from Bradford Hammerton Street depot in September of that year, followed by Healey Mills in March 1973, York in August 1973, back to Healey Mills in July 1976, York in July 1983, and finally Gateshead in December 1983.

It was remarkable in making a total of eight visits to Doncaster Works during its career, the first in September 1967 for an unclassified overhaul. Other attention was executed during August 1968 (general overhaul), April 1974 (unclassified), July 1974 (unclassified), June 1975 (general), May-October 1979 (unclassified), December 1979 (unclassified), and April-August 1982 (general). It also travelled south to Stratford Repair Shops for tyre-turning on 28 November 1967.

The 1958 veteran was the last Class 03 in BR traffic with the old-style conical exhaust stack, and was seen in use as depot shunter as late as 8 January 1988, when it was finally laid up. With No 03063 (qv), it was the final Class 03 to leave Gateshead depot in October 1988.

The loco is now preserved, in working order, at a small private museum within the platforms of Rowden Mill station on the former GWR Worcester-Leominster line. Painted in all-over green as No D2371, it sees regular use on a small section of track.

Class 03 0-6-0 No D2381

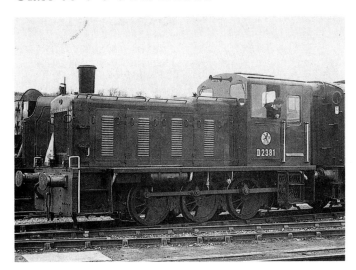

Built: BR Swindon, October
  1961
Number carried: D2381
First allocation: Derby
Final allocation: Derby
Withdrawn: 18 June 1972
Preserved: Steamtown, Carnforth

No D2381 at Steamtown,
Carnforth, on 14 April 1984.
The BR emblem is not as built.
Brian Cuttell

One of the most uneventful working lives of any preserved ex-BR locomotive can be claimed by Carnforth's No D2381, which was delivered new from Swindon Works to Derby in October 1961, and was withdrawn from the same place in June 1972. Deliveries of Class 03s had by this time over-run the original number series of 200, and an additional series was found for 28 of the 1961 build after the Class 04s. The last two numbers, D2370/1, were allocated to the former Departmental Nos 91/2 of 1958 vintage when they were transferred to capital stock (qv D2371).

When No D2381 was withdrawn, a buyer, the late Hon John Gretton, was in the wings, requiring the locomotive for shunting work at the abortive preservation centre at Market Overton, using former British Steel quarry buildings on the redundant High Dyke branch near Grantham. At one time it shared the shed with such illustrious locomotives as Gresley Class A3 'Pacific' No 4472 *Flying Scotsman*, and GWR 'Castle' Class 4-6-0 No 4079 *Pendennis Castle*.

No D2381 moved to Market Overton on 13 April 1973, and was soon restored to all-over lined green livery, without 'wasp' stripes. The Gretton scheme foundered, and No D2381 was duly moved in March 1976 to its present home, Steamtown, Carnforth, where it has seen regular use on passenger shuttles within the confines of the depot.

Class 03 0-6-0 No 03399

Built: BR Doncaster, October
   1961
Numbers carried: (1) D2399,
   (2) 03399
First allocation: Ashford
Final allocation: Norwich
Withdrawn: 5 July 1987
Preserved: Mangapps Farm,
   Burnham-on-Crouch

No D2399 being loaded up at
March depot, 22 March 1989.
David Denton

The highest-numbered Class 03 shunter, No D2399 was secured for preservation from the large dump of withdrawn locomotives accumulated at the former March depot in Cambridgeshire, and formed a working exhibit within a private collection on farmland close to the Essex coast. It was not, however, the most recently built – that record is held by the Colne Valley Railway's No D2184 (qv).

As No D2399, it was delivered new to Ashford in October 1961, and was a Southern Region loco for 11 years with allocations to Weymouth, back to Ashford, and to Bournemouth until it became surplus in 1972. It betrays its Southern parentage by its high-level jumper cables, and would have seen occasional passenger use on the Weymouth tramway which connects with the Channel Islands ferries. It made two visits to Eastleigh Works for repair, being out of traffic from 5 December 1967 to 29 May 1968 for intermediate overhaul, and 24 July to 2 August 1968 for minor attention.

No D2399's survival is owed to its possession of dual air/vacuum brake equipment, evidenced by the large box on the front of the left-hand running plate which houses the compressor. It was returned to traffic with ex-SR sister No D2397 upon transfer to the London Midland Region, based at Derby.

The decision to upgrade the Ipswich Docks Class 03 fleet to dual braked versions saw No 03399, as it had by then become, reallocated to Colchester in February 1977. It was given a final general overhaul at Doncaster Works between March and August 1979, and its final base was at Norwich Crown Point from 18 January 1987. It regrettably suffered theft of parts and vandalism during the two years it took to negotiate a sale from March, and was moved away by low-loader on 22 March 1989 for the journey to Burnham-on-Crouch.

It was quickly returned to full working order on farmer John Jolly's purpose-built quarter-mile stretch of museum line, and sees regular use on public services each summer. Contrary to the general trend of returning preserved diesel traction back to their original liveries, No 03399 has been repainted to the 1970s BR blue applied after the dual brake modifications.

Class 06 0-4-0 No 06003

Built: Andrew Barclay, February 1959
Numbers carried: (1) D2420, (2) 06003, (3) 97804
First allocation: Kittybrewster
Final allocation: Reading Signal Works
Withdrawn: (1) 8 February 1981, (2) June 1985
Preserved: South Yorkshire Railway, Meadowhall, Sheffield

No 97804 at C. F. Booth's scrapyard, Rotherham, with No D2258 (later broken up), 21 November 1986. *Howard Johnston*

Even at the height of diesel preservation in the mid-1980s, it seemed that Class 06 would become extinct when the last survivor of the class was sold to the highest bidder – a scrap merchant. Fortunately that was not the end of the story, because the well-travelled No 06003, at the end of its career renumbered into the departmental series as No 97804, was recognised as a historic vehicle.

C.F.Booth of Rotherham took delivery of the loco in October 1986, but kept it intact until sale to the nearby South Yorkshire Railway was effected on 7 March the following year. With it came a considerable number of parts recovered by BR many years ago from scrapped No 06002.

The last survivor on BR of the 0-4-0 wheel arrangement, No 06003 was new in February 1959 from Andrew Barclay's Kilmarnock works to Kittybrewster depot, Aberdeen, one of 35 powerful short-wheelbase locomotives designed for tightly curved dock lines.

Only ten of the class survived to TOPS renumbering in 1973-74, and No 06003's career seemed at an end in 1978 when it was consigned to store in poor condition as surplus.

It was, however, granted another overhaul at Glasgow Works. Its last duties as a capital stock loco were in Fife, where it was regularly seen in Markinch station yard.

Withdrawal on 8 February 1981 coincided with the sudden need for a new departmental shunter at Reading Signal Works, and No 06003 became the first of the class to work on the Western Region, let alone England. Thus it gained a third identity as No 97804.

Closure of the signal works in 1984 saw No 06003 stabled at first at Reading shed, and it was a working exhibit giving demonstration rides at the following year's Great Western 150th anniversary celebration open day, followed by another outing to Old Oak Common. It was then taken by road to Rotherham, and was started at Attercliffe for the first time on 13 March 1988. However, the cylinder block suffered frost damage while on BR, a complete new radiator needed to be made, and the final drive needed rebuilding or replacement. No 06003 was exhibited at the October 1990 Tinsley Depot Open Day and is now back in full working order.

Class 05 0-6-0 No D2511

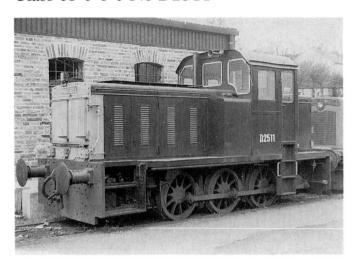

Built: Hudswell Clarke & Co,
    September 1961
Number carried: D2511
First allocation: Barrow-in-
    Furness
Final allocation: Barrow-in-
    Furness
Withdrawn: 30 December 1967
Preserved: Keighley & Worth
    Valley Railway

No D2511 in Haworth yard, 25
September 1983. *Michael
Whatmough*

The second series of Hudswell Clarke 0-6-0s was one of the shortest-lived diesel-mechanical shunting designs, and many will wonder why 10 more of a non-standard class were built when BR was already scaling down production of its own standard Class 03 design at Swindon and Doncaster.

The structural part of the original design could be traced back to LMS days, and 10 awkward-looking examples, Nos 11116-20/44-8, closely following the steam locomotive outline (including steam-style chimney), were built in 1955-56. First allocated to Birkenhead, and later renumbered as Nos D2500-9, they were useful machines but not big enough a class to survive the late-1960s holocaust suffered by minor types.

The facelifted later series, Nos D2510-9, were mechanically identical, but the new superstructure included a mid-body cab with better vision, and the jackshaft drive was moved from front to rear. No D2511 spent most of its short career allocated to Barrow for docks work, apart from the period between October 1966 to June 1967 when it was at Workington for similar work. Withdrawn in 1967, it was one of four sold to the National Coal Board, and operated from Brodsworth Colliery near Doncaster until sustaining cab damage in a collision in early 1977.

No D2511 was nevertheless sold for preservation, and arrived at Ingrow on the KWVR on 8 October 1977. It spent two years at Haworth having the damage straightened out, as well as undergoing refurbishment of tyres, axleboxes, bearings and transmission. Further work was undertaken towards the end of 1991.

Sister loco No D2519 from the NCB's Hatfield Colliery was also at the KWVR for a time from March 1982, but was curiously sold by its owner for scrap. The current level of interest in ex-BR shunter preservation would prevent that happening in 1992.

Class 05 0-6-0 No D2554

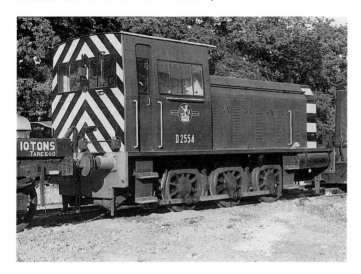

Built: Hunslet Engine Co, May
  1956
Numbers carried: (1) 11140,
  (2) D2554, (3) 05001,
  (4) 97803
First allocation: Parkeston Quay
Final allocation: Ryde
Withdrawn: 25 January 1981
Preserved: Isle of Wight Steam
  Railway, Havenstreet

No D2554 at Havenstreet on
31 August 1989. *Howard
Johnston*

This loco's survival in BR service for 15 years longer than the rest of the class was simply due to its isolation on the Isle of Wight, where it now resides in preservation as a integral part of the island's railway history. It made further history on 1 April 1991 when it was part of the first engineers' train over the Isle of Wight Steam Railway's final mile of track to connect with the BR system at Smallbrook Junction.

The vast over-provision of small diesel shunters in the '50s continued with a series of 69 from Hunslet between 1955-61, incorporating the standard Gardner 204hp engine. The first production series of 24 (Nos 11135-43/61-76, later Nos D2550-73) were followed by a modified larger-wheel version for Scotland (Nos D2574-84) and the North East (Nos D2585-2618). The somewhat tedious mechanical transmission made them unpopular with crews, especially if they were in poor condition, because the time spent in gear-changing would often result in a total loss of acceleration. The only redeeming feature was the spacious, comfortable cab.

The IoW loco was originally numbered 11140 in the steam series, and the search for a diesel shunter for the island resulted in what was then No D2554 being transferred to Eastleigh in June 1966 for its cab height to be reduced to enable it to negotiate the tunnel just south of Ryde Esplanade station. The advent of TOPS renumbering in August 1974 gave it Class 05 all to itself, and it became part of the BR Departmental fleet in January 1981 with a fourth number, 97803. A losing battle with mechanical defects including gearbox trouble dictated its withdrawal in February 1981, when it was replaced by a redundant Class 03 from the mainland.

No D2554's sale for preservation was effected in June 1984. It was restored to green livery during 1987, the condition in which it had arrived on the Isle of Wight, and on Easter Monday 1991 had the honour of being at the rear of the first engineers' train over the new extension to Smallbrook Junction, hauled by former Isle of Wight Central Railway Class A1X steam loco No 11 *Newport.*

Class 05 0-6-0 No D2578 *Cider Queen*

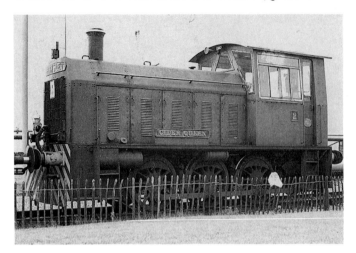

Built: Hunslet Engine Co,
    November 1958
Rebuilt: Hunslet, July 1967
Numbers carried: (1) D2578,
    (2) No 2 *Cider Queen*
First allocation: Thornton
    Junction
Final allocation: Thornton
    Junction
Withdrawn: 7 July 1967
Preserved: Bulmer's, Hereford

No D2578 *Cider Queen* in
Bulmer's sidings, Hereford,
15 September 1990. *Brian
Cuttell*

The need for a working loco as well as a presentable exhibit at the Hereford home for operational main-line steam prompted cider makers H.P.Bulmer Ltd to buy a reconditioned locomotive from Hunslet of Leeds.

No D2578, a 204hp Gardner-engined Class 05, had a singularly undistinguished BR career. Delivered new to Thornton Junction in November 1958 as one of the second series with larger wheels, it shunted in the yard there for a full 9½ years before being declared surplus in July 1967 as part of the decimation of the fleet. No D2578 was then bought back by its

builders at virtually scrap price, and reconditioned for sale to the Hereford cider firm which was by 1968 setting up its own steam preservation centre for such illustrious exhibits as Great Western 'King' Class 4-6-0 No 6000 *King George V*.

Something of a cross between a preserved and working loco, No D2578 now sports a steam-type chimney, and is painted in a modified GWR livery complete with cast brass *Cider Queen* nameplate and cabside numberplate.

Class 05 0-6-0 No D2587

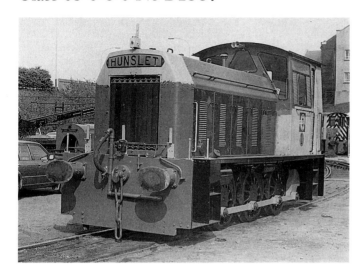

Built: Hunslet Engine Co,
   November 1959
Numbers carried: (1) D2587,
   (2) CEGB No 2
First allocation: Wakefield
Final allocation: Dunfermline
Withdrawn: 30 December 1967
Preserved: South Yorkshire
   Railway, Meadowhall, Sheffield

With repainting in progress, No
D2587 stands at Bury depot yard
25 May 1986. *Howard Johnston*

When they were no longer needed by BR, a small number of Class 05s were bought back by their Leeds-based manufacturers in 1968 for reconditioning and resale to industrial concerns, and the Central Electricity Generating Board ordered two for work at Chadderton power station, Oldham. Happily, both have survived into preservation (see also D2595).

No D2587 was allocated when new to Wakefield, and worked successively at Ardsley, West Hartlepool, Haymarket (from April 1967), Kittybrewster (Aberdeen), Ferryhill and Dunfermline.

Sent back to Hunslet in September 1968, it was fully overhauled with parts taken from other less fortunate members of the class, and was delivered to the CEGB in the following May with a three-year warranty. The order asked for the rear cab-end to be painted with black and yellow bands of alternate 2, 3, 4 and 5 inch widths, but they were in fact done in

orange and black. Likewise the cab interior should have been grey, but actually stayed yellow. In partnership with sister No D2595, No D2587 worked at Chadderton until being made redundant again in May 1980, when it was moved to nearby Kearsley power station for storage on 3 November 1981.

Although official Hunslet records show No D2587 as having been rebuilt as CEGB No 1 with a new works number 7179 of 29 March 1969, it was in fact delivered to Bury Transport Museum on 16 April 1983 bearing CEGB No 2 (works number 7180). Restoration has included repairs to minor collision damage, and by mid-1991 the locomotive had been repainted in non-standard pale green with the bogus cabside number D2477. A deal was concluded in early 1991 to move the loco to Sheffield, realising the museum's ambition to own shunters from Classes 01, 02, 03, 04, 05, 06, 07, 08, 10 and 11 inclusive.

Class 05 0-6-0 No D2595

Built: Hunslet Engine Co,
   December 1959
Numbers carried: (1) D2595,
   (2) CEGB No 1
First allocation: Wakefield
Final allocation: Thornton
   Junction
Withdrawn: 8 June 1968
Preserved: Steamport, Southport

Just repainted, No D2595 is seen
at Bury Bolton Street station on
17 June 1989. *Howard Johnston*

As mentioned on the previous page, there has been a case of mistaken identity in countless railway books and journals for nearly 20 years because everyone thought that the second Class 05 shunter preserved at Bury was No D2593 until restoration during 1985 proved conclusively that it was actually sister No D2595! The confusion arose as a result of No D2595's rebuilding at Hunslet's Leeds factory for the CEGB during 1969, when a small number of components were used from withdrawn and later scrapped No D2593. One person's incorrect observation has been taken seriously too many times.

Because of a general lack of work, the real No D2595 was shunted from pillar to post after its delivery new to York in January 1967 — Ardsley, Bradford Hammerton Street, then to Haymarket in April 1967, followed by stints at Leith Central, Inverness and finally Thornton Junction. The locomotive was then declared surplus in June 1968.

Like sister No D2587 (qv), it was renovated and sold to the CEGB for use at Chadderton power station just north of Manchester until 1980, with new Hunslet works number 7179. Painstaking mechanical restoration and repainting into green livery with black and yellow 'wasp' stripes by a member of the East Lancashire Railway took several years to complete. Incidentally, visitors may be even more confused by the numbers stamped on the loco's wheels and motion, as 1986 saw it equipped with replacements belonging to sister loco No D2607 from Steetley Colliery, retrieved during scrapping in July 1984.

It may have been slow, but No D2595 hauled its first timetabled passenger train on 17 June 1989, the 17.00 Bury-Ramsbottom formed of four well-loaded Mark 1 coaches. A change of ownership saw the locomotive moved to Steamport, Southport, on 19 October 1989.

Unclassed 0-4-0 No D2767

Built: North British Locomotive
  Co, August 1960
Rebuilt: Andrew Barclay, 1968
Number carried: D2767
First allocation: Eastfield
Final allocation: Eastfield
Withdrawn: 29 May 1966
Preserved: East Lancashire
  Railway, Bury

Restored to running order, No
D2767 stands at Bury depot in
1987. *D.H.Swain*

A 225hp shunting locomotive at the head of three BR Mark 1 passenger coaches filled with 105 enthusiasts was not exactly what the manufacturer intended, but it demonstrated the popularity of the East Lancashire Railway's North British 0-4-0 diesel-hydraulic on its maiden passenger run on 1 October 1988.

Preservation of the diminutive shunter No D2767 in 1983 had major significance in that it was then the only representative of the massive but ill-fated fleet of over 250 main-line and shunting diesel locos built for BR by North British at Glasgow between 1953 and 1962. Abandonment of hydraulic transmission in favour of electric, general unreliability, and non-availability of parts after the bankruptcy of NBL meant that all were destined for short lives, and sadly only a handful of shunters sold to industry at the end of the 1960s survived being scrapped.

No D2767 worked its entire BR career from Eastfield, then was one of four sold to Andrew Barclay for rebuilding and resale. Burmah Oil was eager to replace a Barclay fireless steam loco at its Stanlow refinery, and D2767 was secured for £8,686, which included a spark-arrester device. Its sole duty from June 1969 to 1981 was to handle the traffic of 20 crude oil tankers from Nottinghamshire, four at a time, into the loading bay. Mileage at its first service was 13,872, rising to 17,913 before its move to Bury Transport Museum on 12 June 1983. Full restoration to Brunswick green livery was quickly completed, including the provision of vacuum brake equipment for its new role.

Unclassed 0-4-0 No D2774

Built: North British Locomotive
   Co, August 1960
Rebuilt: Andrew Barclay, 1968
Number carried: D2774
First allocation: Grangemouth
Final allocation: Eastfield
Withdrawn: 24 June 1966
Preserved: East Lancashire
   Railway, Bury

No D2774, still in National Coal
Board green livery, at Bury on
26 July 1987. *Howard Johnston*

Like its sister loco No D2767 (qv), No D2774's survival into preservation was only because of its use in industry long after BR had lost interest.

North British was active in the shunting locomotive business throughout the 1950s, and built many dozens for both BR and private use with German-designed Voith hydraulic transmissions. Ninety-four were ordered by BR, eight (Nos D2700-7) with Paxman 200hp engines, 14 (Nos D2900-13) with MAN 330hp units, and 73 (Nos D2708-80) with MAN 225hp systems. Of the last type, both preserved examples are of the most refined version with 3 ft 9 in wheels and a spacious cab with large windows. A handful of similar non-BR machines are still in existence at industrial sites up and down the country.

Mass closure of small North Eastern and Scottish station yards meant none survived beyond 1968. Four (Nos D2738/63/67/74) were sold to Andrew Barclay for rebuilding, and No D2774 passed into NCB ownership, working at Killoch Colliery, Ayrshire, and more recently in South Wales at Celynen South pit, Abercarn, from 1977 onwards.

Although No D2774 was still in full working order, closure of the colliery in 1985 saw it sold to the scrap merchants clearing the site. Fortunately the Bury-based owners of No D2767 stepped in at the eleventh hour. In mid-September 1986 the two locos were reunited after 18 years, and 1991 witnessed the completion of external restoration to 1960s BR livery identical to No D2767.

Class 02 0-4-0 No D2854

Built: Yorkshire Engine
   Company, November 1960
Number carried: D2854
First allocation: Bank Hall
Final allocation: Allerton
Withdrawn: 28 February 1970
Preserved: South Yorkshire
   Railway, Meadowhall, Sheffield

No D2854 when owned by
C. F. Booth of Rotherham,
30 July 1982. *Howard Johnston*

The Yorkshire Engine Company of Sheffield built many successful shunting designs for industry during the 1950s and 1960s, but arrived relatively late on the BR scene, and only secured one production order for 20 short-wheelbase 170hp Rolls-Royce-engined diesel-hydraulic 0-4-0s for dock work. One of them is now preserved in its home city after 18 years in the precarious ownership of one of Britain's best-known and most prolific locomotive scrap merchants.

The well-tried modern design featured a single door at the rear, reached via an enclosed verandah, and although Lancashire was their intended sphere of operation, the locomotives drifted away to Chester, Derby and East Yorkshire. No D2850 was the first of 12 delivered to Bank Hall, Liverpool, in October 1960, to be followed within the month by No D2854.

No D2854 only worked in BR service for 10 years, including spells based at Longsight (November 1960), Speke Junction (October 1966), and Allerton (May 1968) before withdrawal as surplus on 28 February 1970. It was sold on to C.F.Booth of Rotherham in September 1970, but unlike hundreds of steam locomotives and latterly diesel shunters broken up in the yard, was intended for repair and re-use.

No D2854 was in regular use, still carrying its original BR green livery, until the early 1980s, but then saw little use, despite an extensive mechanical overhaul. Although parked at the back of the yard with many other less fortunate locos, its owners recognised both its historic importance and resale value, which was finally realised early in 1988 with its sale to a member of the formative South Yorkshire Railway Preservation Society. Its initial months were spent at the group's Attercliffe base, to be followed in mid-1988 by a move to the more extensive Meadowhall site.

Class 02 0-4-0 No D2860

Built: Yorkshire Engine
   Company, September 1961
Number carried: D2860
First allocation: Fleetwood
Final allocation: Allerton
Withdrawn: 13 December 1970
Preserved: National Railway
   Museum, York

No D2860 at Allerton depot, 27
March 1971. *Norman Preedy*

Yorkshire Engine Company shunters are still considered a modern-looking design, and their compact but powerful format made them a popular choice for industrial concerns away from the BR system, where many still enjoy useful employment.

No D2860, one of the second batch ordered to replace steam in the North West dock areas, was allocated new to Allerton depot, Liverpool, towards the end of 1961. Alternative work was found at Fleetwood, Lostock Hall, Bank Hall and Speke Junction, before a return to Allerton depot in May 1968. Although it was employed in the area for another two years, work finally ran out in April 1970, and on-off activity was followed by withdrawal on 13 December. The

locomotive was then stored for three years while terms were agreed with the National Railway Museum for it to be preserved as a representative of the private-builder diesel shunting fleet.

The next years saw it make spectacular movements – all the way to Brighton's Preston Park Works in March 1973 for storage, up to Thomas Hill at Rotherham in September 1978 for overhaul, and finally to the NRM at York for display the following year. Restored to Brunswick green livery, it is in full working order, and is regularly used to shunt exhibits on the south side of the museum. It also gives brake-van rides on diesel days.

Class 02 0-4-0 No D2866

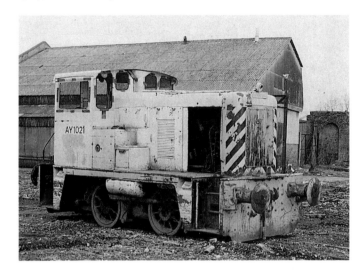

Built: Yorkshire Engine
  Company, November 1961
Numbers carried: (1) D2866,
  (2) AY1021
First allocation: Bank Hall,
  Liverpool
Final allocation: Longsight
Withdrawn: 28 February 1970
Preserved: Brechin Railway

No D2866 at Arnott Young's
yard, Dalmuir, in April 1987.
Harry Needle

The third Yorkshire Engine Company Class 02 to be preserved is the only member of the BR series to have worked in Scotland.

New in November 1961, No D2866's BR career mirrored those of many of its sisters, with availability clearly in excess of actual requirements on the docklands systems in the Liverpool area. It made its first move from Bank Hall to Agecroft in June 1963, to Newton Heath in October 1963 and Longsight in July 1968. It was withdrawn as surplus early in 1970, and moved back to Newton Heath for storage pending sale. It was sold to the scrap firm of Arnott Young of Dalmuir, north of Glasgow,

and moved to the firm's yard in June 1970.

No D2866 arrived at Brechin on 17 October 1987, having been bought by three members of the Brechin Railway Society, and was in somewhat poor physical condition. However, with its cab instruments and windows replaced, it was started within weeks of arrival, and a cosmetic repaint in dark green livery followed. During the last weekend of December 1988, it was employed on engineering work between Brechin and Bridge of Dun with the line's Class 08 No D3059 (qv). Recent attention has involved further cab work and arresting general bodywork corrosion.

Class 01 0-4-0 No D2953

Built: Andrew Barclay, January
1956
Numbers carried: (1) 11503,
(2) D2953
First allocation: Stratford
Final allocation: Stratford
Withdrawn: 19 June 1966
Preserved: South Yorkshire
Railway, Meadowhall, Sheffield

The fully restored No D2953
during its brief stay at Attercliffe,
28 May 1988. *Howard Johnston*

The vast majority of Britain's locomotive builders have gone to the wall over the last 30 years, but Andrew Barclay of Kilmarnock is still manufacturing railway products in 1991, and as part of the Telfos Holdings/Hunslet group has even undertaken modernisation of its Kilmarnock works. Although a successful steam builder, Andrew Barclay co-operated in development of internal combustion as far back as the First World War, and started diesel construction in 1936; No D2953 represents one of its most notable products, as the first ex-BR loco sold out of service back in 1966.

Class 01, a class of only five locomotives, was born out of BR's desire to replace steam over the tight curves of London's docklands, and an 0-4-0 with a Gardner 153hp 6L3 power unit cased within a tiny 23 ft 8 in frame was a good solution. Four were allocated to Stratford depot, and a fifth followed for departmental service (see next page). They first carried black livery, and the five-figure numbers 11503-6.

They were displaced through no fault of their own after only 10 years, and No D2953, Barclay works number 395, was bought by Thames Matex for shunting at their oil refinery beside the river at West Thurrock in Essex. Repainted in pale green livery with all-over yellow ends, the loco was disfigured by cumbersome spark-arresting equipment welded above the left-hand frame. Loaned out to BP and Shellmex at various times, it was finally laid up in about 1980 with a serious gearbox defect which was never repaired.

Its remoteness and the presence of a high-security fence meant that No D2953 had suffered little deterioration by 1985, when John Wade of the South Yorkshire Preservation Society stepped in to purchase and remove the locomotive to the society's then home at Attercliffe, Sheffield, on 15 December 1985. Since transferred nearby to Meadowhall, it has been immaculately restored to late 1960s green livery, and is in full working order.

Class 01 0-4-0 No D2956

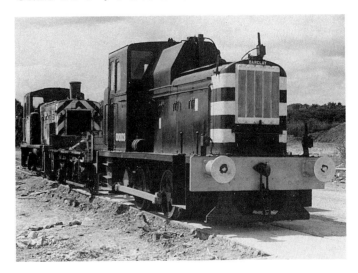

Built: Andrew Barclay, March
  1956
Numbers carried: (1) 11506,
  (2) D2956, (3) 01003
First allocation: Stratford
Final allocation: Doncaster
Withdrawn: 29 May 1966
Preserved: East Lancashire
  Railway, Bury

Cosmetically repainted as No
01003, No D2956 is seen at
Snailwell on departure day, 29
July 1985. *Howard Johnston*

The scrapyard that held Class 01 shunter No D2956 for 19 years gave it to a preservation group in 1985, stipulating that it must never be broken up! Thus it was that Mayer Newman of Snailwell, near Newmarket, bucked the trend by allowing one of the hundreds of vehicles it had inherited from BR for scrapping to be saved for posterity.

No D2956 has led a particularly precarious existence and more than one railway journal has listed it as having been broken up already, confusing it with a Departmental engine of the same design that was given No D2956's number when it became spare.

The real No D2956 was new to Stratford in March 1956 for docklands traffic. When that work ceased, it was sent to Doncaster in February 1966, and formally withdrawn three months later. The second No D2956 was scrapped in South Wales in August 1969.

D2956 was bought by King & Son for work at their Norwich scrapyard. This firm was subsequently absorbed by the Mayer Newman (now Mayer Parry) concern, and No D2956 was moved to Suffolk at the end of 1981, a gearbox fault prompting its replacement in 1983 by ex-BR Class 03 No 03180.

The author succeeded in convincing Mayer Newman manager Arthur Coverdale of No D2956's historical value. Despite the long period of disuse the power unit was easily started up; it was also given a cosmetic black repaint for handing over to the East Lancashire Railway on 29 July 1985. The fictitious number 01003 was chosen to perpetuate the image of the two withdrawn Class 01 shunters Nos 01001 and 01002 which worked the isolated Holyhead breakwater branch from 1967 right up to its closure in 1981.

As a low-priority project at Bury, No D2956 is still in the early stages of being restored to full running condition. The locomotive displays many scars typical of a scrapyard locomotive.

Class 07 0-6-0 No 07001

Built: Ruston & Hornsby, June 1962
Numbers carried: (1) D2985, (2) 07001
First allocation: Southampton Docks
Final allocation: Eastleigh
Withdrawn: 2 July 1977
Preserved: South Yorkshire Railway, Meadowhall, Sheffield

In original green livery, No D2985 stands at Eastleigh depot on 12 June 1965. *Norman Preedy*

Ruston & Hornsby of Lincoln built many hundreds of diesel locomotives for British industry and export, but were poorly represented on the BR system with just 14 locomotives built for Southampton Docks traffic, and a handful built specifically for departmental service.

The short wheelbase and high 275hp power output of the Class 07 0-6-0s, together with the well-designed central cab layout, made them popular machines, but a rapid switch from wagonload traffic to container trains in the early 1970s made them redundant. The first withdrawals were in 1973, and they had all gone within four years.

Only three were sold for scrap, the rest finding valuable use at industrial sites all over the country. The pioneer No D2985, Ruston works number 480686, by then renumbered No

07001, was introduced to Southampton in June 1962, and only had one other official allocation, Eastleigh from January 1966. After withdrawal in 1977, it found a new use at the Peakstone limestone quarry at Dove Holes near Buxton, Derbyshire, in May 1978 via a dealer in Stoke-on-Trent who overhauled it and applied a distinctive yellow livery. It retained is dual vacuum/air brakes and high-level Southern Region air pipes.

It was taken out of use with a minor electrical defect during 1986, and the arrival of a Sentinel shunter meant that repairs were never put in hand. However, great efforts were made by the quarry management to keep it secure for eventual preservation, and it has filled an important gap in the South Yorkshire Railway collection.

Class 07 0-6-0 No D2991

Built: Ruston & Hornsby, July
  1962
Number carried: D2991
First allocation: Southampton
  Docks
Final allocation: Eastleigh
Withdrawn: 6 May 1973
Preserved: Eastleigh

Before restoration, No 2991
stands at Eastleigh Works on
1 March 1986. *Philip Sutton*

Remarkable in retaining its original number 15 years after the introduction of the TOPS computerised system, Class 07 shunter No D2991 was one of the first four taken out of traffic, but was retained as a mobile generator vehicle at Eastleigh Works and survived long enough to attract preservation interest in 1988.

The Southampton Docks traffic for which the 14-strong stylish centre-cab Class 07 fleet was ordered in 1962 was already in steep decline, and the locos were soon to be seen on general duties across a wider area that also took in Poole and Bournemouth. Their special role of being required to shunt passenger stock in their early days caused immediate problems because, unlike their steam predecessors, the USA 0-6-0Ts, they were unable to heat the stock. The cost of equipping the 07s with steam-heat equipment was clearly prohibitive,

so special boiler vans had to be constructed.

Of the first four withdrawn in 1973, Nos D2988/91/2/8, three were scrapped for spares, leaving No D2991 in the yard. The usefulness of the class was demonstrated, however, four years later when the rest of the class were all sold for further use in industry or preservation (see next page).

No D2991, for which TOPS number 07007 was reserved, acquired blue livery in 1968, losing its 'D' prefix, but gained an increasingly decrepit appearance in its support generator role. The loco's value was recognised on 23 May 1982 when it was put on display at the Eastleigh Railway Preservation Society's Open Day at the Works. It was repainted in 1986, and returned to use by society members early in 1988. It was exhibited again at the September 1988 Eastleigh Works Open Day.

Class 07 0-6-0 No D2994

Built: Ruston & Hornsby,
   September 1962
Numbers carried: (1) D2994,
   (2) 07010
First allocation: Southampton
   Docks
Final allocation: Eastleigh
Withdrawn: 4 October 1976
Preserved: West Somerset
   Railway, Dunster

No D2994 after repainting.
Williton, 13 June 1990.
Steve Worrall

It was a decline in rail traffic, not a fault in the design, that meant the end for the 14 purpose-built 0-6-0 diesel-electrics at Southampton Docks. Their pedigree was immaculate, being delivered over a six-month period in 1962 as replacements for the distinctive ex-United States Transportation Corps 0-6-0T steam locos and six ex-LB&SCR Class E2 0-6-0Ts. Several designs were tested before the centre-cab Paxman-engined Class 07 with a wheelbase of only 8 ft 7$\frac{1}{2}$ in was finally settled upon.

The original number series was Nos D2985-98, and No D2994, the tenth of the class, was delivered in green livery with the BR carriage-style emblem on the cabside. It was painted standard blue by 1972 and renumbered No 07010 in 1974 under the TOPS computer scheme. The class was nominally transferred to Eastleigh for maintenance in January 1966, but

withdrawals began as early as 1973. No 07010, further reallocated to Bournemouth (October 1975) and back to Eastleigh (March 1976), was one of the last survivors, and eight were parked in the latter depot's yard for over a year pending sale to private concerns.

No 07010, unserviceable because of faulty piston liners, was moved to Alresford on the Mid-Hants Railway in August 1978 for restoration to its original livery, and after a short spell working on that line it moved to the West Somerset Railway on 19 May 1980. It has been used as Minehead station pilot as well as occasionally on short-haul passenger trains with the line's Class 04 0-6-0 No 2271 (qv), and was given a full repaint over the winter period of 1988-89. The loco moved to a new base down the line at Dunster in 1990.

Class 08 0-6-0 No 13000

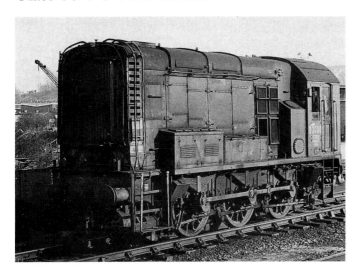

Built: BR Derby, October 1952
Numbers carried: (1) 13000,
    (2) D3000
First allocation: Tyseley
Final allocation: Bristol Bath
    Road
Withdrawn: 11 November 1972
Preserved: Brighton Locomotive
    Works Museum

In later BR days, No D3000
stands at Bristol Bath Road depot
on 16 March 1972. *Norman
Preedy*

An exceedingly worthy preservation candidate, the future of this prototype production 350hp diesel-electric shunter was finally assured at the end of 1986 when its owners agreed to its move from South Wales to the Brighton Locomotive Works Museum project.

No 13000, later D3000, was assembled at Derby Works as the precursor of the standard Class 08/09/10 shunter which ran to a record 1,193 examples, will still be part of the modern BR scene into the 21st century, and is still being updated to handle new types of traffic.

After running-in trials at Toton, No 13000 was allocated to the Birmingham area where it was a popular success. In November 1953 it was moved to Bristol St Philip's Marsh, and although it had a spell at Cardiff Canton, it spent most of its BR career at Bristol Bath Road where it was withdrawn as surplus, still in green livery, in 1972.

No D3000's second career with the National Coal Board in South Wales was almost as long. Originally at Hafodyrynys Colliery near Pontypool until 1975, it also laboured at Bargoed from mid-1978 until it found a home at Mardy Colliery, Maerdy, in 1981. It made two visits to Cardiff Canton for attention in 1975 and 1979.

Although recognised for its historic value, No D3000's worsening mechanical condition gave rise to fears for its future, and a minor collision on 23 September 1985 ended its career. The end of rail traffic at Mardy in 1986, after its underground link-up with Tower Colliery at Hirwaun in the next valley, made the situation even more ominous.

No D3000, still in BR livery, was moved from Mardy by road on 18 March 1987, arriving at Brighton three days later. The completion of restoration work on sister No 13255 (qv D3255) will see a start in earnest on the pioneer loco. Although the power unit is thought to be workable, the main worries are the rebuilding of the control desk, distorted as a result of its collision, and replacement of damaged brakes. The locomotive has nonetheless been smartened up with a single coat of black paint, and the intention is to restore it to as-built condition.

Class 08 0-6-0 No D3002

Built: BR Derby, October 1952
Numbers carried: (1) 13002,
    (2) D3002, (3) No 11 *Dulcote*
First allocation: Tyseley
Final allocation: Bristol Bath
    Road
Withdrawn: 17 July 1972
Preserved: Plym Valley Railway,
    Marsh Mills, Plymouth

Still in Foster Yeoman livery,
No D3002 is seen at Marsh
Mills, 9 August 1986. *Richard
Lewis*

Only the third off the BR Class 08 production line that carried on until December 1962, No D3002 was a virtual copy of the pre-Nationalisation LMS Class 11 shunter except that it followed the SR (Class 12) in having larger diameter 4 ft 6 in wheels, and a more generous loading gauge for all-regions use.

English Electric was formed in 1918 by a merger of Dick, Kerr & Co of Preston and Phoenix Dynamo & Manufacturing Co of Bradford, together with Siemens Brothers of Stafford. It undertook considerable development work on diesel shunters from its inception, and by the late 1930s was interesting all four main-line companies in power units and electrical equipment which could be incorporated into machines assembled at their own works. Of the BR standard type, the initial batch of five, at first numbered 13000-4 in the steam locomotive series, were allocated to Tyseley depot, Birmingham.

It was inevitable that these pioneers should be wanted for trials elsewhere, and No 13002 was drafted to Bristol's St Philip's Marsh depot in December 1953. It moved to Bristol Bath Road in March 1961, and stayed there until withdrawal 11 years later.

Although renumbered No D3002 in February 1960 upon a visit to Swindon Works for overhaul, the loco did not survive long enough to get a TOPS Class 08 configuration (No D3004 was the oldest, as 08001). A new career beckoned for No D3002, however, with Mendip stone firm Foster Yeoman at its Merehead complex, where it was renumbered 11 and named *Dulcote*.

Despite a comprehensive overhaul as late as 1979, No D3002 was rendered spare by a new General Motors Bo-Bo locomotive in mid-1982, and despatched by rail via Westbury and Taunton to the Plym Valley project, which aims to restore passenger services between Marsh Mills and Yelverton. It arrived in full working order.

Class 08 0-6-0 No D3003

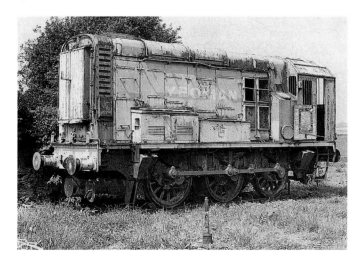

Built: BR Derby, October 1952
Numbers carried: (1) 13003,
   (2) D3003, (3) No 22
   Merehead
First allocation: Tyseley
Final allocation: Bristol Bath
   Road
Withdrawn: 17 July 1972
Preserved: Wanstrow children's
   playground, Somerset

Now a children's plaything,
No D3003 stands at Wanstrow,
28 July 1991. *Brian Cuttell*

It is interesting that yet another of the pioneer Class 08 locomotives has survived, but again it is because of the goodwill of a private company keen to take advantage of the BR fleet reduction of the early 1970s to improve its own motive power situation.

The history of No D3003 closely follows that of No D3002 (previous page), and they were both withdrawn on the same day. For another 10 years they were shedmates at the Foster Yeoman quarry where they had the onerous task of marshalling hundreds of tons of loaded stone hoppers which taxed their ruggedness to the limit.

Clearly past their best by 1982, both Class 08s were pensioned off in favour of a new import from General Motors, USA, the success of which helped pave the way for the Class 59 main-line fleet.

Foster Yeoman's apparent policy of not scrapping redundant locos, although mechanically exhausted, saw the bodyshell of No D3003, minus power unit, gearbox, traction motor and any valuable components, transported to the children's playground in the nearby village of Wanstrow. Painted pale blue, it is visible and accessible from the main road through the village. It must also be the only locomotive to have a basketball frame bolted to the cab-end!

Class 08 0-6-0 No D3014

Built: BR Derby, December 1952
Numbers carried: (1) 13014,
    (2) D3014
First allocation: Hither Green
Final allocation: Eastleigh
Withdrawn: 1 October 1972
Preserved: Paignton &
    Dartmouth Railway, Paignton

Now in red livery, No D3014 at
Paignton on 17 June 1990. *Steve
Worrall*

Certainly the only preserved Class 08 shunter painted red, No D3014 was picked up by the Paignton & Dartmouth Railway from British Coal, which declared it surplus following the rapid run-down of domestic colliery activity in South Wales from 1985 onwards.

Yet another veteran machine preserved almost despite redundancy from BR service at a relatively early stage for the class, No D3014 was a Southern Region locomotive, working from Hither Green, Eastleigh and Norwood Junction between 1952 and withdrawal in 1972. It was delivered in all-over black livery, and carried the five-digit number 13014 until the end of 1960.

The locomotive was sold to the National Coal Board during September 1973 as part of the NCB's policy of finding low-cost but powerful and reliable replacements for steam in

South Wales. After the minimum of attention, it was despatched to Merthyr Vale Colliery, Aberfan. It was never far away from BR during its time in private hands, and made a number of trips back on to BR for repair at nearby Cardiff Canton depot for maintenance, being noted there during December 1974, February 1980, and July 1985. On the last occasion, the NCB was clearly not in any hurry to get the locomotive back, as the repair took six months to complete, after which it spent another six months stabled at Ninian Park.

Sold to the Devon-based private line at the end of 1988, it arrived by low-loader at Paignton on 4 March 1989. The journey from Merthyr Tydfil took three days and was plagued by mishaps, including a burst lorry tyre near Cardiff. No D3014 was repainted red during 1990.

Class 08 0-6-0 No D3019

Built: BR Derby, March 1953
Number carried: D3019
First allocation: Willesden
Final allocation: Allerton
Withdrawn: 10 June 1973
Preserved: South Yorkshire
    Railway, Meadowhall, Sheffield

In Powell Duffryn blue and white livery, No D3019 stands at Gwaen-cae-Gurwen in June 1990. *Harry Needle*

A display of Classes 01, 02, 03, 04, 06, 07, 08, 09, 10 and 11 – that became the proud boast of the South Yorkshire Railway Preservation Society at Meadowhall, Sheffield, following the purchase of Class 08 shunter No D3019 from industrial service in South Wales during June 1990.

As has already been remarked, the survival rate of the earliest examples of the 15 mph 350hp English Electric 6KT-engined Class 08 has been assisted by their sale in some numbers to industry after withdrawal in the early 1970s. Although No D3019 never carried a TOPS number, it was actually allocated No 08012, but this was not applied before it was taken out of traffic at Allerton depot, Liverpool, as surplus during the early summer of 1973.

No D3019's BR career was generally unspectacular. New to Willesden in March 1953, it moved to Crewe South in December 1957, Speke Junction (Liverpool) in October 1958, back to Crewe South in December 1959, Liverpool Edge Hill from March 1963 until the depot's closure, and finally Allerton in May 1968. Moved to Bescot after condemnation as surplus, it was sold to the National Coal Board subsidiary Powell Duffryn Fuels in December 1973, for work at Gwaun-cae-Gurwen disposal point, painted in the company's house colours of light blue and white, and named *Gwyneth*. It is reported to have visited Cardiff Canton depot during 1978 and 1987 for maintenance, but a further overhaul during 1989 was ruled out by the company because it already had two younger Class 08 locomotives, Nos 08113 and 08598, both in better condition as a result of comparatively recent main works overhauls.

No D3019 represents the early design of Class 08 equipped with a 90-volt electrical system, and the owner has now expressed interest in acquiring two other types, a mid-series version to paint in green livery, and a later-build dual braked version in BR corporate blue.

The move to Sheffield reunites No D3019 with its old Powell Duffryn Gwaun-cae-Gurwen shedmate, Blackstone-engined Class 10 shunter No D4092 (qv).

Class 08 0-6-0 No D3022

Built: BR Derby, May 1953
Numbers carried: (1) 13022,
    (2) D3022, (3) 08015
First allocation: Cricklewood
Final allocation: Tinsley
Withdrawn: 21 September 1980
Preserved: Severn Valley
    Railway, Bewdley

No D3022, Bewdley station pilot,
on 7 May 1988. *Howard
Johnston*

The acquisition in 1983 of the first Class 08 shunter for preservation was treated with a considerable degree of scepticism, but few large private lines are now without at least one nowadays. The demands of the Severn Valley Railway's engineering department outgrew the line's fleet of Ruston 165hp 0-4-0 ex-industrial shunters, and the acquisition of this heavy-duty ex-BR 350hp 0-6-0 diesel-electric machine solved the problem.

One of the first batch of 25 standard shunters (Nos 13000-24) ordered from Derby Works as order number 6232, No 13022 was the first of a series of three delivered to the former Midland Railway depot at Cricklewood, North London, moving on to Kentish Town in September 1963.

By then renumbered to No D3022, it migrated eastwards to Stratford in June 1972, up to Shirebrook in January 1974, and finally to Tinsley, Sheffield, in August 1977. The decision taken in 1979 to phase out overhauls of early vacuum braked examples meant withdrawal of No 08015 (its TOPS number was applied in January 1974) and, in common with many other recession victims, it was towed to Swindon Works in October 1980 for breaking up.

It was stored there for some considerable time before the Severn Valley Railway's Bewdley area members had sufficient funds to justify a professional inspection of the large number of locos in the works yard. The superior condition of this loco was recognised, and it arrived at Bewdley on 6 June 1983. Restoration to 1950s green livery as No D3022 took place within a year and, although intended for general duties at the southern end of the line, it has found itself pressed into main-line passenger use on a number of occasions, deputising for steam shortages.

Class 08 0-6-0 No D3029

Built: BR Derby, November
 1953
Numbers carried: (1) 13029,
 (2) D3029, (3) 08021
First allocation: Tyseley
Final allocation: Leicester
Withdrawn: (1) 2 April 1986,
 (2) 11 December 1986
Preserved: Birmingham Railway
 Museum, Tyseley

No 3029 in black livery at
Tyseley on 25 March 1990. The
number style is not authentic.
Fastline Promotions

Tyseley depot acquired its first batch of four Class 08 shunters, Nos 13026-9, at the end of 1953, and the last of them, No 13029, has, coincidentally or otherwise, returned to the same location for preservation.

This locomotive was remarkably long-lived, but little-travelled, in its 33 years of BR service. The only recorded transfers were to Stourbridge Junction in August 1960, Bescot in April 1967, and finally Toton in July 1968. It was renumbered 08021 in April 1974, the TOPS numbers not quite matching the original numbers because several earlier locomotives had by that time been withdrawn.

The official withdrawal date of 2 April 1986 did not take effect because Toton continued to use the locomotive! It was officially reinstated to Leicester the following November, but only lasted one more month before being laid up for the last time.

Since movement to Tyseley in May 1987, No 13029 has been returned to full working order and repainted from corporate BR blue to its original all-over black with steam-size cabside number transfers.

Class 08 0-6-0 No D3059 *Brechin City*

Built: BR Derby, August 1954
Numbers carried: (1) 13059,
   (2) D3059, (3) 08046
First allocation: Wellingborough
Final allocation: Burton-on-Trent
Withdrawn: 18 May 1980
Preserved: Brechin Railway
   Society

No D3059 shunting at Bridge of
Dun, 7 May 1990. *R.D. Allison*

It was the generosity of a Glasgow firm that led to the unexpected preservation of a Class 08 shunter on Tayside. It is now back in its original BR green livery as No D3059 and named after the local Scottish League Division 2 football team.

It was an early 1950s convention to allocate a small batch of Class 08s to depots as the first stage of steam replacement, and Wellingborough's turn came when Nos 13057-9 were delivered new from Derby Works in the summer of 1954. No 13059, the preserved example, was interesting in that it experienced three successive allocations to Woodford Halse on the former Great Central, always returning to Wellingborough. Depot reorganisations saw it become the responsibility (on paper at least) of Leicester Midland in April 1965,

Wellingborough in April 1966, and Leicester again in November 1967. The loco moved north to Derby Etches Park within a few days, to Toton in March 1969, and finally Burton in February 1970 for the rest of its career. It became No 08046 in 1974.

Withdrawn as surplus in May 1980, No 08046 was put into store at Derby Etches Park depot until sold to Associated British Maltsters for re-use, being towed to ABM's Airdrie base on 28 January 1981. It carried a strange-looking orange and maroon livery for a time.

No 08046 had a shorter than expected life in industry, despite mechanical overhaul, and arrived at its final home early in 1986. Now No D3059 again, it sees regular use on the Brechin-Bridge of Dun line, and is generally mechanically trouble-free.

Class 08 0-6-0 No 13079

Built: BR Darlington, January
   1954
Numbers carried: (1) 13079,
   (2) D3079, (3) 08064
First allocation: Hull Dairycoates
Final allocation: York
Withdrawn: 23 December 1984
Preserved: National Railway
   Museum, York

No 08064 undergoes overhaul
and repaint at the NRM
workshops in September 1991.
Murray Brown

It is fitting that the National Railway Museum should consider a 350hp 0-6-0 shunter worthy of preservation, and No 08064 made the short journey from nearby York Clifton depot at the end of 1985. Although questions were inevitably asked as to why this particular example was chosen, one explanation may be that while the 1968 Transport Act dictates that the NRM has the right to claim any exhibit from BR without payment, the same does not apply to movement costs.

Darlington Works switched production from the LMS design to the BR standard version after the completion of (Class 11) No 12138 in 1953, and an initial order (Nos 13060-81) was intended for the Eastern and North Eastern Regions. The NRM's example was little-travelled during its 31 years in revenue service – the first 16 were spent at Hull Dairycoates, interrupted only by overhauls at Doncaster Works, including one during October/November 1969. No D3079 was reallocated to nearby Botanic Gardens in September 1970, Doncaster in December 1975, Healey Mills in May 1976 (with general overhaul and repaint at Derby in the November), Knottingley in July 1978, and finally to York in August 1981, where it was withdrawn as surplus a few days before the end of 1984.

Although externally extremely shabby in its ex-BR condition, No 08064 was used by the NRM for shunting exhibits until 1990, when a blowing exhaust valve prompted its withdrawal for a top-end overhaul of the power unit. The work, undertaken by the Friends of the National Railway Museum, also includes full external restoration to all-over black livery with the cabside number 13079. The project is due to be complete by the summer of 1992.

Class 08 0-6-0 No D3101

Built: BR Derby, February 1955
Numbers carried: (1) 13101,
  (2) D3101
First allocation: Norwood
  Junction
Final allocation: Ashford Chart
  Leacon
Withdrawn: May 1972
Preserved: Great Central
  Railway, Loughborough

Minus rods, No 3101 stands at
Amey Roadstone, Loughborough,
26 September 1984. *A.J. Booth*

Lack of both vacuum and air brakes proved eventually to be a severe handicap for ten Class 08 shunters in the D3092-D3101 series built for the Southern Region, and they were among the first of the design to be withdrawn in two batches during 1972. Four of them, Nos D3092/4/8 and D3100, were reconditioned at Derby Works and sold to the LAMCO mining concern in Liberia, while the final example, D3101, was sold in February 1973 to Amey Roadstone for shunting in the firm's yard at Loughborough.

D3101's career had hitherto been somewhat unspectacular, consisting simply of movement between Brighton (April 1955), Norwood Junction (June 1955), Hither Green (October 1955), Ashford (August 1958), Eastleigh (September 1964), and finally Ashford Chart Leacon (May 1969).

At ARC it exchanged its blue livery for a khaki green, and lost its connecting rods, but was otherwise intact when work there came to an end at the close of 1984. The proximity of the Great Central Railway made the loco an obvious preservation candidate, and restoration saw a return to BR green livery with yellow and black 'wasp' stripes. It has latterly been partly dismantled at the back of Loughborough shed awaiting volunteer help for its restoration.

Class 08 0-6-0 No D3167

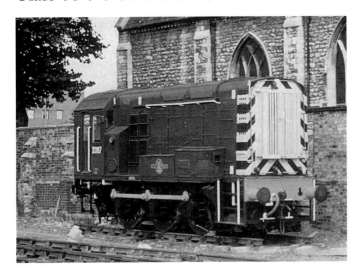

Built: BR Derby, August 1955
Numbers carried: (1) 13167,
    (2) D3167, (3) 08102
First allocation: Saltley
Final allocation: Doncaster
Withdrawn: (1) 17 June 1964,
    (2) 17 March 1985,
    (3) 14 March 1988
Preserved: Lincoln station

No D3167 at Lincoln Central
station on 8 August 1990.
Howard Johnston

The immaculately restored green Class 08 0-6-0 on a short section of track just to the west of Lincoln Central station is a lasting memorial to the city's railway history, and significant as the very last BR diesel shunter to be allocated within the county of Lincolnshire.

Built at a time when BR was experimenting (unsuccessfully) with a variety of different power unit designs within the same bodyshell, No D3167 was the first of a batch of conventional locomotives with English Electric 350hp engines assembled at Derby Works for the London Midland and Western Regions. New to Saltley in August 1955, No D3167 stayed in the West Midlands for two decades before transfer to Doncaster depot in December 1975. It then did the rounds of local depots, with a spell at Immingham from March 1979, and Lincoln in September 1980.

Its two most recent works visits were both to the former Midland Railway headquarters at Derby. It arrived there on 30 May 1969 for a general overhaul, and was back in traffic by 2 July. A later intermediate overhaul took longer, from 1 April to 14 May 1976. Destined for early withdrawal anyway because of its relative age and lack of air brake equipment, No 08102, as it had by then become, was actually condemned at Lincoln in June 1984, and again in March 1985. It was, however, quickly reinstated on both occasions for further work.

Upon closure of Lincoln depot on 27 September 1987 for maintenance, No 08102, a victim of changed working practices associated with the arrival of modern DMUs, was transferred to Doncaster depot for a short time, although Lincoln City Council was keen for its return after final withdrawal. The repaint was executed at Doncaster Works.

The council has been very wise in its choice of preservation plinth for D3167 – well out of harm's way sandwiched between the Lincoln-Newark running lines and within full view of the main road crossing and signal box. In 1991 the council was also seeking to buy a Lincoln-built Ruston & Hornsby locomotive for display elsewhere in the city.

Class 08 0-6-0 No 08108

Built: BR Derby, September
 1955
Numbers carried: (1) 13174,
 (2) D3174, (3) 08108
First allocation: Crewe
Final allocation: Cambridge
Withdrawn: 8 July 1984
Preserved: East Kent Railway,
 Shepherdswell

No 08108 at the now-closed
Dower Wood yard at Newmarket
on 9 November 1990. *Ray King*

Railfreight's decision to withdraw from the wagonload Speedlink service in July 1991 was good fortune for the recently formed East Kent Light Railway, which was able to negotiate the purchase of a fully operational and well-maintained Class 08 shunter at a bargain price from a private operator in Cambridgeshire.

New from Derby Works in September 1955 and painted all-over black as No 13174, the loco spent its first six months working out of Crewe South steam shed before being sent south to Willesden, its base until February 1966 when Rugby assumed control. (It had been one of the last shunters to gain a D number, not being altered until early 1962.) A month later it was off to Holyhead.

A visit to Derby Works for general overhaul in February 1972 saw the loco repainted into blue livery, and retained for use at Derby depot. It was renumbered 08108 in February 1974, and reallocated to the Western Region's Old Oak Common depot the same November. A surplus of shunters at that depot in January 1976 meant another transfer, and a third region, for No

08108, this time to Stratford for examination and a brief trial before a final trip north to Cambridge a week later. The loco underwent a final intermediate overhaul, again at Derby, in March 1976.

The Newmarket firm of Dower Wood approached BR in July 1984 for a shunter to work at its grain terminal to the east of the station on the Cambridge-Bury St Edmunds line, and hand-picked No 08108 from a selection of possibles at Cambridge (those rejected included Nos 08083 and 08100). The loco was delivered under tow in August 1984, and an agreement was reached with BREL Doncaster and later RFS Industries for it to be maintained in good order. A repaint was even undertaken in BR colours.

Redundant again in 1991, No 08108 was offered for sale to the East Kent group who undertook testing before movement to Shepherdswell in August. It was the first loco to reach Aythorne, 3 miles from base, since the clearance of the line, and is to retain its blue paint style.

Class 08 0-6-0 No D3180

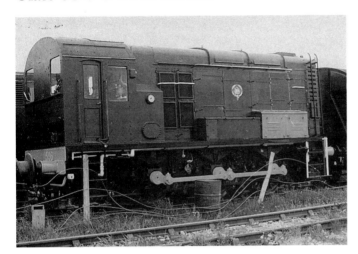

Built: BR Derby, October 1955
Numbers carried: (1) 13180,
   (2) D3180, (3) 08114
First allocation: Derby
Final allocation: Doncaster
Withdrawn: 6 November 1983
Preserved: Great Central
   Railway, Loughborough

No D3180 during its term at
Blunsdon, May 1985. *Harry
Needle*

Vast numbers of Class 08 shunters became victims of a sudden loss of rail business at the beginning of the 1980s. BREL's Swindon Works not only became a mass storage area and breaking-up site, but also a shopping venue for preservation lines looking for cheap but reliable motive power. Thus it was that No 08114 was singled out for a second career, originally with the Gloucestershire Warwickshire Railway at Toddington.

This example was new as No 13180 in October 1955, part of a Derby Works order for the London Midland Region. Its career generally lacked headlines, working in yards at Derby until December 1955, Saltley until March 1956, Cricklewood until November 1967, Derby Etches Park until October 1967, and finally Doncaster for the rest of its working life. The final general overhaul was completed at Swindon in March 1980.

Within a fortnight of its withdrawal on 6 November 1983, No 08114 (as it had become) was on its way to Swindon for scrapping. Bought from the long scrap-lines because of its generally good condition, the loco was moved by road to Toddington early in October 1984, and has been repainted from its BR blue livery into a dark shade of green similar to Great Western colours. A subsequent move was made to Blunsdon on the Swindon & Cricklade Railway.

The beginning of 1991 saw the loco on the move again, this time to the Great Central Railway at Quorn. The intention, however, is to transfer it to the northern extension line where it can run some of the early trains between Ruddington and East Leake; it will be able to return to Loughborough Central when the gap is bridged between the two lines. No D3180, in full working order, spent its early GCR days shunting in all-over black livery without any identifying numbers, but the intention was to put it back into green livery as No 13180. Engine repairs were effected during 1991.

Class 08 0-6-0 No 08123 *George Mason*

Built: BR Derby, November
   1955
Numbers carried: (1) 13190,
   (2) D3190, (3) 08123
First allocation: Severn Tunnel
   Junction
Final allocation: Crewe
Withdrawn: 20 March 1984
Preserved: Cholsey &
   Wallingford Railway, Oxon

CWR No 08123 in use near
Wallingford in the summer of
1988. *P.Warrington*

The arrival of former Crewe Works pilot No 08123 by road on 8 June 1985 represented the first fully operational motive power for the Cholsey & Wallingford preservation group, and within hours was the first loco to traverse the line since it closed to BR traffic in 1981. Analysis of several dozen redundant Class 08 shunters at the nearby BREL Swindon Works had left society members pondering over a choice of Nos 08121 and 08123, and the latter was eventually chosen for its better condition, having been given a general overhaul as recently as December 1979.

No 08123, as it continues to be known at Wallingford, started life new from Derby as black-liveried No 13190 in 1955, working from Severn Tunnel Junction. It moved little in its 20 BR years, going to Newport in June 1968, and north to Crewe in October 1980. It was

withdrawn as surplus in March 1984, but was stored for 11 months before being sent to Swindon Works for scrapping.

In preservation, No 08123 was named *George Mason* as a tribute to a late CWRPS founder member at a ceremony at Wallingford station on 26 October 1985, and has also received cast GW-style cabside numberplates which it carries on operating days. BR corporate blue livery has given way to a domestic style of dark green, including 'C&WR' in Great Western style on the bodysides.

The arrival of steam has seen No 08123 used less on passenger services over the last couple of years, although it is always on standby and is regularly called upon for permanent way duties. Although starting is sometimes a problem, the locomotive has required little but essential maintenance since arrival.

Class 08 0-6-0 No D3255

Built: BR Derby, May 1956
Numbers carried: (1) 13255,
  (2) D3255
First allocation: Bristol St
  Philip's Marsh
Final allocation: Gloucester
Withdrawn: 30 December 1972
Preserved: Brighton Railway
  Museum

A visitor for repair, No D3255 at
Cardiff Canton depot, 24 April
1982. *Norman Preedy*

The first of the three ex-National Coal Board 350hp Class 08 diesel-electric shunters preserved at Brighton Locomotive Works was nearing the completion of restoration at the end of 1990. It has been repainted black to meet the museum's general plan to maintain its fleet of locomotives as they were in the mid-1950s; the NCB had retained the final BR Brunswick green carried at withdrawal, and had arguably never cleaned it during nearly two decades of use in South Wales.

No 13255 was ex-works from Derby in May 1956 to Bristol St Philip's Marsh depot, and also worked out of Bristol Bath Road (October 1961), Cardiff Cathays (March 1963), Landore, Swansea (July 1964), Oxley, Wolverhampton (April 1967), Bristol Bath Road again (September 1969), and finally Gloucester (February 1972).

No D3255 was written off BR's books as early as December 1972 – too early even to acquire a computerised TOPS number which might have otherwise been somewhere in the 08180-08200 region. It was moved from Gloucester depot to Blaenavon Colliery near Abergavenny in March 1974, and then on to Bargoed Colliery within a few weeks; Mardy Colliery took it over during 1984.

The locomotive had not seen the inside of a locomotive works for almost 20 years when it was moved to Brighton, and despite having no radiator elements was successfully started up during 1988. Recent work has been devoted to the electrical circuitry, power unit, auxiliary generator and compressor. Superficial damage inflicted on No 13255 during rough colliery use has also had to be straightened out, including footsteps and handrails. This work complete, attention was then due to be turned to Brighton's more celebrated No 13000 (qv).

Class 08 0-6-0 No D3261

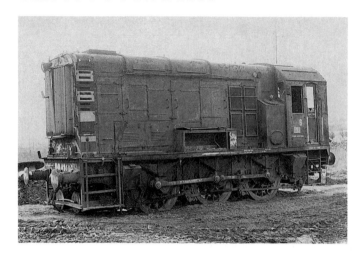

Built: BR Derby, July 1956
Numbers carried: (1) 13261,
  (2) D3261
First allocation: Llanelli
Final allocation: Cardiff Canton
Withdrawn: 30 December 1972
Preserved: Brighton Railway
  Museum

No D3261 at Tower Colliery,
23 April 1988. *Michael
Whatmough*

How many preserved locomotives can claim to have been stolen? The story of how No 13265 came to be loaded onto a lorry owned by unscrupulous scrap merchants is one of the most remarkable in this book. Indeed, it was only a sharp-eyed National Coal Board employee who noticed that the low-loader which arrived to collect it from Tower Colliery, Hirwaun, South Wales, was not the one booked by Brighton Railway Museum.

That obstacle overcome, worse was to follow. No 13265 was unloaded into pit slurry, well away from a set of rails. Apart from the obvious damage, it took considerable planning to first dig it out and then find a way of lifting it on to stable ground for it to be moved away. Minor vandalism left the volunteers wondering whether it was in fact worth all the bother to save it. Including negotiations, the whole exercise took two years to complete.

New from Derby Works to Llanelli depot in June 1956, it was also on the books of Neath (November 1956), Llanelli again (August 1957), Cardiff Cathays (October 1962), and finally Cardiff Canton (November 1964). It was withdrawn without being allocated a TOPS number, one of only a small handful of Class 08 shunters to miss out. It was stored at Landore depot, Swansea, for several months prior to sale.

The National Coal Board first placed Class 08 shunters on its shopping list as steam replacements in the early 1970s, and BR released No D3261 for use at Tower Colliery, at the extreme end of the Aberdare branch. The transaction was one of the earliest such sales, but the locomotive repaid its investment by putting in over 15 years of service before closure of the colliery ended its active role.

Road movement to Brighton took place on 11 December 1988, and the locomotive was originally put into store in the upper goods yard engineering siding until space was made available at the former Preston Park Pullman Works. The plan is eventually to restore it to early BR livery as No 13261.

Class 08 0-6-0 No 08195

Built: BR Derby, August 1956
Numbers carried: (1) 13265,
  (2) D3265, (3) 08195
First allocation: Duffryn, Port
  Talbot
Final allocation: Cardiff Canton
Withdrawn: 25 September 1983
Preserved: Llangollen Railway

In pre-preservation days, No
08195 is seen at Radyr depot,
Cardiff, on 19 August 1979.
Norman Preedy

The Llangollen Railway's Class 08 shunter No D3265 is one of a batch 'hit-listed' from 1980 when an excess of numbers meant that overhauls would cease on locomotives which were not considered suitable for dual braking. Thus the outshopping of the final overhaul, No 08254, from Glasgow in December 1980 preceded wholesale scrapping of all Class 08 locomotives numbered below No 08388.

Bought from the Swindon dump of withdrawn 08s in 1986, No D3265 had enjoyed a generally unspectacular 27-year career on BR, working out of South Wales depots. A new batch of Class 08s for the Western Region began with the delivery of No 13255 from Derby in May 1956, followed by No 13265 three months later, destined for the yards at

Port Talbot. It moved on to Neath (November 1956), Llanelli (August 1957), Cardiff East Dock (August 1957), and nearby Cathays (October 1957). Cardiff Canton took customary possession in November 1964, and only parted with it upon withdrawal as No 08195 in September 1983. The loco's last major overhaul had been at Derby in November 1975, and it arrived at Swindon on 12 October 1984 for breaking up, but was purchased for yard duties at Llangollen. It departed from Swindon on 25 March 1986 for its new home in North Wales.

It is now back in service after a two-year programme of renovation, which included replacement of the most recent BR corporate blue livery by a coat of BR Brunswick green.

Class 08 0-6-0 No 13290

Built: BR Derby, December 1956
Numbers carried: (1) 13290,
(2) D3290, (3) 08220
First allocation: Nottingham
Final allocation: Crewe
Withdrawn: 28 March 1986
Preserved: Steamtown, Carnforth

No 08220 at Stoke depot on
14 November 1981. *Norman
Preedy*

A little-publicised locomotive in preservation, Class 08 shunter No 08220 arrived at Steamtown, Carnforth, in July 1990 aboard a low-loader. It had spent a number of years in a yard at Wakefield, having been bought from BR from store at Chester. It is in full working order, and was repainted in black livery with yellow and black nose and cab end chevrons at the end of 1991 for Christmas specials at the Lancashire depot, but had yet to acquire its pre-September 1962 number of 13290.

New English Electric-engined 350hp shunters were being turned out in such numbers in the mid-1950s that large batches were often allocated to one depot. It was unusual, therefore, that No 13290 should go to Nottingham when the rest of the 13288-93 batch went to Sheffield. The loco stayed in the area until September 1963, and is only credited with one other base in its 30-year life, moving to Crewe in November 1966. In that year over 20 Class 08s were required for the area's yards, and there were also separate allocations for the Stoke, Chester and Shrewsbury areas. By 1986

all of these duties were managed by Crewe, and it is likely that this loco would have be used on such diverse duties at Crewe as Basford Hall trip pilot, shunter at the Gresty Lane wagon shops, or BREL Works loco. Duties at Stoke included the still-open Cockshute yard, while Shrewsbury provided work at the station carriage sidings and in Coton Hill yard on the east side the Gobowen line.

The loco was renumbered No 08220 in August 1974, and was a relatively early recipient of blue livery with the number transfers positioned over the BR emblems which were also carried on its cabsides. Its final overhaul was at Doncaster Works, completed in March 1978. Equipping with dual brakes was never considered.

Even BR finds it more economical to use road transport to shift slow-moving locomotives, and No 08220's owner chose this method to move the loco from Wakefield to Carnforth. It was seen on the M6 Motorway on 30 June 1990, arriving at its new home a week later.

Class 08 0-6-0 No 08238

Built: BR Derby, May 1956
Numbers carried: (1) 13308,
 (2) D3308, (3) 08238
First allocation: King's Cross
Final allocation: Gloucester
Withdrawn: 18 March 1984
Preserved: Swindon Heritage
 Centre

No 08238 at Gloucester depot on
6 May 1984. *Norman Preedy*

The locomotive which is used for shunting at the troubled Swindon Heritage Centre complex was obtained third-hand after a scheme to develop mining interests in the Dean Forest area of Gloucestershire failed to get off the ground, even though the prospecting company had already acquired two locomotives for the expected rail traffic generated by its activities. One of was No 08238, which was conveniently withdrawn from Gloucester depot and was parked in the yard for several years in serviceable condition.

This particular Class 08 shunter was a Derby Works product for the London area of the Eastern Region. Originally numbered 13308, it was one of six delivered new to King's Cross Top Shed over a four-week period in May/June 1956. The subsequent opening of the purpose-built diesel depot down the line at Finsbury Park saw all the locos transferred there in January 1961. They were subsequently progressively dispersed, and the replacement programme for Blackstone-engined Class 10s saw No 13308 transferred to Tinsley (Sheffield) in February 1969. Further ER moves were to Langwith (November 1972) and Shirebrook (May 1973). The loco was renumbered No

08238 in February 1973.

No 08238 retained its green livery until a visit to Derby Works for a general overhaul, completed in June 1976. Already earmarked for transfer to Laira (Plymouth), further Western Region transfers were to Newton Abbot (November 1976), Bristol Bath Road (October 1977), Newton Abbot again (from May 1980 until closure), Bristol (March 1981), and finally Gloucester (July 1982). By that time the effects of a recessional down-turn in freight business meant that vacuum-brake-only locomotives numbered below No 08388 were not technically suitable for dual-brake conversion, and No 08238 was withdrawn as surplus in March 1984.

It was purchased in August 1984, along with another Class 08, Derby-built No 08320, withdrawn in December 1982 from Toton, by the Free Forest Mining Company of Tetbury, but in the event neither was ever required. After five years of inactivity, No 08320 was resold to English China Clays to shunt at Fowey Docks. No 08238 moved to Swindon, where it has been returned to full working order to shunt preserved stock. It latterly retained its BR blue livery.

Class 08 0-6-0 No D3336

Built: BR Darlington, February 1957
Numbers carried: (1) 13336, (2) D3336, (3) 08266
First allocation: Darnall
Final allocation: Shirebrook
Withdrawn: 17 March 1985
Preserved: Keighley & Worth Valley Railway, Haworth

No D3336 at Haworth yard on 7 November 1989. *Howard Johnston*

Darlington Works was building 350hp shunters at an average of one a week during 1957, producing English Electric-engined (Class 08) and Blackstone-engined (Class 10) versions side by side.

No 13336 was the last officially outshopped from Darlington Works in black livery with the obsolete five-figure number, the next loco, 12 weeks later, appearing in green as No D3454. No 13336 is also reported to have uniquely carried the carriage-type BR emblem instead of the lion and wheel. It later carried standard blue livery, and the computerised No 08266 from February 1974.

Preservation on the Worth Valley Line is not far removed from the locomotive's original working environment. New to Darnall depot,

Sheffield, with Nos 13331-5, it did, however, work out of King's Cross Top Shed for 11 months from May 1957 before returning north for the rest of its career based variously at Tinsley, Darnall, and Shirebrook. Its final overhaul was completed at Derby Works in May 1976.

Surplus to the Eastern Region's needs, No 08266 was towed to Swindon for scrapping in June 1985, but five months later was on its way north again for preservation at Haworth. Since arrival there by road on 21 November 1985, it has been restored to BR green as No D3336. The locomotive is primarily required for works trains, but has been known to make the occasional appearance on passenger duty.

Class 08 0-6-0 No D3358

Built: BR Derby, June 1957
Numbers carried: (1) D3358,
  (2) 08288
First allocation: Llanelli
Final allocation: Swindon
Withdrawn: 21 January 1983
Preserved: Mid-Hants Railway,
  Ropley

The Mid-Hants's No D3358
under repair in Ropley yard on
2 February 1990. *David Warwick*

The decision to number the BR diesel fleet into a separate series from steam took effect at Derby Works in June 1957, and this loco was the first to be outshopped with a 'D' prefix.

No D3358 became part of the domestic WR fleet, and was later allocated to a succession of South Wales depots, first Llanelli, then Neath a month later, and back to Llanelli in July 1959. It was transferred to Landore in April 1964, Cardiff in September 1967, and Swindon in May 1969. Its furthest journey was to Newton Abbot for a spell from February 1978 until March 1981, following which a month at Bristol preceded its final transfer to Swindon.

No 08288 was stored out of use for two years until withdrawal in January 1983, and it was moved into the works on 14 April for scrap. Rescue came in the shape of the Mid-Hants Railway, which was searching for motive power to handle tracklaying to Alton. No 08288 was bought by the line's Woking and Guildford Regional Group, and moved on 1 November 1984. After some initial problems with vandalism whilst parked at Farnham *en route* to the line, the loco is now in full working order. Its colour scheme is early BR green.

Class 08 0-6-0 No 08350

Built: BR Crewe, December
   1957
Numbers carried: (1) D3420,
   (2) 08350
First allocation: Cardiff East
   Dock
Final allocation: Cardiff Canton
Withdrawn: 17 January 1984
Preserved: North Staffordshire
   Railway, Cheddleton

No 08350 at Radyr depot,
Cardiff, on 19 August 1979.
Norman Preedy

Crewe Works was late to join in the Class 08 production programme, and is only credited with construction of 135 of BR's biggest class of locomotives. No D3420, preserved at the North Staffordshire Railway centre at Cheddleton, was only the second off the production line there at the end of 1957, when steam locomotives were still being assembled alongside in some numbers.

No D3420's BR career could not be regarded as spectacular, working from Cardiff East Dock until a short move to Cathays in October 1962. It was then at Canton from November 1964 until the end of its career. The last major works overhaul was completed at BREL Swindon in August 1976.

Like many of its sisters, No 08350 was occasionally hired out to the National Coal Board, and was noted in this capacity at Abercwmboi in mid-1983. It was withdrawn in January 1984, and moved within two months to Swindon for scrap.

The North Staffordshire Railway acquired two Class 08s for its Cheddleton base, and No 08350 arrived there on 18 September 1984. Since then the locomotive has spent some considerable time out of use with a defective wheelset after slipping a crank, a relatively common fault on BR which normally required a visit to works or a major repair centre. The loco had to be lifted to roll the wheelset out from underneath the nose-suspended traction motor, no mean feat as the motor weighs around a ton!

The wheelset was then transported to BREL Crewe for the offending wheel to be pressed off the axle, realigned and reassembled. The North Staffs group established a target of having the loco back in service by the end of 1991 after another repaint to BR Brunswick green livery.

The second Class 08 to have been part of the Cheddleton fleet was No 08359/D3429 – see next page.

Class 08 0-6-0 No D3429

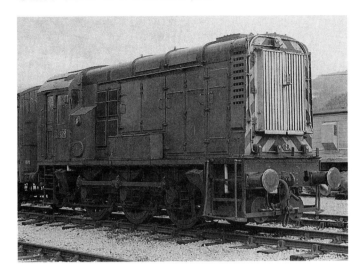

Built: BR Crewe, March 1958
Numbers carried: (1) D3429,
  (2) 08359
First allocation: Bristol St
  Philip's Marsh
Final allocation: Cardiff Canton
Withdrawn: 7 March 1984
Preserved: Peak Railway, Buxton

No D3429 in Darley Dale yard,
15 April 1990. *Steve Worrall*

The Peak Railway's Buxton site is the latest home for Class 08 shunter No D3429, which was originally acquired for the North Staffordshire Railway's motive power fleet at its Cheddleton site.

Another product of Crewe Works, the loco's stay in the Bristol area was short, being transferred to Swansea Danygraig depot in January 1960, followed by spells at most major South Wales depots – Neath in January 1962, Margam in March 1964, Landore in August 1980, Newport Ebbw Junction in July 1981, and finally Cardiff Canton from November 1982. Its withdrawal was followed by a tow to Swindon Works for removal of spares and breaking up, arriving on 7 March 1984.

Although notable achievements of mass-production machines are inevitably scarce, No D3429 is credited with working the last train over the Cymmer-Glyncorrwg section of the South Wales Mineral Railway on 22 May 1970

to collect the empties from the closed Glyncorrwg Colliery. The loco's last major works overhaul was at Swindon in June 1976, and it was loaned to the NCB Wernos Colliery for part of December 1979.

Sale with sister No 08350 (see previous page) was effected that same July, and it arrived at Cheddleton by road on 20 September. Restoration to BR green with black roof and red buffer-beams was completed in time for a naming ceremony on 15 September 1985 as *Signal Radio*, after the local broadcasting station.

It was transferred by low-loader to Peak Rail's headquarters at Buxton on 9 January 1987, and has since moved on to the line's southern headquarters at Darley Dale. Renumbered No D3429, it sports green livery again, and is fitted with non-standard cast metal numberplates with a red background.

Class 10 0-6-0 No D3452

Built: BR Darlington, November
    1957
Number carried: D3452
First allocation: New England,
    Peterborough
Final allocation: Toton
Withdrawn: 22 June 1968
Preserved: Bodmin & Wenford
    Railway

No D3452 as a working loco, at
Fowey Docks in 1983.

English China Clays bought three non-standard Blackstone-engined Class 10 shunters from BR in 1968. They proved to be good buys – ECC operated the extensive system at Fowey Docks in Cornwall with them for a full 20 years before more modern and reliable Class 08 replacements came their way.

No D3452 was new to the once vast East Coast Main Line steam depot at New England, Peterborough, in November 1957, but moved to Doncaster in July 1962, on to Sheffield Darnall in December 1964, Tinsley in October 1965, and finally Toton in October 1966.

A vast surplus of even its larger 350hp diesel-electric shunting locomotives prompted BR to cut the fleet by some 15 per cent between 1967 and 1972, and the obvious candidates for withdrawal were some of the troublesome early types with non-standard Crossley power units and Crompton-Parkinson traction motors, plus all those with Blackstone power units and either GEC or BTH motors. The decision seemed harsh, since some of them had only been delivered from Darlington Works as late

as 1962. No D3452 was withdrawn in June 1968 when Class 08 substitutes arrived from the Scottish and Western Regions.

The National Coal Board picked up several examples at bargain prices, but had disposed of them all by the mid-1980s; only one NCB Class 10, No D4067, survives in preservation (qv). English China Clays needed to replace steam in Cornwall, and opted to buy a total of three Class 10s, two to work and one ostensibly as a source of spare parts; two have since been bought for new careers.

No D3452 still bore its original BR green livery when it was delivered to the nearby Bodmin & Wenford Railway on 5 March 1989. It was quickly put into running order, being started for the first time in preservation on 23 January 1990. Spares were obtained from derelict sister No D3497 (new to Stratford, London, in December 1957) before it was broken up. Renovation and repainting was completed during 1991, and the loco double-headed with Class 08 No D3559 (qv) at the diesel gala on 5-6 October.

Class 08 0-6-0 No D3462

Built: BR Darlington, June 1957
Numbers carried: (1) D3462,
    (2) 08377
First allocation: Hither Green
Final allocation: Plymouth Laira
Withdrawn: 26 June 1983
Preserved: Dean Forest Railway

No D3462, restored to its
original number style, on the
Dean Forest Railway on 6 May
1990. *Fastline Promotions*

It was the Southern Region that gained a series of 14 new shunters, Nos D3459-72, between June and October 1957, and most of them were destined to have shorter lives that the rest of the class because of the unsuitability of their 90-volt electrical systems and lack of dual brakes. Most of the series were in fact altered to run at 20 mph for use on electrified lines, but this example was not changed from the original design.

No D3462 was certainly well-travelled during its time with BR. After periods at Hither Green, Norwood Junction and Selhurst, it migrated north to Crewe in December 1968, and by May 1972 was at Wigan Springs Branch. Renumbering as No 08377 coincided with a

major overhaul in February 1974, and the same June it discovered pastures new with transfer to Bristol Bath Road.

This was far from the end of the story, however, as No 08377 worked out of the Cornish China Clay depot of St Blazey from February 1975, and its final move was to Laira in September 1980 for three years before withdrawal on 26 June 1983. Towed to Swindon Works for scrap, it laying there for a long period in the cutting-up line before being sold to the Dean Forest Railway. It departed the Works on 12 March 1986, arriving at Lydney seven days later. Restoration has taken place since then to 1950s BR livery with old-style large cabside numbers.

Class 10 0-6-0 No D3476

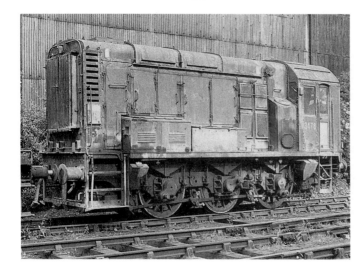

Built: BR Darlington, December 1957
Number carried: D3476
First allocation: King's Cross
Final allocation: Toton
Withdrawn: 1 June 1968
Preserved: South Yorkshire Railway, Meadowhall, Sheffield

No D3476, a recent arrival at Meadowhall from Fowey Docks, on 28 May 1990. *Brian Cuttell*

A total of 171 'large' shunters built at Crewe and Darlington between 1955 and 1962 were equipped with non-standard power units and transmissions – Crossley/Crompton Parkinson, and Blackstone/GEC – and were classified as Class 10. Some had very short lives indeed, especially the Crossley variants, and reductions in freight traffic saw even the relatively modern Blackstone examples eliminated by 1971. But even if BR didn't want them, there was a brisk trade for re-use by industry, especially in colliery areas.

BR allocated all the Blackstone-engined Class 10s to either the Eastern Region or the Nottingham area, so the sale of three to English China Clays to displace steam at Fowey Docks in West Cornwall was all the more surprising.

They proved a worthwhile buy, however, working for a further two decades before replacements arrived.

No D3476, the second oldest Class 10 to survive, was new to King's Cross Top Shed in December 1957, and stayed in the London area for a further four years, working the yards around Hatfield from January 1958, and Hitchin from January 1961. Then followed a transfer north to Tinsley in April 1961, and subsequent transfers to Retford (July 1962), Lincoln (June 1965), Langwith (March 1966), Toton (August 1966), Colwick (November 1967), and finally Toton again in December 1967 for its last six months of operation on BR.

No D3476 arrived at Meadowhall on 2 October after a long period of transit from Fowey.

Class 08 0-6-0 No D3559

Built: BR Derby, November
 1958
Numbers carried: (1) D3559,
 (2) 08444
First allocation: Polmont
Final allocation: Cardiff
Withdrawn: 2 November 1986
Preserved: Bodmin & Wenford
 Railway

No D3559 restored to green
livery at Bodmin, 22 June 1990.
Steve Worrall

For a Class 08, No D3559 was remarkably well-travelled during its BR career, covering three regions. New from Derby Works to Polmont in southern Scotland in November 1958, it moved on to Grangemouth in January 1964 and Haymarket in February 1969. The biggest move thus far took place in June 1969 when it was despatched to Doncaster as part of the general nationwide redistribution of shunters to allow for the withdrawal of the Blackstone-engined Class 10s. A further major change in this loco's life took place in September 1983 when its lack of air brakes made Cardiff a more useful base.

These moves also ensured that the locations of its overhauls were also diverse – an intermediate repair at St Rollox, Glasgow, during October 1963, a general at Doncaster Works in April/May 1971, and another general at Swindon in December 1978. Two more visits were made to Swindon for minor attention, in June 1979 and November 1980, but not being selected for dual braking inevitably shortened

the locomotive's life.

In February 1987 No D3559 was sold to Fitzgerald Lighting Ltd, a firm actively supporting the Bodmin Steam Railway, and actually earns its keep there. It is expected to handle a regular weekly freight service of four of five wagons, which started between the company's sidings and a BR exchange siding at Bodmin Parkway on 2 December 1989, conveying products to other plants at St Helens, Basildon and Edinburgh.

The loco lost its distinctive TOPS number upon completion of the repaint into 1960s BR green as No D3559 in April 1990, and it has already been involved in passenger haulage on the expanding preserved line. On 5 July 1991 it came to the aid of its former owners when it was sent to Bodmin Parkway before the start of normal traffic to collect a defective English China Clays bogie slurry wagon which was towed up the hill to be pumped out prior to repairs.

Class 08 0-6-0 No 3586

Built: BR Crewe, November
1958
Numbers carried: (1) D3586,
(2) 08471
First allocation: Burton-on-Trent
Final allocation: Leicester
Withdrawn: 9 September 1985
Preserved: Severn Valley
Railway, Bridgnorth

No 3586 at Bridgnorth shed on
12 May 1991. *Howard Johnston*

The Severn Valley Railway's second Class 08 shunter did not turn a wheel during its last two years on BR's books – it was held in store at Swindon pending availability of finance for a full overhaul and dual braking, but cutbacks ordered during 1985 saw it withdrawn instead.

No D3586 was little-travelled during its BR career, being delivered to Burton-on-Trent in November 1958, following which only one move was made, to Leicester in November 1967; it was regular sight at the sub-shed at Wellingborough for the next three years. The loco's final intermediate overhaul was at Swindon Works in May 1980, but lack of air brake equipment severely hampered its activities. It was put into store first at Leicester on 29 May 1983, and was later moved to

Swindon pending conversion.

Purchased for use by the SVR Holdings Company for use as the Bridgnorth shed and station pilot, No 08471 left Swindon on 26 March 1986 by rail to Gloucester, thence to the Severn Valley line by road transport. Still in final BR blue livery in contrast to the line's other Class 08, No D3022 (qv), it has been renumbered back to post-1968 style as No 3586; BR policy was to drop the 'D' prefix in that year when there ceased to be the possibility of a number clash with a steam locomotive. The loco required minimum maintenance before being fit for service. Unlike the line's sister loco, No D3022, it had by 1991 still to achieve the honour of passenger service on the main line to Kidderminster.

Class 08 0-6-0 No D3591

Built: BR Crewe, December
  1958
Numbers carried: (1) D3591,
  (2) 08476
First allocation: Newton Heath
Final allocation: Thornton
  Junction
Withdrawn: 8 September 1985
Preserved: Swanage Railway

In BR green livery with a white
roof, No D3591 is seen at
Swanage on 23 May 1990.
Howard Johnston

Another locomotive which should have been overhauled for a further spell of use in Scotland but was condemned on economy grounds was No 08476. The work was never carried out, and it has since found a new home in preservation in Dorset.

Unlike its London Midland contemporaries, Crewe product No D3591 was transferred away to Scotland after spells at Newton Heath and Longsight. It went north to Polmadie in November 1971, and there were also transfers to Eastfield (March 1972) and Ayr (May 1973). A clear indication that its final general overhaul was completed at Glasgow Works (in November 1980) was that it carried the characteristic Scottish paint variation of 'barbed wire' emblems on the battery boxes instead of the bodysides. Running out of work, it operated spasmodically from Dunfermline after June 1982, and finally Thornton Junction in October 1984.

It was towed all the way to Swindon two months later for storage pending overhaul. Bought by the Swanage Railway, it departed on 21 March 1986, and by the end of the year was back in full working order and repainted in the old-style green livery as No D3591. It has been heavily involved in the Swanage Railway's 3-mile northward extension to Harman's Cross, which was reached with passenger coaches on a crew training trip on 3 December 1988. Corfe Castle is next.

Class 08 0-6-0 No 08490

Built: BR Horwich, November
1958
Numbers carried: (1) D3605,
(2) 08490
First allocation: Old Oak
Common
Final allocation: Thornton
Junction
Withdrawn: 24 November 1985
**Preserved: Strathspey Railway,
Aviemore**

No 08490 was based at Croes
Newydd depot, Wrexham, on
17 October 1981. *Norman
Preedy*

The Strathspey Railway's Class 08 shunter No 08490 has surely had the most prestigious roster of any 350hp shunter during 1991 – it was regularly used at the head of the 'Royal Scotsman', a luxury nine-coach train of vintage stock whose passengers are quite prepared to pay £1,000 for the privilege of a tour over Scotland's scenic lines. No 08490 only worked 11 miles in 1990, but then serious mechanical failure of the line's Class 27 main-line locomotive and an early morning commitment to haul the special between Aviemore and Boat of Garten meant use of the 08 or a crew rising before dawn to fire up a steam locomotive!

A maximum speed of 15 mph has not proved too much of a restriction for the preserved railway, although serious consideration was being given at the end of the year to purchasing a more suitable 1,000hp Class 20 Bo-Bo loco as standby.

One of the last active vacuum-brake-only shunters on the Scottish Region, No 08490 is one of the widest travelled of preserved Class 08s, having also worked on the Western and London Midland during its career. It is significant in being the only diesel locomotive product from the former Lancashire & Yorkshire Railway works of Horwich so far saved for preservation

New to Old Oak Common depot in November 1958 as No D3605, it was moved on to South Wales the following year, working out of Cardiff East Dock (January 1959), Cardiff Cathays (October 1962), Neath (October 1963), Port Talbot (March 1964), Landore (March 1968), and back at Old Oak (April 1969). February 1970 saw it moved up to Birkenhead Mollington Street, Allerton the following month, Chester in April 1977, and then to Scotland, based at Dundee (July 1982), Dunfermline Townhill (July 1982), and Thornton Junction (October 1984). Granted a final works overhaul at Derby, completed during August 1981, it was out of use at Perth depot from the beginning of 1986.

Its sale for preservation at Britain's most northerly standard gauge site was concluded in January 1987 after long-term store at Perth. It still carries final BR blue livery.

Class 10 0-6-0 No D4067

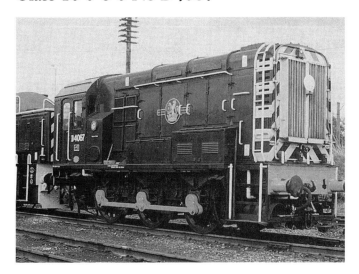

Built: BR Darlington, May 1961
Number carried: D4067
First allocation: Darnall
Final allocation: Shirebrook
Withdrawn: 13 December 1970
Preserved: Great Central
    Railway, Loughborough

No D4067 in Loughborough
yard, 11 April 1987. *Howard
Johnston*

Apart from providing employment for the former North Eastern Railway locomotive works at Darlington in the last decade of existence, and the Blackstone engineering company of Stamford, there could be little satisfaction in building 171 locomotives that were only to survive in BR service for a maximum of 14 years.

No D4067 was typical of the final series of 45 Class 10s, Nos D4049-94 constructed between January 1961 and June 1962. They provided vast over-capacity for Eastern Region depots in the Sheffield area, North London, Doncaster, Peterborough and across Lincolnshire, and were withdrawn from the summer of 1968 onwards either as surplus or when replacement Class 08s arrived from the run-down of Scottish and Western Region allocations.

New to Sheffield in May 1961, No D4067 spent its entire BR career in that area, was bought by the National Coal Board for steam replacement in the Kent coalfields, and arrived at Betteshanger in April 1971. The loco moved on to the nearby Snowdown Colliery in May 1976, and, by good fortune, to Nailstone Colliery in Leicestershire the following month. A full overhaul at Derby in November 1976 seemed somewhat wasteful as rail traffic ended at Nailstone on 23 August 1979 with the installation of a rapid-loading conveyor system, but a new owner in the shape of a Great Central member was on hand.

Delivery to Loughborough took place on 5 February 1980. No D4067 was restored to full working order, repainted in green livery, and celebrated its 25th anniversary on 5 May 1986 with due ceremony. It has most recently been seen stabled at Rothley shed, the midway point of the Great Central line.

Class 10 0-6-0 No D4092

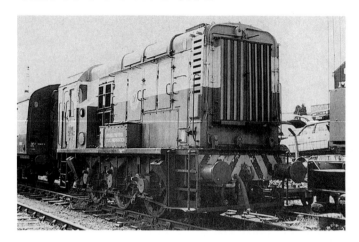

Built: BR Darlington, May 1962
Number carried: D4092
First allocation: Tinsley
Final allocation: New England,
    Peterborough
Withdrawn: 1 September 1968
Preserved: South Yorkshire
    Railway, Meadowhall, Sheffield

No D4092 in blue and grey
industrial colours at Meadowhall,
18 June 1989. *Howard Johnston*

Class 10 shunter No D4092 returned to its old stamping ground on the outskirts of Sheffield in 1988 after a 20-year career that took it into West Wales as part of the motive power stable of Duffryn Powell Fuels of Gwaun-cae-Gurwen, an opencast coal disposal site, where it had worked since purchase from BR in October 1968. A traction motor fault ended its career.

The final series of Blackstone-engined Class 10s, Nos D4049-94, were completed at Darlington between January 1961 and June 1962, and it was indicative of the volume of work radiating from Darnall depot that all 46 were initially allocated there.

No D4092 itself worked in the Sheffield area for most of its six-year career, including Tinsley and Staveley, although the last three months were spent at New England, Peterborough, by then in its death throes.

It took nearly eight months of negotiations for the Barclay Locomotive Group to negotiate the purchase of No D4092 from Powell Duffryn Fuels. The intention is to restore No D4092 to its original BR green livery after repair. It presently carries the Powell Duffryn colours of blue and white with the name *Christine*. It has carried its original number throughout its working life.

Class 24 Bo-Bo No D5032 *Helen Turner*

Built: BR Crewe, July 1959
Numbers carried: (1) D5032,
    (2) 24032
First allocation: March
Final allocation: Crewe
Withdrawn: 17 July 1976
Preserved at: North Yorkshire
    Moors Railway

No D5032 during its initial two-tone green era, at Grosmont on 14 February 1982. *Howard Johnston*

BR's love affair with the Sulzer-engined Type 2 design lasted only 30 years, even though a vast total of 594 locomotives were produced from BR workshops and private builders. The Class 24 was the original version from BR Derby between 1958 and 1961 (others came from Crewe and Darlington) before a revised and uprated Class 25 design came off the drawing-board. No D5032's survival is interesting because it took place so early and needed a complex series of circumstances to bring it about.

Delivered from Crewe Works to March depot on 28 July 1959, No D5032 moved on to Stratford in January 1960, and in December transferred to Willesden. It spent the rest of its 16-year career on the London Midland Region: after transfer to Bletchley in December 1965, it followed the LM vogue of divisional (not depot) allocation to London (Western), then in April 1966 to Birmingham, August 1967 to Stoke, and finally 6 May 1973 to Crewe, being renumbered No 24032 the following year.

Although the Class 24s by that time could be seen anywhere from Wick and Thurso to Tyne Dock and Bristol, No 24032 would have been more at home on the Cambrian Coast. It was repainted blue in late 1972, and the last major

overhaul was completed at Derby in October 1974. Although put into store on 2 May 1976, withdrawal on 17 July did not see No 24032 despatched with its sisters to Swindon or Doncaster Works for scrap, but instead it moved under its own power from Bescot five days later to Stockton-on-Tees metal dealer T.J.Thompson.

The North Yorkshire Moors Railway seized the opportunity to borrow No D5032 during the 1976 drought when steam locos were a fire hazard; it was later able to secure it on a long-term loan, and it remained one of the railway's most reliable performers for the next 10 years.

In 1982 it acquired a steam-heat boiler from scrapped Class 25 No 25056. At first repainted from BR blue to two-tone green, it was later restored to a more acceptable Brunswick green, and named on 30 October 1982 after the daughter of a director of the Thompson firm. No D5032 covered 100,000 miles before being side-lined for major overhaul and the fitting of new tyres, and returned to service on 1 December 1990. A repaint includes the addition of an orange safety stripe around the roof line, used on BR to warn of 25,000-volt overhead wires!

Class 24 Bo-Bo No D5054

Built: BR Crewe, December
  1959
Numbers carried: (1) D5054,
  (2) 24054, (3) TDB968008,
  (4) ADB968008
First allocation: March
Final allocation: Cambridge
Withdrawn: (1) 17 July 1976,
  (2) December 1982
Preserved: East Lancashire
  Railway, Bury

No D5054, Crewe Works Open
Day, 4 July 1987. *Howard
Johnston*

Since restoration, former Class 24 train heating unit No D5054 has been a consistently good performer, and a visitor to many exhibitions and diesel days.

New to March depot in 1959, No D5054 was displaced in January 1961 by the arrival of more powerful Brush Class 31s to Great Northern lines out of King's Cross. Reallocated to Finsbury Park in January 1961, the locomotive was used on general suburban duties such as King's Cross-Moorgate, and North London line freights.

Another re-organisation banished the Class 24s to the London Midland and Scottish Regions, and No D5054 moved to Eastfield (October 1966). Subsequent transfers were to Carlisle (March 1968), Longsight (April 1968) and Crewe (September 1968). Its final duties were in Wales and the North West, and its final overhaul was at Derby in June 1974.

Although No 24054 was condemned as surplus in July 1976, the need for two electric train heat generators on the WR saw two superior examples, Nos 24054 and 24142, resurrected from the Crewe Basford Hall scrapline a month later, and renumbered in Departmental stock as Nos TDB968008/9. Apart from the isolation of traction motors and

minor rewiring, No 24054 was otherwise unaltered. It saw service at Exeter, Penzance and Worcester before being used and then stored at Newton Abbot from March 1979 to September 1982.

By then very shabby, the former No D5052 was resurrected again for further use at Norwich and Cambridge, and a visit to Stratford repair shops included a full external repaint! Complaints at Cambridge about late-night engine noise speeded its replacement by a landline in December 1982, and the locomotive was stored at March depot prior to movement to the East Lancashire Railway on 13 October 1983.

It ran at first in blue livery as No 24054 with a small yellow panel, and made its debut run to Ramsbottom on 25 January 1987. Since then it has been repainted in the original all-over green, and has been displayed at the 1987 Crewe Works Heritage Exhibition, and a Coalville Open Day. Its first revenue passenger run was between Bury and Ramsbottom on 1 October 1988, and it has also worked over the Keighley & Worth Valley Railway. April 1991 saw it taken by road to Heywood as part of the ELR's scheme to promote the rebuilding of the westward link from Bury to Rochdale.

Class 24 Bo-Bo No 97201 *Experiment*

Built: BR Derby, January 1960
Numbers carried: (1) D5061,
  (2) 24061, (3) RDB968007,
  (4) 97201
First allocation: March
Final allocation: Derby Technical
  Centre
Withdrawn: (1) 10 August 1975,
  (2) 18 December 1987
Preserved: Midland Railway
  Centre, Butterley

A pre-preservation visitor to
Butterley, No 97201 stands at
the Midland Railway Centre on
21 July 1991. *Robin Stewart-
Smith*

It was always thought that the longer Derby Technical Centre kept its distinctive red and blue liveried Class 24 Bo-Bo training locomotive No 97201 *Experiment*, the better chance it would stand of being preserved. In June 1989, some 14 years after withdrawal from BR capital stock, the future of this '50s survivor was finally safeguarded.

The urgent need to replace worn-out steam locomotives in East Anglia saw 75 new Class 24s, Nos D5020-94, delivered to Ipswich and March depots from 1959 onwards. As one of these, No D5061's career was unremarkable. New in January 1960, it worked domestic East Anglian services until transferred to Scotland in August 1966, based at Haymarket, Edinburgh. It was allocated to Longsight depot, Manchester, from January 1968, and from September 1968 until withdrawal it was based at Crewe.

As one of the earliest Class 24 withdrawals in 1975, it was selected for transfer to the departmental fleet as No RDB968007. Sent to Derby RTC at the end of 1978, it needed a visit

to Doncaster Works the following August for a replacement power unit courtesy of late survivor No 24063, in for breaking up. RDB968007 was renumbered No 97201 in the operational departmental series in June 1980.

The loco is the only Sulzer-engined Type 2 still equipped with nose-end communicating doors. Its survival into the late 1980s was despite lack of air brake equipment, shortage of spares, and crewing problems, but amongst the reasons was an abortive changeover to Class 31 traction when replacement loco No 97203 (31298) was written off with fire damage, and another Class 31 had to be procured and commissioned in its place.

Strict new Government health and safety regulations covering the presence and removal of asbestos insulation dictated No 97201's inspection by qualified private contractor Vic Berry of Leicester, to whose yard it ran under its own power in July 1988. It stayed in the yard for over three years, but moved to Butterley on 19 July 1991, where it is planned to keep it in red and blue Research Department livery.

Class 24 Bo-Bo No 24081

Built: BR Crewe, March 1980
Numbers carried: (1) D5081,
  (2) 24081
First allocation: March
Final allocation: Crewe
Withdrawn: 5 October 1980
Preserved: Steamport, Southport

The last survivor – No 24081 at
Crewe Works on 22 September
1979. *Norman Preedy*

The last operational Class 24 on BR outlived the rest of the class by some 18 months, by which time it had become a favourite with both enthusiasts and staff at Crewe depot. In the end No 24081 arrived at Southport for preservation a month before the London Midland Region caught up with it and issued the paperwork for its withdrawal!

Commissioned from Crewe Works to March depot early in 1960, No D5081 was transferred to the London Midland Region within a few days and, apart from a short spell on loan to Rugby, stayed in the London area at Willesden, Watford (November 1960), Willesden again (January 1965) and the D01 (London) pool (April 1966) until transfer to the Crewe area in December 1966 for the rest of its career. It was unusual in being renumbered No 24081 in February 1974 while still in green livery, acquiring standard blue when overhauled in mid-1975.

One reason for No 24081's retention was its serviceable steam-heat boiler, useful on overnight parcels duties, and it became a regular sight on railtours and 'farewell' specials. By the time withdrawal actually came, large numbers of the more modern and more powerful Class 25s were also going for scrap.

Preservation of No 24081 at Steamport, Southport, has been in its final BR condition, although the 1984 season saw it converted to push-pull operation, using nine of the spare circuits in the 27-way electrical jumpers on the loco. It has been decided to maintain it in the BR blue livery with full yellow ends in the style that it was best remembered in its final year in BR traffic.

May 1989 saw No 24081 haul its first revenue passenger train since preservation when it was loaned to the East Lancashire Railway for its Bank Holiday diesel weekend. It also provided the special opportunity for double-heading with another Class 24, the line's green-liveried resident No D5054 (qv).

Class 25 Bo-Bo No D5185

Built: BR Darlington, May 1963
Numbers carried: (1) D5185,
  (2) 25035
First allocation: Toton
Final allocation: Crewe
Withdrawn: 15 March 1987
Preserved: Northampton &
  Lamport Railway, Pitsford

Thirteen days before withdrawal, No 25035 stands at Llandudno Junction depot on 2 March 1987. *Larry Goddard*

The modest increase in power available from a new charge-air-cooled 1,250hp Sulzer engine was the inspiration behind the Class 25 locomotive, introduced to BR from April 1961 onwards. The ability to increase the maximum speed from 75 to 90 mph also provided greater versatility, although in later years very much at the expense of overall reliability. The transition to long-haul bulk freight, and the need for higher power in one machine, eventually caught up with the Class 25s, which were reduced from over 300 to none in less than a decade. Vast numbers were moved to Swindon, Derby and Doncaster Works for scrapping, but a change in policy saw the last handful sent to the private contractor's yard, Vic Berry at Leicester.

As the next few pages will demonstrate, however, several were still in running order at the end and, after removal of blue asbestos, were sold on to a large number of eager buyers within the preservation movement.

The plan to reopen part of the Northampton-Market Harborough line has been strengthened by the acquisition of two BR Type 2 diesels, one of which being boiler-fitted No 25035, which had the distinction of being the last Darlington-built main-line locomotive in BR service. No 25035 also has other distinctive attributes as the oldest survivor of the class – it was also the last Class 25 to haul a rostered BR service, the 1V05 07.09 Holyhead-Cardiff on 15 March 1987, for 21 miles between Chester and Crewe after a Class 47 failure.

Brand new to Toton on 25 May 1963, No D5185 worked from a variety of London Midland Region depots until July 1972, when it was moved to Leeds Holbeck. October of the same year saw a move to Tinsley, and then, in February 1965, Haymarket. It was overhauled and fitted with dual brakes at Derby in July 1978, then a period of storage from July 1979 to June 1980 was spent at Polmadie. It was a visitor to Derby Works during August 1982 for main generator repairs. No D5185's lengthy sojourn at Crewe began in November 1980, making it a regular performer on the Cambrian routes from Shrewsbury.

Class 25 Bo-Bo No D5207

Built: BR Derby, June 1963
Numbers carried: (1) D5207,
   (2) 25057
First allocation: Toton
Final allocation: Crewe
Withdrawn: 12 March 1987
Preserved: North Norfolk
   Railway, Sheringham

No 25057 shunts stone wagons
at Witton after arrival from
Caldon Low, 26 February 1987.
Chris Morrison

The Class 25 design evolved as it appeared from BR works in vast numbers from 1963 onwards and, apart from cosmetics such as a cleaned-up bodyshell, included such important changes as a different type of traction motor (from No 25027 onwards), electrical control gear, and dual air/vacuum brakes.

No 25059, actually one of the last 15 of the class of 327 to remain in traffic, was one of a series of 35 boiler-fitted examples delivered from BR Derby to the new depot at Toton, Nottingham, to accelerate the replacement of steam from mixed traffic duties radiating from the Midland Main Line. One of the earlier series with the Class 24-style body, it carried all-over Brunswick green livery until the mass alteration to corporate blue in the late 1960s/early 1970s. As a multi-purpose machine, No D5207 was allocated to a variety of former Midland Railway depots until a transfer to Wigan in December 1967 released it into to the common-user pool. By then renumbered to No 25057, it actually spent from May 1978 to November 1980 based at Plymouth Laira depot on the Western Region, and because of an intermediate overhaul and dual braking at Derby in February 1980 survived the depot's clear-out of that year which saw most of the WR Class 25s sent direct to the scrap-heap.

After some time allocated to Longsight, No 25057 became a Crewe locomotive in its final

months, and was laid up at Llandudno Junction on 15 March 1987. Although BR can be slow in disposing of its redundant assets, it seemed keen to rid itself quickly of its remaining 25s, and the lines of withdrawn machines soon were moved from Crewe to Vic Berry's scrapyard at Leicester for breaking up. At the same time recognising the demand from preserved lines, a deal was struck whereby the best examples would be put up for sale by tender, part of the deal including the removal of blue and brown asbestos from the bulkheads.

No 25057 was thus put up for sale by tender at the end of 1987, but the sale to a consortium of members of the Great Central Railway at Loughborough fell through, and it was at first thought that it would be broken up along with other scrap Class 25s in Vic Berry's yard. In the event, the BR Director of Supply accepted an alternative offer from the Buckinghamshire Railway Centre at Quainton Road, where it arrived on 5 August and where immediate attention was given to preventative maintenance, cleaning, and rectifying vandalism. It was successfully started on 3 January 1989, and used on demonstration trains during the 1990 season.

A need for additional Type 2 motive power on the North Norfolk Railway's Holt extension saw the loco moved to Sheringham during April 1991. It was only partly restored, but due to be repainted green.

Class 25 Bo-Bo No D5209

Built: BR Derby, June 1963
Numbers carried: (1) D5209,
    (2) 25059
First allocation: Toton
Final allocation: Crewe
Withdrawn: 20 March 1987
Preserved: Keighley & Worth
    Valley Railway, Haworth

No stranger to the KWVR, No D5209 is seen at Oxenhope on 6 November 1988. *Howard Johnston*

The KWVR's resident Class 25 actually worked the line in its BR days at the head of a weed-killing train.

New to Toton as No D5209 in June 1963, this locomotive did the rounds of the London Midland Region like its sisters – Cricklewood, Longsight, Preston and Wigan – before a term on the Western Region from January 1972 as a direct replacement for Class 22 and 35 diesel-hydraulics. Sent first to Newport Ebbw Junction, it moved on to Bristol and Cardiff before May 1976 saw a new sphere of operation from Edinburgh's Haymarket depot. Its final major overhaul at Derby in November 1979 included dual braking. Back on the LMR in September 1982, No 25059 ended up at Crewe with the rest of the class. When the final call came for condemnation, it was one of two Class 25s — the other was No 25213 (D7563) – north of the border on the last full day of Class 25 operation. It was based in the Motherwell area, but managed a few more journeys to Carnforth, Crewe and Buxton, where its snowploughs came in useful during blizzard conditions.

The deadline for withdrawal of all Class 25s on BR was 15 March 1987, but No 25059 was game to the last, actually being restored to life a full four days after the end to haul two damaged locomotives from Buxton to Crewe Works. The locomotive's reliability was never in doubt even at the end, and its possession of a steam-heat boiler and dual air/vacuum brakes made it an excellent buy for a preserved line, where steam does have inevitable disadvantages with modern rolling-stock.

Secured by the KWVR from Vic Berry's compound at Leicester, No 25059 has since been repainted in its original green livery. The loco technically broke BR's diesel ban on 4 June 1988 when it was allowed half a mile on to the main line to rescue a Derby-Carnforth steam special stranded after the breakdown of LMS 'Jubilee' 4-6-0 No 5593 *Kolhapur*. The crew wanted the 25 to go the whole way to Carnforth!

The winter of 1990/91 saw the installation of a reconditioned power unit bought from the Derby Training School. No D5209 was noted at Leeds on 13 April 1991 behind Class 47 No 47370, destined for Neville Hill depot for tyre-turning.

Class 25 Bo-Bo No D5217

Built: BR Derby, August 1963
Numbers carried: (1) D5217,
   (2) 25067
First allocation: Toton
Final allocation: Cricklewood
Withdrawn: 13 December 1982
Preserved: Mid-Hants Railway

No D5217 in Ropley yard on
2 February 1987. *Howard
Johnston*

The Mid-Hants Railway was the first off the mark in saving a Class 25 locomotive, and No D5217 was the only one of almost 150 of the type – half of the class – broken up at Swindon Works between 1976-86. Since then it has repaid its investment many times over with a consistent reliability record on the Alton-Alresford line, where the backbone of motive power is still steam.

Built at Derby Works to works order 4600, No D5217 was delivered new to Toton in August 1963 as one of final Derby examples to sport nose-end doors and the untidy collection of bodyside grilles.

Although many Class 25s has 20 or more allocations in their careers, No D5217 was much more restrained in its movements. Once run in, it was transferred almost immediately to Cricklewood, went across to Willesden in June 1968, returned to the London end of the Midland Main Line in May 1973, Toton in January 1981, and back to Cricklewood the following February. An interesting working involving No 25067, as it had by then become,

was on 11 March 1982, when it arrived at Cardiff with the 16.02 service from Crewe, towing failed Class 33 pioneer No 33001 which had failed south of Shrewsbury.

After withdrawal and a long period in store at Bescot, a final use for No 25067 was found at the end of 1983 as an exhibition symbol. On 11 October it was towed to Wellington, Shropshire, for display during the local rail week. Later it was given a cosmetic blue repaint for exhibition at the new Sandwell & Dudley station, and it was also parked at the former GWR Wolverhampton Low Level station for a number of weeks.

By then very shabby, No 25067 finally arrived at Swindon Works for breaking up in July 1984, but was selected from the vast numbers by then accumulated there as the most suitable for purchase. Since arrival at Ropley on 26 November 1985, it has been fully restored to a 1963-style green livery with half yellow warning panel, and is a regular sight on all types of Mid-Hants passenger and permanent way duties.

Class 25 Bo-Bo No D5222

Built: BR Derby, September
  1963
Numbers carried: (1) D5222,
  (2) 25072
First allocation: Cricklewood
Final allocation: Crewe
Withdrawn: 5 December 1985
Preserved: Swindon & Cricklade
  Railway, Blunsdon

In undercoat before the
application of GWR green livery,
No D5222 stands at Cricklade
depot on 23 May 1988. *Mike
Goodfield*

Although the rush to buy redundant BR Class 25s had slowed down by the end of 1987, the availability of Toton training loco No 25072 generated considerable interest from preservationists seeking a boiler-fitted locomotive. The successful bidder was Terry Bird of the Swindon & Cricklade Railway, who in turn sold on sister no-heat locomotive No 25313 (qv), the former D7663, to Llangollen.

No D5222's career follows similar lines to the rest of the class. New in September 1963, it was one of the last batch of Derby-built Class 25s built to the original body-style specification with nose-end communicating doors, bodyside ventilation grilles, and plain Brunswick green livery with white bodyside stripe. Only another nine would be produced like this over the next eight weeks before the re-styled No D5233 in two-tone green made its appearance (see next page).

No D5222's first allocation was Cricklewood in September 1963. It worked specific services at the London end of the Midland Main Line until June 1968, when it had a two-year spell on the LM's Western Lines based at Willesden,

returning to Cricklewood in May 1973. Back to Willesden in August the following year, No 25072, as it then was, returned again to Cricklewood in June 1975 before heading off to Scotland in October 1976. It enjoyed its last major overhaul at Derby Works during the summer of 1977, was transferred to Haymarket (Edinburgh) in January 1980, Eastfield again in March 1982, and finally to Crewe in October 1982.

After inspection for asbestos at Vic Berry's yard at Leicester, the locomotive arrived at Blunsdon by low-loader on 18 March 1988. The next day, after only two hours spent checking if the systems were OK, it was fired up at the first attempt — putting other Class 25 owners to shame for the high prices they paid for locomotives which were not even runners.

In preservation the loco was used over the Easter weekend 1988, and has since been repainted in a controversial livery of dark green with Great Western-style lining out and cast cabside No 5222 numberplates. Certainly not as Derby Works intended!

Class 25 Bo-Bo No 25083

Built: BR Derby, December 1963
Numbers carried: (1) D5233,
   (2) 25083
First allocation: Toton
Final allocation: Crewe
Withdrawn: 9 July 1984
Preserved: Crewe Heritage
   Centre

No D5233 in two-tone green at
Leeds Holbeck depot on 10 May
1964. *Gavin Morrison*

The external appearance of Class 25s changed significantly from No D5233 onwards, when a smartening-up process was instituted from lessons learned with the similar, privately-built Birmingham RC&W Class 26s, 27s and 33s. By little more than chance, the first revised Class 25 has survived as an exhibit at Crewe's growing Heritage Centre.

The front end was cleaned up by the abandonment of the unnecessary connecting doors, and installation of a large centre windscreen. The mass of small bodyside ventilation panels were also dispensed with in favour of grilles at cantrail height. The livery was altered from one-shade Brunswick green to a two-tone style, dark green lower panels and light green above the central waistline. (Darlington Works, however, continued to build to the old design and livery for the rest of its existence.)

Class 25s were being delivered in increasing numbers by 1963 for freight work across the central belt of England, and only five of this later body design, Nos D5233-7, were actually fitted with a train heating boiler. No D5233

was new to Toton depot on 21 December of that year and, in common with other Class 25s, moved freely around the system according to traffic demands – reallocations were to Derby in January 1964, Bescot in April 1964, Midland Lines in April 1966, Toton in March 1968, Midland Lines again in May 1968, Toton in June 1968, Haymarket in September 1963, Eastfield in the same month, Tinsley in October 1963, Bescot in March 1975, Eastfield again in July 1975, Inverness in June 1976, Eastfield once more in May 1978, Haymarket in December 1978, Wigan Springs Branch in December 1980, and finally Crewe in April 1982. No 25083 was withdrawn there on 9 July 1984 after a serious electrical flashover, but survived after being selected for staff and apprentice training. It had been given a general overhaul at Derby Works as recently as January 1980.

It was moved across the tracks from Crewe Electric Depot to the Heritage Centre early in 1988 and, pending what needs to be a major repair, was allowed a cosmetic repaint in blue livery in its renumbered guise of No 25083.

Class 27 Bo-Bo No 27001

Built: Birmingham Rail Carriage
& Wagon Company, June
1961
Numbers carried: (1) D5347,
(2) 27001
First allocation: Thornton
Junction
Final allocation: Eastfield
Withdrawn: 8 July 1987
Preserved: Brechin Railway

No 27001 undergoing
refurbishment at BREL Glasgow
Works, 16 August 1983. *Howard
Johnston*

Although the contract to construct 214 medium-powered locomotives for British Railways was small in comparison to those given to large firms such as English Electric and Brush, the products of the Birmingham Rail Carriage & Wagon Company of Smethwick are destined to be some of the last examples of the 1955 Modernisation Plan fleet in BR use. The first of the three BRC&W designs eliminated was the 1,250hp Sulzer-engined Class 27, which once numbered 70 examples; it was even then a surprising decision considering the heavy expenditure incurred for refurbishment of many of the class for up to ten years' more service.

Forty-six Type 2s (Class 26) had been produced with the 6LDA28 power unit rated at 1,160hp, supported by Crompton Parkinson traction motors, when BR pressed for an engine of higher output and, after experience with modifications to the BR 'Peak' Type 4s, an intercooled 6LDA28B unit was employed from No D5347 onwards, this time with GEC traction motors. The more powerful Class 27s were capable of 90 mph, and were allocated to the Midland, North Eastern and Scottish Regions.

No D5347, the first Class 27, was commissioned at Thornton Junction depot at the end of June 1961, and was allocated to depots in Southern Scotland for its entire career – Eastfield (July 1961), Haymarket (February 1970), Eastfield (January 1972), Haymarket (March 1972), and finally Eastfield again (May 1973). It was given an intermediate overhaul in March 1979, but was out of use again at first Dundee then Perth from September 1982 and June 1983 pending further repair. Yet the locomotive owes it survival to refurbishment at Glasgow Works during the early part of 1983, wasteful considering its short subsequent life.

No 27001 worked the Scottish Railway Preservation Society's Class 27 Farewell railtour with No 27046 between Glasgow Central and Inverness on 9 May 1987 and while enthusiasts always hoped that it would be preserved, it was condemned after suffering a traction motor defect on 8 July of that year. Although other members of the class were mechanically more sound, the Class 27 Group stepped in with an offer, and No 27001 was moved by road to Brechin on 27 February 1988 (it was actually driven onto a low-loader at Montrose), since when it has worked engineering trains to Bridge of Dun. A replacement traction motor was fitted from scrapped No 27054 (No D5399) in May 1989.

Class 27 Bo-Bo No D5351

**Built: Birmingham Rail Carriage
& Wagon Company, August
1961
Numbers carried: (1) D5351,
(2) 27005
First allocation: Eastfield
Final allocation: Eastfield
Withdrawn: 10 July 1987
Preserved: Scottish Railway
Preservation Society, Bo'ness**

**When still in blue livery and
before removal to Bo'ness,
No 27005 stands at Falkirk on
21 February 1988.** *Tom Noble*

The Scottish Railway Preservation Society's Class 27 locomotive No D5351 has to be considered as another bargain buy considering BR's expensive rebuild of the mechanical and electrical equipment only three years before it was declared surplus and withdrawn for scrap.

The Class 27s held sway on the Scottish Region for a quarter of a century up to 1987, but then quickly fell from favour in the face of reduced and reorganised traffic flows, and the general surplus of more reliable Class 20 and Class 37 motive power from other regions, plus of course the highly favoured Sprinter DMUs.

The Class 27 was immediately distinguishable from the earlier Class 26 design by the addition of a headcode panel, although this fell into disuse from 1 January 1976 when two white marker spots were placed in the roof panel instead. The BRC&W decision to group the engine compartment ventilator grilles in the roof section was later copied in BR's conceptually similar Class 25 design. The early deliveries, Nos D5347-69, were originally fitted with a recess for tablet-catcher apparatus on the driver's cabside, but this was later plated over.

No D5351 only had two allocations in its entire career. New to Eastfield at the end of

August 1961, it stayed for 19 years before being moved to Inverness in March 1980, during which time it was renumbered No 27005. Its last works visit was in April 1984 for refurbishments and dual braking, and it later returned to its Eastfield base. Apart from its survival to the last few weeks of Class 27 operation, it is also credited with the type's final working over the West Highland Line, which it visited with No 37033 on 3 July 1987 with alumina tanks to Fort William. It returned with the following day's freight to Mossend yard, and was eventually withdrawn on the 10th with nothing more than a triple pump defect.

No 27005 was purchased with the proceeds of two enthusiasts' railtours, and was moved by rail from St Rollox to Falkirk on 14 February 1988, and thence by road to Bo'ness, which at that time was awaiting its connection to the BR main line. It has since undergone restoration to its original livery as No D5351. It failed in service on 23 September 1989 but, after complete main generator replacement, was successfully restarted in February 1990. It has also been fitted with authentic snowploughs courtesy of M.C.Metals at Glasgow BRML Works.

Class 27 Bo-Bo No D5353

Built: Birmingham Rail Carriage
& Wagon Company,
September 1961
Numbers carried: (1) D5353,
(2) 27007
First allocation: Eastfield
Final allocation: Inverness
Withdrawn: 21 January 1985
Preserved: Mid-Hants Railway,
Ropley

Restoration re-starts on No
27007 after a long break. Ropley
yard, 2 February 1990. *David
Warwick*

Although BRC&W locomotives have been part of the Southern scene for the last 30 years, the Type 2 version has not been seen in action since the mid-1960s when Class 27s worked the odd excursion from the Midlands to the South Coast. When eventually restored to working order, the Mid-Hants Railway's No D5353 will change all that.

The arrival of surplus English Electric Class 37s from the Eastern Region in the mid-1980s spelled a rapid run-down of the lower-powered Class 27 fleet, especially those only equipped with vacuum brakes. No D5353, one of the early casualties, devoted its entire BR career to Scottish duties, and was a familiar sight in the Lowlands and on the West Highland Line for 19 years from delivery until transfer from Eastfield to Inverness in March 1980. It was renumbered No 27007 in April 1984, and on 4 May of that year double-headed No 27006 on a BR-sponsored railtour from Fort William to Eastfield. Its last general overhaul was at Glasgow Works in October 1979.

No 27007's career was marred by two incidents. First, it caught fire while working in multiple with Class 25 No D7620 on coal empties to Waterside colliery, Ayrshire, on 29 February 1968. The second, more serious, accident was on 3 February 1983 when it was in charge of the five-coach 13.50 Aberdeen-Inverness, derailed by a broken rail 2 miles east of Elgin. One passenger was killed and eight injured. The loco's withdrawal in 1985 followed a minor fire in the battery-charging circuits.

It was stored at Motherwell depot until sale and movement south on 31 October 1985. It took two weeks to reach Swindon Works, where a special movement by a Class 33 loco with fellow preserved No 25067 (qv D5217) was arranged for transfer to Alresford on 26 November.

Externally No D5353 has only suffered one noticeable alteration since construction – the sealing up of the redundant nose-end doors to avoid draughts. The headcode panel blinds were also removed in the early 1970s in favour of two simple circular white marker lights. Bodywork repairs and restoration to green livery started immediately, but was halted by a serious fire in Ropley shed on 10 July 1986. Work resumed at the end of 1989, and the power unit was successfully started on 17 June 1991.

Class 27 Bo-Bo No 27024

Built: Birmingham Rail Carriage
  & Wagon Company, January
  1962
Numbers carried: (1) D5370,
  (2) 27024, (3) ADB968028
First allocation: Thornaby
Final allocation: Eastfield
Withdrawn: 2 July 1987
Preserved: Northampton &
  Lamport Railway, Pitsford

No 27024 outside Glasgow
Works, 15 April 1979. *Norman
Preedy*

A late arrival on the preservation scene was Eastfield training loco No 27024 in February 1990. Nine Class 27s were built specifically for freight work in the North East during 1962, and it is appropriate that the final example to be saved should be one of them. The principal difference between Nos D5370-8 and the rest of the class was the omission of a steam-heat boiler, which reduced the overall weight by 2 tons. They worked Newcastle and York local duties, but were exchanged at the end of 1965 for Nos D5248-56 (later 25098-106) from Leicester.

Although the Class 27 will always be remembered as a significant part of the Scottish scene, it is interesting to recall that it was in fact only a minor player until mid-1966, with just 23 of the 69 examples working out of Eastfield depot. The desperate need to improve affairs by scrapping the troublesome centre-cab Clayton Class 17 D85xx and North British Class 21 D61xx Bo-Bos included transferring the entire English allocation of 46 BRC&W locomotives to Eastfield and Haymarket between June 1968 and April 1970. Scottish Class 20s also went south to Toton, and dual braked Class 25s crossed the border for the first

time to help out on passenger services.

No D5370 was at Toton in October 1969 when the call came, and spent the rest of its 25-year career based in Glasgow. Its sphere of operation would still be wide, West Highland Line duties to Mallaig and Oban, freight through Ayrshire, and a variety of work in the Glasgow-Dundee/Aberdeen corridor. Large-scale withdrawals of Class 27s did not take place until 1985, although a refurbishment of dual braked examples took place for a life of up to five years; this policy was reversed after several major overhauls had taken place. No 27024, whose final intermediate repair was at Glasgow Works in January 1979, was refurbished in April 1984, but condemned at Eastfield on 2 July 1987.

While other Class 27s were quickly towed away for scrap, the opportunity was taken to replace the by then decrepit Class 27 training locomotive No ADB968024 (ex-No 27207) with a refurbished example. No 27024, later No ADB968028, was originally intended as a source of spares for the Northampton Steam Railway's No 27056 (qv D5401), although it may be put back into running order eventually.

Class 27 Bo-Bo No D5386

Built: Birmingham Rail Carriage & Wagon Company, May 1962
Numbers carried: (1) D5386, (2) 27103, (3) 27212, (4) 27066
First allocation: Cricklewood
Final allocation: Eastfield
Withdrawn: 29 July 1987
Preserved: North Norfolk Railway, Sheringham

In just one of its many guises, No 27212 at Eastfield depot on 11 June 1975. *Norman Preedy*

There is no question that BR had its money's worth out of this locomotive, whose 25-year career was both varied and hard-working. The North Norfolk Railway has already justified its purchase with two years' trouble-free use on the new extension to Holt where steam locomotives have been considered a dangerous fire risk during the summer season.

The final D5379-D5415 series of Class 27s were sent new to the London Midland Region for local services radiating from St Pancras, Leicester and Nottingham. Birmingham, March, Leeds, the South Coast, even Bristol and Gloucester were reached on occasions.

However, the opportunity was seized to convert the Edinburgh-Glasgow service to push-pull operation, and 24 Class 27s were duly fitted with the equipment to allow one to be used at each end of a six-coach Mark 2 rake. They were re-designated Class 27/1, and No D5386 duly became No 27103 in April 1974. However, the rapid changeover to electric-heat coaches saw 12 of the special Class 27s supplied with a small Deutz engine to power an ETH generator. No D5386 was one of them, and was again renumbered 27212 in a new series in March 1975. Interestingly, it is virtually unheard of for two locomotives to carry the same number, but loco No 27118 was renumbered 27103 to fill the gap created by No D5386's changed circumstances.

The high-speed capability of the Class 27s meant good service in this new role, although after six years of slogging between the two capitals the arrival in 1979 of Class 47/7s was met with some relief amongst operating staff. No D5386 was relegated to more mundane domestic duties, and a heavy overhaul in October 1982 saw it returned to the conventional Class 27 fleet with another new number, 27066.

The penultimate Class 27 retired at the end of July 1987, and it was towed to Leicester for scrap or resale. The North Norfolk Railway were eager purchasers, and No 27066 moved to Sheringham by road on 14 March 1988. It hauled the first test trains over the 2^1/$_2$-mile extension to Holt on 5 March 1989, and a repaint in green has been carried out.

Class 27 Bo-Bo No D5394

Built: Birmingham Rail Carriage
& Wagon Company, June
1962
Numbers carried: (1) D5394,
(2) 27106, (3) 27050
First allocation: Cricklewood
Final allocation: Eastfield
Withdrawn: 6 July 1987
Preserved: Strathspey Railway,
Aviemore

No D5394 restarts the 'Royal
Scotsman' private charter out of
Aviemore Speyside station on
12 August 1988. *Mike Haddon*

Many historic Scottish locomotive designs which survived to the end of steam on the region were tragically lost because of the lack of finance, and the seemingly panic desire of BR to consign them to the breakers. When their replacement diesels disappeared in 1987, the preservation groups were far more organised, and no fewer than eight Class 27s were saved for further use. The Strathspey Railway's choice from those available at Eastfield depot was No 27050, one of the last few in traffic, and practically rebuilt during a heavy overhaul at Glasgow Works as recently as November 1982. The owners also paid for the same works to restore it to exhibition finish as No D5394, in original green livery with white bodyside stripe, small yellow warning panel, and four-character headcode blinds restored.

No D5394 was certainly worked hard during its life. A Midland Lines locomotive from new, it would have been a common sight on empty stock workings out of St Pancras, and freight workings up to Leicester and Nottingham. A particularly unusual duty for No D5394 on 15 August 1964 was to work a ten-coach holiday special ex-Yarmouth along the

Kettering-Higham Ferrers branch which had closed to normal services five years previously.

No D5394 spent a year at Toton from August 1967 before heading to Eastfield in July 1968. Selected for conversion for the 24-strong Edinburgh-Glasgow push-pull fleet, it became No 27106 in April 1974. Locomotives were required at each end of six Mark 2 coaches; dual brakes, automatic fire-fighting equipment and driver-guard communication equipment were fitted, and the generator and traction motors were given special attention in anticipation of problems with the high level of 90 mph running expected from them. They were stretched to maintain the service, and it was a relief to the operators to receive a fleet of more powerful replacement Brush Class 47/7s from 1979 onwards.

Returned to the conventional fleet, No 27106 moved to Inverness in August 1981, for use on Aberdeen line services until displaced again by Class 47s. The locomotive gained a third identity after its final works visit in November 1982, and had two more transfers, Haymarket from May 1986 and Eastfield from September of that year.

Class 27 Bo-Bo No D5401

Built: Birmingham Rail Carriage
& Wagon Company, July 1962
Numbers carried: (1) D5401,
(2) 27112, (3), 27056
First allocation: Cricklewood
Final allocation: Eastfield
Withdrawn: 10 February 1987
Preserved: Northampton &
Lamport Railway, Pitsford

No 27056 parked at Eastfield
depot, 18 April 1987. *Norman
Preedy*

The Northampton Steam Railway's Class 27 locomotive can genuinely be described as a royal loco as a result of its selection to haul the Royal Train containing Prince Charles from Glasgow to Fort William on 20 November 1983. Eastfield even added a white stripe to the lower bodyside to celebrate the occasion, a significant variation in the days when practically every locomotive was painted in all-over blue.

The refurbishment of Class 27s in 1982-85 has to be considered a waste of money since reduced motive power needs north of the border meant that they went for scrap with years of life still left in them. No 27056 was the first to be outshopped from Glasgow Works in August 1982.

When new as No D5401, it was another example built for the Midland Lines, delivered new to Cricklewood in 1962. It left for Toton in July 1968, and Eastfield in June 1969. Three years later it was one of the 24 selected for the Edinburgh-Glasgow push-pull workings, and redesignated Class 27/1 No 27112. When more

powerful motive power came along, it was downgraded to Class 27/0, gaining a third identity, No 27056, in August 1982.

No 27056 unwittingly found itself on top link West Coast Main Line duties on 15 June 1983 when catenary problems at Law Junction prevented the rostered Class 86 electric loco taking forward the 07.27 Nottingham-Glasgow/Edinburgh north of Carlisle. No 27056 made it over Beattock summit at just over 25 mph with its 11-coach train, but time was made up by losing five coaches at Carstairs for a 70-minute late arrival at Glasgow Central.

After withdrawal and removal to Vic Berry, Leicester, it was offered for sale in October 1987, and secured for the new preservation project at Pitsford, geographically the closest of the class to its original haunts. It was transported there by road on 12 March the following year, and was successfully started on 25 May 1988 after a number of small faults were rectified. It has seen regular use since then, and is being restored to green livery.

Class 27 Bo-Bo No D5410

**Built: Birmingham Rail Carriage
& Wagon Company,
September 1962**
**Numbers carried: (1) D5410,
(2) 27123, (3) 27205,
(4) 27059**
First allocation: Cricklewood
Final allocation: Eastfield
Withdrawn: 6 July 1987
**Preserved: Severn Valley
Railway, Bridgnorth**

No 27059 at Basingstoke during
the Rail Weekend, 26 September
1987. *Chris Wilson*

The Smethwick works of the Birmingham Rail Carriage & Wagon Company was only a few weeks away from total closure when No D5410 emerged in September 1962. It meant the end of a business founded in 1855, and strongly associated with vehicle exports worldwide and Pullman car manufacture before the decision was taken to enter the field of diesel locomotives in the early 1950s. The first order came from CIE in Eire, quickly followed by BR Classes 26, 27 and 33, and large numbers of DMU cars. The early 1960s were, however, dogged by industrial relations problems, and merger talks with Charles Roberts & Co of Wakefield were not in the event proceeded with.

No D5410 was new to Cricklewood in September 1962, and apart from work on the Midland Main Line out of St Pancras it might also have reached the South Coast on summer holiday excursions. Transferred north in February 1969, it was one of 24 examples modified for use on top link Edinburgh-Glasgow push-pull duties, renumbered first as No 27123, then No 27205. Given a heavy general overhaul as late as January 1983, it was repainted at Eastfield depot after withdrawal from BR service in July 1987, nominally for display at open days and exhibitions.

It ran south under its own power to Crewe on 22 August destined for the following month's Basingstoke Open Day. It was also rostered for a Birmingham-Derby-Manchester main-line special, but this was halted on the directive of InterCity. It was, however, permitted to haul trains at the Severn Valley Railway's Gala Weekend on 10-11 October.

After a long period of storage at Tyseley, good news in April 1988 was that Sandwell Council, the local authority for Smethwick, had agreed to buy the locomotive for display, initially at the Birmingham Railway Museum. It was moved to Leicester for asbestos removal on 15 June 1988 by No 31413 *The Severn Valley Railway*, and April 1990 saw the completion of the restoration of No D5410 to BR green livery. It was displayed at the 29 September 1990 Cambridge Depot Open Day, and at Coalville on 26 May 1991, before transfer to the its new home on the SVR.

Class 31 A1A-A1A No D5500

Built: Brush, October 1957
Numbers carried: (1) D5500,
    (2) 31018
First allocation: Stratford
Final allocation: Stratford
Withdrawn: 10 July 1976
Preserved: Steamtown, Carnforth

No D5500 at Thornaby depot for
tyre turning, 10 May 1986.
Philip Sutton

The Brush Type 2 is still an active part of the BR scene over 30 years after No D5500 emerged from the Brush Works at Loughborough, although the current version running on BR is a far cry from the original design, and represents millions of pounds of investment in re-engineering. The new English Electric power unit, electric train heating and dual vacuum/air brakes are a far cry from the original specification.

No D5500 narrowly missed being the first private-builder loco delivered under the 1955 Modernisation Plan (English Electric No D8000 beat it by four months). It ran trials in Derbyshire on 10 October 1957, and was formally handed over to BR at Loughborough on 31 October. Modifications to the design were made at regular intervals; electro-pneumatic control gear replaced electro-magnetic after the first 20 units, leaving Nos D5500-19 non-standard and restricted to Great Eastern lines for their entire lives, and candidates for early withdrawal in the mid-1970s as a useful source of spares for the rest of the class. All by then had lost their troublesome

Mirrlees JVS12T power unit for a down-rated EE 1,470hp 12SVT as used in the Class 37.

New to Stratford, D5500 stayed there all its life apart from a short spell at March (June 1959) and Ipswich (June 1959 to June 1962). No 31018, as it had then become, was put into store in May 1976 and withdrawn in July along with five others, Nos 31001/9/10/1/6; it was chosen for preservation to reflect the private-builder influence in the 1955 Modernisation Plan.

No 31018 worked to Doncaster under its own power on 8 January 1977, went to York museum the following month, and then back to Doncaster in March for external restoration to green livery with white bodyside stripes. It was loaned to the North Yorkshire Moors Railway for three years' operation between Grosmont and Pickering from 7 April 1978, but has since been out of public view because of unsatisfactory external condition. It was moved by road to Steamtown, Carnforth, on 16 June 1989 for storage during the NRM's rebuilding operation.

Class 28 Co-Bo No D5705

Built: Metropolitan-Vickers,
    December 1958
Numbers carried: (1) D5705,
    (2) S15705, (3) TDB968006
First allocation: Derby
Final allocation: Preston Division
Withdrawn: 7 September 1968
Preserved: Peak Railway,
    Matlock

Freshly repainted, No D5705 was
on show at the last Coalville
Open Day, in 1991. *Steve Knight*

The builders' desire for a high starting tractive effort in their two-stroke design while sticking to BR's design specification resulted in the unique five-axle machine that was nicknamed the 'Co-Bo' after its odd wheel arrangement. The design was, however, destined for a short life because of the notoriously unreliable Crossley two-stroke engines. The initial duties for the class of 20 included double-heading the prestigious 500-ton 'Condor' container train between Hendon and Glasgow Gushetfaulds goods depot, as well as domestic Scottish turns. Manchester-St Pancras expresses also employed the Class 28s, although by the 1960s the LM was replacing them with more reliable Sulzer Class 24 and 44 designs.

An agreement for rebuilding at Dukinfield, Manchester, was drawn up in 1961, but it had little effect, and the fleet was transferred to Barrow-in-Furness for dedicated local duties. After consideration had been given to re-engining with the same English Electric unit going into the Class 31, they were instead all withdrawn by the end of 1968, and sold for scrap, with one exception – D5705.

Allocated new to Derby, the locomotive was stored at Cricklewood for most of 1961 before transfer to Barrow in February 1962, Carlisle in December 1966, and finally to the general Preston Division pool. It had received a major overhaul during 1967, and after withdrawal was accepted by Derby Railway Technical Centre for various running tests. It never carried BR blue livery.

By then numbered S15705, it was booked to be towed from Derby to Gloucester on 18 September 1974, and on to Swansea Danygraig repair shops. It was moved to Bristol Bath Road depot in February 1986 for conversion to a train heating unit, but the work was never carried out and it suffered an underbody fire in the hot summer of that year. Swindon's CCE yard was its home from 11 June 1980, and its future was settled on 20 March 1986 when it was re-sold and moved to Matlock on 7 April. Although some restoration by the Pioneer Diesel Locomotive Group has taken place, progress is being hampered by a shortage of skilled fitters and electricians. The major tasks of power unit overhaul and re-wiring have yet to be tackled. After cosmetic but impressive external restoration, the loco made its first public appearance in over a decade at the 26 May 1991 Coalville Open Day.

Class 33 Bo-Bo No 33034

Built: Birmingham Rail Carriage & Wagon Company, April 1961
Numbers carried: (1) D6552, (2) 33034
First allocation: Hither Green
Final allocation: Stewarts Lane
Withdrawn: 25 January 1988
Preserved: Ludgershall

In BR days, No D6552 as 33034 on the scrap-line at Eastleigh depot on 4 June 1987. *David Warwick*

No 33034 is an unexpected survivor from the long lines of withdrawn Class 33s accumulated at Eastleigh during the late 1980s, and despite the absence of many vital components is still seen as an operational prospect. It is also the first of the larger BRC&W products to be saved for preservation. The Class 33s, the locomotive type the Southern Region seemingly cannot do without, have been running since 1960, and a new wave of overhauls should ensure that many of them survive into the 21st century in BR revenue service. The entire class of 98 was initially allocated to Hither Green, but from June 1962 onwards made appearances on the South Western Division, culminating in half the class being based at Eastleigh by 1967.

No D6552 entered service in April 1961. Until recent times there was a desire to allocate the fleet in strict numerical sequence between Eastleigh and Hither Green depots, but changing traffic patterns meant that those numerically halfway would often be reallocated, and this loco was often on the move – to Eastleigh in October 1966, Hither Green in May 1968, Eastleigh again in January 1969, back to Hither Green in May 1971, to Eastleigh in October 1971, Hither Green in May 1973,

and Eastleigh yet again June 1983. The final reallocation was to Selhurst on 7 December 1987, seven weeks before withdrawal. No 33034's most recent overhauls were a general in September 1982, and an intermediate in December 1985.

The Southern Region was the slowest to apply yellow warning panels, and No D6552 retained the basic green livery at least until 1966. While a Hither Green locomotive, it would until 1968 have been a regular sight on the East Coast Main Line as far north as York on through block cement trains for Uddingston. In the 1980s its off-region activity would have been most wide, regular diagrams taking it as far as Manchester Piccadilly, the North Wales Line, Swansea, and even Plymouth.

No 33034 was withdrawn having suffered crankshaft damage and being denied a visit to Eastleigh Works for repair. Three traction motors and other electrical equipment were also removed to repair sisters Nos 33012/38, and there are no immediate plans for their replacement. The loco was moved to a private siding at Ludgershall in May 1990.

Class 35 B-B No D7017

Built: Beyer Peacock, January 1962
Number carried: D7017
First allocation: Bristol Bath Road
Final allocation: Old Oak Common
Withdrawn: 13 March 1975
Preserved: West Somerset Railway, Williton

No D7017 at Williton on 3 February 1984.
Howard Johnston

The demise of the Western Region's popular 'Hymek' diesel-hydraulics gave the modern traction movement real impetus, and a farewell railtour of 22 September 1973 prompted the first purchase of a main-line diesel loco by public subscription. Although mass withdrawals of the 101-strong class had taken place during the years 1971-72, a small number survived on domestic duties for another three years.

No D7017, the oldest survivor, was delivered from Beyer, Peacock of Gorton to Bristol Bath Road depot in January 1962, and stayed there until transfer in October 1971, soon after overhaul and repairs to minor collision damage. Although withdrawn in May 1973 as surplus, it was rapidly returned to use to replace another 'Hymek' which had expired after major failure, and in March 1974 No D7017 actually received a replacement power unit. After a repaint, it was the only member of the class to carry new-style cabside number transfers.

The end came on 13 March 1975. The newly formed Diesel & Electric Group's attempts to save No D7026 failed, and No D7017 was secured instead. It was towed away to Taunton on 30 July by No 25162, and stored in the down yard for nearly a year before transfer was allowed to its present home, Williton depot on the West Somerset Railway. The first passenger run was on 19 March 1977, after which the problem of being too heavy for the line was solved by removal of the steam-heat boiler. The loco achieved apparent immortality by appearing in the BBC TV comedy 'Some Mothers Do 'Ave 'Em' which is repeated on a regular basis.

Initial repainting was from blue to original green livery with small yellow warning panels added, although the entire cab ends are now yellow. Replacement of damaged intercoolers, fuel pumps, filters, heat exchangers and electric fittings has been necessary, and No D7017 successfully hauled an 11-coach train at the WSR's Open Week in 1986. Weight restrictions have limited its use to just a few days per year, and it did not work at all from 1988 until 24 March 1990.

Sporting a full yellow end, it left the WSR for the first time to attend the 1 July 1990 Open Day at Gloucester, followed by visits to Barry and Newport, and worked specials over the Torbay & Dartmouth line on 15-16 June 1991.

Class 35 B-B No D7018

Built: Beyer Peacock, January
  1962
Number carried: D7018
First allocation: Cardiff Canton
Final allocation: Old Oak
  Common
Withdrawn: 18 March 1975
Preserved: West Somerset
  Railway

While in blue livery with a small
yellow panel, No D7018 is seen
at Didcot on 4 February 1984.
Howard Johnston

A long-time stablemate of No D7017, 'Hymek' No D7018 had the distinction of being the last of the class in BR service, outliving its 100 sisters by the short space of five days.

Already in terminal decline by the time it secured the 'Hymek' building contract, the Manchester firm of Beyer, Peacock was banking for orders of up to 500 of their medium-sized 1,700hp Maybach MD870-engined product with Mekydro transmission (hence the 'Hymek' name) and the early decision by the Western Region of BR to discard diesel-hydraulic transmission in favour of the then standard diesel-electric was a body-blow to the company.

No D7018, new to Bristol Bath Road, was sent to Cardiff for two months from January 1966, Bristol again two months later, and was finally transferred to Old Oak in November 1971. It was involved in early experiments with an anti-wheelslip device, and a replacement power unit ensured its survival beyond 1973.

Following withdrawal, its new owner, a Derby businessman, arranged for its stabling at the hitherto steam-only bastion of the Great Western Society at Didcot, but little work was carried out. The threat of scrapping again hung over it until the Diesel & Electric Preservation Group took an interest in 1977.

Originally intended as a source of spares for the group's No D7017, it was eventually decided to restore it to running condition. Severe frost damage suffered in the 1979 winter meant a complete and protracted engine removal and rebuild, culminating in a successful start-up on 24 August 1985. Initial external restoration was to late-1960s style, BR blue with white cab surrounds and small yellow panel, but this was changed to all-over Brunswick green for the 1985 Old Oak Common Open Day. It has also been exhibited at Tyseley.

Electrical faults dogged its return to service in 1987 at the autumn open day. In early 1988 a campaign was launched to provide the group with its own maintenance shed at Didcot, but in the event it was decided to move to Somerset. The move took place via the 22 June 1991 Open Day at Cardiff Cathays and Bristol Bath Road seven days later, where it met up with No D7017 for the first time in 16 years.

Class 35 B-B No D7029

Built: Beyer Peacock, April 1962
Number carried: D7029
First allocation: Cardiff Canton
Final allocation: Old Oak
  Common
Withdrawn: 28 February 1975
Preserved: North Yorkshire
  Moors Railway, Grosmont

No D7029 at Levisham with
'Deltic' No 55019 on
28 September 1985.
Gavin Morrison

Without doubt one of the major crowd-pullers on the North Yorkshire Moors Railway, No D7029 has seen regular service on the preserved line since its arrival there in Easter 1981.

New to Cardiff in April 1962, No 7029 saw allocations to Bristol (September 1965), Plymouth Laira (August 1967), Bristol Bath Road (November 1967), and finally Old Oak Common (April 1968). Its power range enabled it to replace GWR 'Castle' Class 4-6-0 steam locos, including 'numbersake' No 7029 *Clun Castle*, which it would follow into preservation a decade later.

Although complex machines, the 35s' robust design and generous working space (it was one of the few main-line loco types to have bodyside engine-room doors) made them easier to carry out maintenance on than most designs. Nonetheless, 'Hymek' withdrawals began in October 1971, but No D7029's good condition ensured its survival until 28 February 1975, when it was withdrawn with a cracked cylinder

liner in the power unit.

In this non-runner condition it was bought by members of the Diesel Traction Group, whose own operating experience was to prove useful during a lengthy rebuild. No D7029 was moved from Old Oak to a siding beside the WR main line at Reading on 20 November 1975 with 'Warship' No D821 *Greyhound* (qv), and later at the safe haven of the Swindon Works turntable for restoration to working order, and repainting from BR blue livery to the original green.

The 'Hymek' departed Swindon by rail on 16 April 1981, arriving at Grosmont the following day. NYMR diesel days have seen No D7029 in regular use, and one of the most bizarre workings of its career so far must have been to double-head Class 55 'Deltic' No 55009 (qv D9009) on the line's Members' Day specials in 1985. It has recently been out of use pending mechanical overhaul.

Class 35 B-B No D7076

Built: Beyer Peacock, May 1963
Number carried: D7076
First allocation: Old Oak
    Common
Final allocation: Bristol Bath
    Road
Withdrawn: 6 May 1973
Preserved: East Lancashire
    Railway, Bury

No D7076 after restoration, at Bury running shed on 31 July 1988. *Howard Johnston*

The restoration of 'Hymek' No D7076 has been a Herculean task for members of the East Lancs Railway because it was purchased in virtually derelict condition after ten years out of use as a BR Departmental dead-load vehicle.

No D7076 was new to Old Oak Common, but that year was also involved in crew-training on the type at Worcester. It started a short stay at Cardiff Canton in January 1968, and its final depot was Bristol from January 1972 onwards, when it would be seen on workings as varied as North Devon, Portsmouth and Birmingham. After withdrawal, it was dumped with other hydraulics at nearby Marsh Junction for many months.

However, Nos D7076 and D7096, instead of being consigned to Swindon for scrap, were requisitioned by Derby Technical Centre for experiments. They moved from Bristol Bath Road to Saltley on 24 August 1974, and thence to the Old Dalby test location on 11 October. No D7076 was also seen on the Edwalton test track being hauled short distances to measure locomotive performance.

Although disused after 1979 and heavily robbed for parts, sufficient potential was seen by the East Lancs Railway to make one good locomotive from the pair of 'Hymeks', and the more complete example was purchased in 1983. Thus No D7076 was towed first to Leicester and then northwards, arriving at Bury on 25 February. Although a complete engine rebuild and rewire has been necessary, the presence at Bury of other diesel-hydraulics with identical power unit and electrical equipment has been a great help to the team. The other 'Hymek', D7096, has since been sold by BR for scrap.

A significant day for the restoration team was 1 May 1988 when the overhauled Maybach MD870 engine fired up for the first time in 15 years. The loco made its inaugural test run to Ramsbottom on 18 September, and has been a regular performer on the railway since then. Restoration has been carried out to the mid-1960s paint style of BR green with small yellow warning panels and cast bodyside numbers.

Class 25 Bo-Bo No D7523 *John F.Kennedy*

Built: BR Derby, January 1965
Numbers carried: (1) D7523,
 (2) 25173
First allocation: Toton
Final allocation: Crewe
Withdrawn: 19 March 1987
Preserved: Crewe Heritage
 Centre

Immediately after withdrawal,
No 25173 heads the scrap-line at
Crewe Gresty Lane on 25 March
1987. *Philip Sutton*

Derby Works was turning out Class 25s at the rate of two per week when No D7523 was delivered to Toton depot at the start of 1965, a year that saw London Midland Region steam locomotives cast aside in their hundreds, and inter-regional diesel workings take the Sulzer 1,250hp Type 2s to virtually every part of the country.

No D7523, visually attractive in the new body design with two-tone green livery, was actually one of the simpler Class 25 versions for purely freight traffic radiating from the East Midlands, hence the lack of a steam-heat boiler and fittings. The vast numbers of common-user Class 20s, 24s, 25s, 40s and 47s caused the LMR to abandon specific depots from 1965 in favour of pools administered by the central administrative centres of London (West Coast), London (Midland), Birmingham, Leicester, Nottingham, Stoke, Manchester, Liverpool and Preston, although this was also abandoned in 1971 for a return to the old system.

No D7523 spent most of its career as a common-user loco, and survived to be one of the last five 25s in service, courtesy of a final overhaul and dual braking at Derby Works in

June 1978. On 18 March 1987, three days after official withdrawal, it journeyed from Manchester to North Wales to work the 3J04 05.08 Bangor-Manchester Red Bank parcels train, and the next day the 6Z40 07.30 Glazebrook-Parkeston Quay tanks as far as Crewe, where it was taken off and removed to the lengthening lines of withdrawn locomotives in Gresty Lane yard.

Its superior condition by comparison with many others of the same class prompted preservation interest. No D7523 was tripped to the BREL Crewe Works in September 1987 for repairs, and it also visited Leicester at the end of 1988 for asbestos removal. Its first public showing in two-tone green livery with small yellow warning panels was at BREL Crewe Works Open Day on 21 July 1990, albeit with marker lights still in place, and non-authentic cabside numbers. The locomotive has also been named *John F. Kennedy* after its owner, with plates on the lower bodysides behind the right-hand cab door. No D7523 visited the Hereford BR Rail Festival on 5 May 1991 and Laira four months later.

Class 25 Bo-Bo No D7535 *Mercury*

Built: BR Derby, March 1965
Numbers carried: (1) D7535,
    (2) 25185
First allocation: Toton
Final allocation: Crewe
Withdrawn: 5 November 1984
Preserved: Torbay & Dartmouth
    Railway, Paignton

In BR blue livery, No 25185 was
photographed at Manchester
Victoria on 25 March 1982.
Norman Preedy

No D7535 avoided the almost monotonous convoys of withdrawn locomotives despatched to Swindon Works in 1985 because Toton needed a workable example for apprentice training on the Sulzer power unit which in various forms occupied almost the depot's entire vast allocation.

The single-bank version of the LDA 28B power unit, half the size of the Class 45 'Peak' main-line version then still in active use on the Midland Main Line and Trans-Pennine routes, was successful if generally unspectacular in overall performance, but standardisation of many parts did assist with overall availability.

No D7535 represented the later, simpler, body design, with AEI 253AY traction motors, GEC Series 2 electric equipment, blue star coupling for multiple working, and 500-gallon fuel tanks. The lack of a steam-heat boiler made it simpler to maintain, but did not preclude it from taking summer passenger turns which as late as 1980 could be a double-header over the Cambrian Coast Line from Shrewsbury to Aberystwyth, or Derby to Yarmouth, Leicester to Skegness, and even Sheffield to Llandudno.

New to Toton, it was based variously at Willesden, Bescot, Toton, Longsight, Carlisle and Wigan during its career. Dual braked and given a final overhaul at Derby in March 1978, it was declared surplus at the end of 1984. It soon became an obvious preservation candidate, and attracted several bidders when put out to tender. The successful purchaser was the Torbay & Dartmouth Railway, which had a need for a loco for permanent way and standby duties from Paignton and, as first intended, at Buckfastleigh on the Dart Valley line.

No 25185, as it then was, arrived at Paignton on 14 February 1986 in full working order, and was quickly restored to its original two-tone green livery. It was named *Mercury* during 1987.

Class 25 Bo-Bo No 25191

Built: BR Derby, April 1965
Numbers carried: (1) D7541,
    (2) 25191
First allocation: Toton
Final allocation: Crewe
Withdrawn: 15 March 1987
Preserved: North Yorkshire
    Moors Railway, Grosmont

The last Class 25 on the
Cambrian, No 25191 tows the
Crewe Inspection Saloon at
Trewern near Welshpool on
17 March 1987. *Geoff Bannister*

A very high five-figure bid was required by the North Yorkshire Moors Railway to successfully secure No 25191 for preservation, because it was recognised as arguably the best-condition Class 25 at the time of withdrawal of the survivors in March 1987. Vic Berry's yard at Leicester, the holding yard for Class 25s offered for sale by tender, was visited by dozens of potential purchasers in the middle of the year.

New to Toton as No D7541 in April 1965, it was transferred to Cricklewood's books in October 1965, Longsight in May 1968, Liverpool Division in October 1971, Wigan in May 1973, and Carlisle in January 1975. Dual braked in June 1978 during its last overhaul at Derby Works, it had by this time lost its smart two-tone green livery for all-over blue with full yellow nose-ends.

The locomotive moved to Crewe on 11 May 1986 when the survivors were concentrated there, and was a regular sight over the North and West route from there to Cardiff. It had a dubious reputation for being involved in mishaps. It was involved in a fatal accident at Leominster on 24 June 1985, and at Hereford on 21 January 1987. Another claim to fame was its selection on 2 October 1986 to haul the brand new Brush Class 89 electric prototype from BREL Crewe to Derby Litchurch Lane, from where it was moved by low-loader to Loughborough. No 25191 was one of the last of the type to reach the depths of the Western Region when, on 20 January 1987, it worked a nuclear flask train from Bridgwater for Sellafield.

No 25191 was in use again three days after its planned withdrawal date. On 15 March 1987 it was recorded on an overhead line train between Kidsgrove and Longport, and the following day made a final trip over the North Wales line to collect a Llandudno Junction-Crewe Gresty Lane permanent way train. It turned out to be the perfect way to get it back to base for final withdrawal.

No 25191 was moved to the NYMR at the end of January 1988, and made its first revenue-earning run at the NYMR's Diesel Day on 22 April 1988, with No D7628 (qv), a first in preservation. So far, however, it has seen little general use.

Class 25 Bo-Bo No D7585

Built: BR Darlington, February 1964
Numbers carried: (1) D7585, (2) 25235
First allocation: Toton
Final allocation: Crewe
Withdrawn: 13 March 1985
Preserved: Scottish Railway Preservation Society, Bo'ness

No 25235 stabled at Stonebridge Park, Willesden, on 13 October 1984. *Philip Sutton*

The 20th Class 25 to be preserved was a thoroughly late starter, being one of the long-withdrawn, unsold examples parked in Bescot yard for almost five years before being secured by Bo'ness and Kinneil Railway members looking for a compatible Sulzer-engined companion to their BRC&W Class 27. One reason for the choice of No D7585 was its possession of a steam-heat boiler right to the end of its working life, although now in need of considerable repair. Another tenuous reason might have been that it spent six years of its 21-year life based on the Scottish Region, including actual employment on a Scottish Railway Preservation Society railtour from Glasgow to Fort William on 22 April 1978.

One of the last main-line locomotives to be constructed at Darlington, No D7585 sported the by then obsolete bodyshell with nose-end communicating doors, multiplicity of bodyside ventilation grilles and all-over Brunswick green livery. Its first allocation was to Nottingham in February 1964, but within the next six years it had also been based at Derby (from October 1964), Toton (January 1965), Bescot (June 1965), Midland Lines (April 1966), Allerton

(April 1968), Liverpool Division (June 1968), Preston Division (September 1968), Manchester Division (November 1968), and Longsight (May 1973). By now renumbered to No 25235, it was despatched to Scotland, to Eastfield, in July 1975, followed by moves to Haymarket (February 1978), Eastfield (May 1978), back to Toton (February 1981), Wigan Springs Branch (May 1982), and finally Crewe (October 1982). Its final major overhaul is officially recorded as having been conducted at BREL Derby Works in March 1978, although the location of its number transfers behind the cab doors indicates it must have also visited Glasgow Works after that for attention.

Three years after the end of Class 25 operation and its attendant wave of preservation activity, it could not have been imagined that anyone would have wanted to embark on the heavy restoration programme required by No 25235. However, it arrived at Bo'ness at the end of 1990 via M.C.Metals at St Rollox, Glasgow, for asbestos removal. The power unit was removed for overhaul, and it has been successfully operated during 1991.

Class 25 Bo-Bo No 7594

Built: BR Darlington, June 1964
Numbers carried: (1) D7594,
(2) 25244
First allocation: Toton
Final allocation: Crewe
Withdrawn: 28 July 1986
Preserved: Nene Valley Railway,
Wansford

Destined for the Swanage
Railway, No 25244 crosses the as
yet un-relaid trackbed near Corfe
Castle. *Andrew Wright*

The former North Eastern Railway works at Darlington ceased locomotive construction in August 1964, a year before total closure, and the final order was for 20 Sulzer-engined Class 25s, Nos D7578-97. They were also the final series to be fully equipped with oil-fired steam-heat boilers, and, somewhat out of sequence, followed the old body style with bodyside grilles and nose-end doors. No D7594 was therefore a versatile machine amongst the Toton fleet, and might have been seen on all types of mixed traffic work on the Midland Main Line. It drifted to Manchester in June 1968, to Eastfield in August 1985, back to Longsight in October 1982, Cricklewood in May 1984, and finally Crewe the following November. Already in blue livery and dual braked, it was last overhauled at Glasgow in January 1978, easily proved because the Scottish works applied its locomotive numbers on the bodysides instead under the driver's cabside window.

Condemned at Crewe in July 1986 with a number of defects, No 25244, as it had been renumbered, was stored with many others of the same type for several months before being despatched with later withdrawals to Vic Berry's Leicester yard in the early summer of 1987. The purchasers had originally hoped to buy the first-built Class 25/1, No 25027, which was towed up from Swindon to Leicester when the former BREL works closed, but were discouraged by its inferior condition and the cost of asbestos removal.

No 25244 was released from Leicester and received a quick repaint for display at the 26-27 September 1987 Basingstoke exhibition, renowned for featuring practically every design of surviving BR locomotive type in one long line. A curious further repaint was executed for the Eastleigh Works Open Day on 18 September 1988 – the all-yellow ends were retained, but one side was left in BR blue as No 25244 while the other was in 1960s BR green as No 7594. Although then stranded from the rest of the BR system, the locomotive was one of the growing modern traction fleet at the Swanage Railway, where it arrived on 26 May 1989. It changed ownership in January 1992, being moved to Peterborough in a complex exchange arrangement also involving No D9521 (qv) from Cottesmore.

Class 25 Bo-Bo No 25262

Built: BR Derby, April 1966
Numbers carried: (1) D7612,
    (2) 25262, (3) 25901
First allocation: Eastfield
Final allocation: Crewe
Withdrawn: 16 March 1987
Preserved: East Lancashire
    Railway, Bury

Battle-scarred No 25901 soon
after arrival at Bury, 9 October
1989. *Howard Johnston*

No 25262 is credited with the last Class 25 duty on BR, outliving the rest of the class by several days because of the lack of a suitable locomotive to work local trip freights out of Carlisle at the end of March 1987, a full two weeks after it was due to be laid up. Sadly the exact date is not officially recorded, although the locomotive did actually cross the Scottish boundary to traverse the Longtown branch.

No D7612 was new to Eastfield (Glasgow) from Derby Works in April 1966, but transferred south in September 1967 for a varied career in the Nottingham and Birmingham area for next 20 years. Its last major overhaul was at Derby in May 1977, but it paid a number of further visits for minor attention.

Withdrawal of the Class 25 fleet was close to completion in November 1985 when the need arose for a small dedicated fleet of locomotives based at Carlisle for a specially identified chemicals contract. They would be needed until the end of 1988, and it prompted BR to inspect the survivors to segregate the 12 best of the final series in terms of engine life, electrical

condition and tyre wear. They were renumbered Nos 25901-12 to denote their different status and a 60 mph maximum speed was specified to ensure a longer traction motor life. The scheme was, however, quickly abandoned because the chemical contracts never materialised. The 25/9s thus ended up in the same Crewe pool, and withdrawals were not delayed beyond the rest of the fleet.

Unlike the rest of the final operational fleet, No 25901 stayed at Carlisle for many months after disposal, and was taken to Glasgow Works, not Leicester, for asbestos inspection prior to being offered for sale in November 1988. After arrival at the East Lancashire Railway at Bury on 17 September 1989, it was running within a fortnight on test runs to Ramsbottom, but is in need of some work before it can be considered a fully operational locomotive. Still in blue but renumbered back to No 25262, it was the first locomotive for nine years to travel over the ELR north from Ramsbottom to Ewood Bridge station on 28 October 1989, hauling three coaches for Territorial Army track-laying volunteers.

Class 25 Bo-Bo No 25265

Built: BR Derby, May 1966
Numbers carried: (1) D7615,
  (2) 25265
First allocation: Toton
Final allocation: Crewe
Withdrawn: 18 March 1987
Preserved: Peak Railway, Darley
  Dale

No 25265, recently transferred
to Darley Dale, on 15 April
1990. *Steve Worrall*

Thirteen Class 25s, Nos D7611-23, were delivered new to the Scottish Region between April and September 1966 for freight work in the Glasgow area, but they were standard Derby Works fare apart from the provision of a recess in the driver's side cabside for single-line token equipment; this recess was later plated over.

No D7615 is the oldest in preservation of the final Series 3 sub-class with revised electrical control equipment, which were generally the longest survivors. Of the later body style with three same-size front windows and no connecting doors, they were not boiler fitted, but were more favoured for fitting with air brakes until work ceased in 1978.

No D7615, which would have been regularly seen as far north as Inverness and Oban as well as Ayrshire, was sent south to Allerton in August 1968, and then did work from all main LMR depots before settling down at Crewe in January 1984. It acquired dual brakes in 1974, and was one of the last of the class to be granted a general overhaul at Derby Works, not being returned to traffic until June 1980.

In its final weeks in traffic, No 25265, as it then was, carried the bilingual unofficial name *Castell Harlech/Harlech Castle*, typical of the legend applied to Class 25s when they arrived at Aberystwyth with oil trains from Stanlow. No 25265 worked its last BR train on 15 March 1987, a local freight to Holyhead, where it also performed domestic shunting before being switched off and towed back to Crewe for condemnation. It was sold through the agency of Vic Berry at Leicester, where it was taken for removal of asbestos.

Preservation on the Peak Railway is appropriate considering the level of Class 25 activity once present for the incessant limestone traffic generated from the local quarries. They were direct successors to the Stanier Class 8F 2-8-0s which dominated the routes to Manchester until they too were eliminated at the end of the 1960s. No 25265 is also ideal to haul four- or six-coach passenger trains over the revived Midland Railway route from Buxton to Matlock. It was moved from Buxton to Darley Dale at the end of 1989.

Class 25 Bo-Bo No D7628

Built: Beyer Peacock, August
 1965
Numbers carried: (1) D7628,
 (2) 25278
First allocation: Tinsley
Final allocation: Crewe
Withdrawn: 15 March 1987
Preserved: North Yorkshire
 Moors Railway, Grosmont

A smart No 25278 in Gloucester
yard on 27 May 1983. *Norman
Preedy*

Derby Works' association with the 478-strong Class 24 and 25 locomotive fleet ended in January 1981 with the completion of the final general overhaul on No 25278, a member of the then substantial allocation at Cricklewood at the southern end of the Midland Main Line. The North Yorkshire Moors Railway had to make a substantial bid for this particular engine when it was put up for sale in mid-1987. No 25278 was in fact in use to the end of Class 25 operation on BR, running out of time on 17 March 1987, two days after official withdrawal, after working a Bescot-Crewe Basford Hall freight turn.

The interesting decision was taken in 1964 to sub-contract the construction of the final 54 Class 25s to Beyer, Peacock – the first BR design to go a private builder – in an attempt to keep the Manchester firm in business during a lull. In the event, only 36 were built there before the firm asked for release from its contract and ceased trading. It was, however, generally accepted later that the Beyer, Peacock examples were the soundest built.

This locomotive was new to the Eastern Region as No D7628 in August 1965, when a need for 1,250hp motive power was identified for the first time at Tinsley, Sheffield, although the depot was already familiar with the type from a maintenance point of view. After a short spell based at Wath, it joined the London Midland Region's Midland Lines fleet in August 1967, and became a common-user machine for the rest of its career with additional spells at Toton, Bescot, Longsight, Wigan, Cricklewood, Carlisle and finally Crewe in March 1986. It lost its two-tone green livery for blue in October 1974.

With its new number, 25278's most important working was on 25 November 1982, when it double-headed No 25259 on a Wolverhampton-Tywyn Royal Train. It carried the unofficial name *Castell Powys/Powis Castle* during its final weeks in traffic, and was moved from Vic Berry's Leicester yard to the NYMR with No 25191 (qv) in January 1988. Restored to two-tone green livery, it covered 2,695 miles during the 1990 season.

Class 25 Bo-Bo No D7629

Built: Beyer Peacock, September
  1965
Numbers carried: (1) D7629,
  (2) 25279
First allocation: Tinsley
Final allocation: Crewe
Withdrawn: 15 March 1987
Preserved: Llangollen Railway

Ex-works after a repaint, No
D7629 in Llangollen yard on
25 August 1990. *Steve Worrall*

The eagerness of BR to sell off as many Class 25s as it could to preserved line operators in 1987 saw No 25279 towed to Vic Berry's yard at Leicester for storage pending the issuing of a tender list. Ironic though it may seem, a scrapyard was the best place to store the engines because it was more protected from vandalism and theft than the sidings at Crewe Gresty Lane or Bescot.

Beyer, Peacock-built No 25279's career started at Tinsley as No D7629 in September 1965. Although identical to sister No D7628 on the previous page, its moves between depots were more frequent – no fewer than 16 transfers in 22 years. It was an early candidate for dual braking in the early 1970s, and visited Derby Works for its last general overhaul in 1979, returning to traffic in the September. One of its more interesting duties was to work the 08.35 service from Birmingham New Street into Paddington on 25 August 1982 in the absence of a more powerful main-line locomotive.

In its final year, when the survivors were all concentrated at Crewe diesel depot, No 25279 would have still been employed on a variety of duties varying from Ayrshire trip freights to Sellafield nuclear flask traffic (which involved a regular trip to Bridgwater in Somerset); Cambrian freights, trips down the Blaenau Ffestiniog branch, and even outings to East Anglia were also relatively commonplace.

The last weekend's activities for No 25279 were departmental duties around Carnforth and Lancaster before movement to Wigan Springs Branch depot on 15 March 1987 for condemnation and removal to the Crewe scrap-line.

Sold to the Llangollen Railway for use on the Ruabon-Corwen line then under reconstruction, it was started for the first time in preservation on 9 April 1989, and apart from a minor air leak no major problems were discovered. Its first full outing was on a civil engineer's train on 23 July, and it worked its first passenger train, a 'Santa Special', on 24 December of the same year. Restoration has been to original two-tone green livery with small yellow warning panel.

Class 25 Bo-Bo No D7633

Built: Beyer Peacock, September
 1965
Numbers carried: (1) D7633,
 (2) 25283, (3) 25904
First allocation: Tinsley
Final allocation: Crewe
Withdrawn: 15 March 1987
Preserved: Severn Valley
 Railway, Bridgnorth

Carrying its second number, No
25283 is under repair at Tyseley
on 30 March 1985. *Philip Sutton*

The Severn Valley Railway expressed interest in buying a Sulzer Type 2 as early as 1979, but its efforts to secure one of the last boiler-fitted Class 24s retained for Cambrian mail traffic were stifled by lack of time to raise the necessary finance. The end of the Class 25s eight years later gave them renewed determination, and No 25904 was secured as one of the best examples from amongst the last survivors.

Delivered brand new from Beyer Peacock at Gorton to Tinsley depot as No D7633 in October 1965, it was regarded as a purely freight engine from the very beginning because of the lack of a steam-heat boiler. It moved to Wath in April 1966, Wigan Springs Branch in October 1967, Bescot in August 1972, Willesden in December 1972, Wigan again in February 1973, Crewe in October 1982, Carlisle Kingmoor in October 1985, and finally Crewe the following year. Renumbered first to No 25283, it visited Glasgow Works for a final major overhaul in December 1978, hence the bodyside numbers as opposed to cabside as on Derby overhauls.

The renumbering to No 25904 took place in November 1985 as part of the general scheme

to retain the 12 best examples of the final series until the end of 1988 to fulfil a special contract, which did not materialise. In addition their reliability turned out to be no better than the rest of the class, despite increased mechanical supervision.

Every one of the final batch of survivors had to perform a 'last' working of some description, and No 25904 made the final trip over the Western Region on 17 March 1987, two days after it was due to be taken out of traffic. The duty was to collect the nuclear flask from Bridgwater, and the usefulness of the Class 25, by now only one of two still in service, continued right through to the 23rd when it was used on ballast duties from Chester and Connah's Quay before being retired to Crewe with a minor turbocharger fault, and lined up for disposal.

Via asbestos removal at Vic Berry's Leicester yard, No 25904 arrived at Tyseley BR depot on 1 January 1988 for tyre-turning, and was then moved to its new home on the Severn Valley Railway. It was repainted in two-tone green in the spring of 1988 as No D7633, with four-character headcodes restored. It is normally stabled at the Kidderminster end of the line.

Class 25 Bo-Bo No 25909

Built: Beyer Peacock, July 1966
Numbers carried: (1) D7659,
  (2) 25309, (3) 25909
First allocation: London Midland
  Control, Derby
Final allocation: Carlisle
  Kingmoor
Withdrawn: 9 September 1986
Preserved: East Lancashire
  Railway, Bury

A livery never carried in BR
days, No 25909 sports a small
yellow panel only at Bury on
17 June 1989. *Howard Johnston*

The 8,069th and final locomotive from the works of Beyer, Peacock of Gorton, Manchester, before its closure in 1966 has been saved for working preservation at Bury, only a few miles from its birthplace. Beyer, Peacock started locomotive building in 1855, enjoying outstanding success with exports of steam locomotives all over the world. It was, however, late off the mark with diesel and electric locomotive designs, until the BR fleet was nearing completion and the world market was dominated by other established builders of modern traction.

One of the final orders was the assembly of 54 standard BR Type 2s, although only 36 were completed before Beyer, Peacock asked to be released from its contract. The last pair, Nos D7658 and D7659, were taken on test to Chinley on 12 July 1966 before delivery without ceremony to Willesden depot.

No D7659 was also the last of the class built in two-tone green livery, and worked from 15 depots during its career. After Willesden, it travelled to Toton (December 1968), Wigan Springs Branch (May 1970), Longsight (January 1971), Bescot (August 1972), Carlisle Kingmoor (October 1972), Wigan (May 1973), Longsight (July 1973), Willesden (August 1973), Cricklewood (June 1975), Toton (November 1977), Cricklewood (April 1979), Toton (September 1979), Cricklewood (March 1980), and finally Carlisle (January 1984). It received its last general overhaul at Derby Works in May 1980.

One of 12 Class 25s earmarked for life extension, it was renumbered No 25909 in late 1985, but only survived another year. After a long period of open storage at Carlisle, it was sold to pop music producer Pete Waterman, and returned to working order at the depot in March 1988. It actually ran on test down the West Coast Main Line to Crewe, and was towed by Class 31 loco No 31311 from Crewe to Bescot in a special freight on 22 April. After asbestos removal at Vic Berry, Leicester, it arrived at Bury via display at the 5 June 1988 Coalville Open Day. It has most recently been repainted in BR blue but with non-standard small yellow panels, but still as No 25909. It had its first passenger outing on the ELR on 1 October 1988.

Class 25 Bo-Bo No 25313

Built: BR Derby, November
  1966
Numbers carried: (1) D7663,
  (2) 25313
First allocation: Willesden
Final allocation: Crewe
Withdrawn: 18 March 1987
Preserved: Llangollen Railway

With restoration barely started,
No 25313 stands at Llangollen
on 29 August 1988. *Mike
Goodfield*

Derby Works had planned to cease diesel locomotive building with Class 25 No D7623 in September 1966, but had to set up its production lines again at the end of the year to assemble the final series of 18 after Beyer, Peacock of Gorton, Manchester, asked to be released from their construction contract. No D7663, preserved at Llangollen, is one of this final Derby series, emerging in November 1966 when all-over blue livery with 'barbed wire' BR emblems had superseded two-tone green. Dual-braked from new, it was one of only 12 allocated new to the London end of the West Coast Main Line at Willesden, where its duties would have included empty stock workings in the newly electrified Euston station; its revamped colour scheme would have blended in well with the high-tech image projected by the blue electric locos and new blue and grey rolling-stock.

In later years No D7663 migrated to Bescot (December 1968), back to Willesden (May 1971), Cricklewood (May 1973), Toton (November 1977), Wigan Springs Branch (February 1978), Cricklewood (July 1978),

Longsight (January 1984), Bescot (July 1984), and finally Crewe (September 1985). Renumbered from No D7663 to 25313 in March 1974, it was given its final major overhaul at Derby Works in March 1977.

One of the final members of the class in traffic at the end of Class 25 operation on BR, No 25313 was still busy three days after the official withdrawal date, and its last recorded duty of all was the 05.26 Barrow-in-Furness-Manchester Red Bank empty newspaper vans, after which it was moved to Crewe for condemnation.

After inspection at Vic Berry's Leicester yard and subsequent asbestos removal, No 25313 was sold to the Swindon & Cricklade Railway for hauling passenger trains out of Blunsdon on the former M&SWJ line, but it was quickly recognised that the lack of a steam-heat boiler would be a severe winter handicap. It was subsequently sold on to the Llangollen Railway, where it is has hitherto been regarded as an easy source of spares for the restoration of mechanically superior sister Class 25 No D7629 (qv). It arrived in North Wales on 1 June 1988.

Class 25 Bo-Bo No D7671

Built: BR Derby, February 1967
Numbers carried: (1) D7671,
  (2) 25321
First allocation: Willesden
Final allocation: Crewe
Withdrawn: 29 September 1986
Preserved: Midland Railway
  Centre, Butterley

No D7671 on freight duty at
Butterley, 31 August 1991.
Robin Stewart-Smith

Derby Industrial Museum made known its intention to buy a Class 25 in mid-1987, but it was not until December of that year that No 25321 was secured direct from the BR Technical Centre, where it had been for some time for safekeeping.

No D7671 represents the final development of the Sulzer-engined Type 2 locomotive for the British market, not having appeared from Derby Works until 1967 (the original Beyer, Peacock assembly contract having been cancelled). Consideration was also given to preserving the last-built No 25327 which was still extant in 1987 at Vic Berry's scrapyard, but its derelict condition after three years out of use meant it was beyond economic redemption.

New to Willesden in February 1967, No D7671 also saw service from the full range of London Midland Region depots, Toton, Carlisle Upperby and Kingmoor, Allerton, Bescot, Wigan, Cricklewood, Longsight, and finally Crewe. Its final works overhaul was at Derby in May 1978.

D7671 was repainted in 1960s two-tone green livery with small yellow ends (a livery it never actually carried in BR service but which has always been considered more visually attractive) at Derby RTC during the summer of 1988 prior to handover. The original intention was to display the locomotive on a plinth in the city centre, although this was happily quickly abandoned in favour of running at the Midland Railway Centre, Butterley.

It made trial runs on 21 January 1989, and made its passenger debut at the Midland Railway Centre on 21 April, the first such use for $2^1/_2$ years. Since then it has been in regular use on the short preserved line from Pye Bridge on both passenger and engineering trains, and has made several BR open day visits, including Derby and Coalville during 1990.

Class 25 Bo-Bo No D7672 *Tamworth Castle*

Built: BR Derby, February 1967
Numbers allocated: (1) D7672,
  (2) 25322, (3) 25912,
  (4) ADB968027 (never
  carried), (5) D7672
First allocation: Toton
Final allocation: Crewe
Withdrawn: (1) 29 January
  1984, (2) 15 March 1987,
  (3) 30 March 1991
Preserved: North Staffordshire
  Railway, Cheddleton

No D7672 at Appleby with No
47407 on 23 June 1990. *Howard
Johnston*

Every class has its celebrity machine, and newest-built No D7672 is certainly the star of the Class 25s. Still BR-owned and maintained, it was actually allowed out on the main line during 1990/91 before lack of a sponsoring sector forced its withdrawal and sale for preservation. *Tamworth Castle*'s fame dates back to 12 May 1984, when Tyseley depot staff undertook a complete repaint for display at a week-long rail festival at Tamworth, for which it was adorned with hand-painted 'Tamworth Castle' lettering on its bodysides. The non-standard paint style, full yellow cabsides with black numbers and black window surrounds, while not exactly attractive, captured widespread attention at a time when BR locomotive liveries had still to break out of the blue and yellow mould. Nicknamed the 'ice-cream van', No 25322 soon gained a substantial following.

As plain No D7672, it was the 1,005th diesel locomotive built at Derby Works, and was delivered new to Toton in February 1967, only two months before the BR/Sulzer Type 2 design was completed with a total of 478 examples, Nos D5000-D5299 and D7500-D7677. In blue livery from new with full yellow ends, it also worked at most LMR depots. Given a final overhaul at Derby in May 1977 while a Wigan loco, it was transferred to Carlisle in July 1978. The official reason for No 25322's withdrawal at the end of January 1984 was that it was life-expired, but it subsequently survived long enough to be selected as one of 12 for long-term retention as Class 25/9s. Renumbered as No 25912, it then worked until 23 March 1987.

It was then commandeered by the ER Training Engineer at Leeds Holbeck depot for apprentice training, arriving on 6 May, and was restored to full running order in two-tone green (it was actually new in blue), with cast nameplates. Spares came from withdrawn sisters Nos 25202 and 25206. The first outing on the main line was on test to Carlisle on 24 February 1990, and it was officially reinstated to BR capital stock on 15 September 1990, to be withdrawn six months later after a requiem railtour from Leeds to Holyhead. It visited Glasgow for asbestos inspection before immediate sale to the North Staffordshire group, arriving at Cheddleton on 18 May 1991.

Class 20 Bo-Bo No D8000

Built: English Electric, June 1957
Numbers carried: (1) D8000, (2) 20050
First allocation: Devons Road, Bow
Final allocation: Toton
Withdrawn: 14 December 1980
Preserved: National Railway Museum, York

No D8000 stands in a precarious state at Swindon Works on 5 December 1980. *Howard Johnston*

The 30-year careers of the Class 20s, BR's first main-line design, are fast drawing to a close with the delivery of Class 60s for coal and metals traffic. Even so, the single-cab 1,000hp English Electric locomotive can still be regarded as an outstanding investment. Of the 228 built between 1957-68, few were still in service by 1991, but until recently they were regarded as indispensable in the Midlands, North West of England, and southern Scotland, most often seen in pairs, nose-to-nose, on duties where substantial braking power was most needed.

Withdrawn as long ago as 1980, it is remarkable that the pioneer, No D8000, has been preserved. As works number D735/2347 it was handed over with due ceremony at Vulcan Foundry, Newton-le-Willows, to run trials at various depots before moving to the now closed Devons Road, Bow (London), depot to replace LMS 3F 0-6-0Ts. Flexibility of operation is evident in a long list of transfers since then – Toton (August 1957), Devons Road again (September 1957), Toton (July 1958), Crewe South and Toton (September 1958), Camden (October 1960), Willesden (September 1965), London (Western) Division (April 1966), Nottingham Division (August 1969), Tinsley

(October 1970), Haymarket (October 1971), Eastfield (February 1973), Haymarket (April 1973), and finally Toton again (November 1973).

The inability of the TOPS computer to handle the number 20000 saw D8000 renumbered in February 1974 as No 20050, at the end of the first production series. During a lull in freight business, it spent August to November 1975 in store at Westhouses. Then a major restructuring of BR freight business saw large numbers of vacuum-braked Class 20s consigned to store pending a crash dual braking programme, but No 20050, stored at Swindon, was condemned instead. It was claimed by the NRM for restoration at Doncaster to the green livery lost late in 1972, and was towed north on 7 October 1981.

It was exhibited at the NRM from 7 July 1985, sporting non-original features such as round buffers and fluted bogie struts, and lacking bodyside ladders and cabside emblems. It is not operational because its traction motor cables were severed before arrival at York, but is a popular exhibit because its easily removable bodyside doors are considered a boon for educational tours of a diesel locomotive.

Class 20 Bo-Bo No 20001

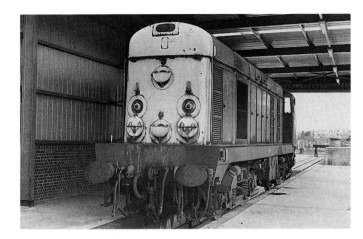

Built: English Electric, July 1957
Numbers carried: (1) D8001,
(2) 20001
First allocation: Devons Road,
Bow
Final allocation: Toton
Withdrawn: 20 April 1988
Preserved: Midland Railway
Centre, Butterley

No 20001 inside Toton training
compound on 28 May 1988.
Howard Johnston

The survival of the second oldest Class 20 is due in the most part to staff at Toton TMD, who persuaded depot management to keep it as a departmental training locomotive after it was withdrawn as surplus, but in full working order. When others were being robbed for spares and lined up for the breakers, No 20001 was moved to the security of a covered and fenced area at the rear of the depot. It then took fully 3^1/2 years for the locomotive to be offered for sale, and even then it was thought that the Class 20 Society would be outbid by a commercial enterprise looking to export serviceable examples to work in France.

No 20001, the former No D8001, was new to Devon's Road, Bow, in July 1957, and was used for a variety of familiarisation work across the London Midland Region. It moved to Crewe in September 1958, and went back to the London area (Willesden) in October 1960. It was one of the first Class 20s to be repainted from green to blue livery with full yellow ends, being noted ex-works in this style as early as July 1967. A further stock switch-round saw No D8001 moved on to Toton in August 1969, Tinsley in

October 1970, and Edinburgh Haymarket in October 1971. Returned to Toton March 1973, it was stored at Westhouses in July 1975 as surplus, and moved to Derby Works the following month pending a decision on its future.

An overhaul was, however, granted, and the loco was returned to service at Toton at the end of October that year. Two more transfers took place, to Tinsley in November 1978, and finally back to Toton in September 1984 to join the Nottinghamshire general coal fleet. Its final general overhaul was completed at Glasgow Works in April 1980, but it was another four years before it was to be fitted with dual brakes and slow-speed control gear.

Although still a BR locomotive, No 20001 was taken to the Midland Railway Centre at Butterley for the 1990 summer season, received a blue repaint for the occasion, and hauled a number of special trains. Like No D8000 on the previous page, any restoration project will have to take into account a large number of non-original fittings, including the wrong type of bogies.

Class 20 Bo-Bo No 20020

Built: English Electric, October 1959
Numbers carried: (1) D8020, (2) 20020
First allocation: Hornsey
Final allocation: Toton
Withdrawn: (1) 21 December 1982, (2) 12 December 1990
Preserved: Bo'ness & Kinneil Railway

No 20020 at Gloucester Rail Day, 1990. *Philip Sutton*

The English Electric Type 1 design was undoubtedly one of the most successful of the early Modernisation Plan designs, and the first of the main production series has also survived into preservation after sale during 1991. It has, however, been substantially rebuilt during its career, and the story of its remarkable survival after withdrawal in 1982 with serious accident damage is recorded here.

There was an 18-month lull in production after the delivery of No D8019 to the London Midland Region in March 1958 but, once mobilised, the Lancashire works of English Electric turned out the next series of 30 at the amazing rate of one every three days. Notable differences from the first series included round buffers, fluted bogie struts and lack of a right-hand bodyside ladder. The first eight, Nos D8020-7, were allocated to Hornsey for empty stock and cross-London freight workings, moving on to Finsbury Park when the purpose-built depot was commissioned in April 1960. The unreliable nature of other early types based at the southern end of the East Coast Main Line often saw them deputising on services to Hitchin and occasionally Cambridge. All this ended for No D8020 in November 1960 when

it was transferred to Sheffield Darnall, beginning a long association for the class with the South Yorkshire area.

The loco returned to Finsbury Park in September 1962, but was off to Immingham in April 1966. Further reallocations were to Tinsley (October 1966), Polmadie (January 1967), Gateshead (June 1967), Tinsley (October 1970), Eastfield (July 1977), Inverness (June 1979), and Eastfield (February 1980). It was laid up first at Eastfield and later Aberdeen from April to September of that year, then was returned to use at Haymarket. Moved back to Eastfield in October 1981, it went into store again the following year, and after sustaining serious body damage was withdrawn in December 1982 and sent to Glasgow for scrap.

Eighteen months later, however, it was merged with the cab and superstructure of collision-damaged No 20036, and put back into traffic at Eastfield. Further allocations were to Haymarket (August 1984), Motherwell (October 1984), and finally Toton (January 1985). It retained the green livery as late as 1978, one of the last to do so.

Class 20 Bo-Bo No 20031

Built: English Electric, January 1960
Numbers carried: (1) D8031, (2) 20031
First allocation: Kittybrewster, Aberdeen
Final allocation: Toton
Withdrawn: 14 September 1990
Preserved: Keighley & Worth Valley Railway

Still with cabside tablet-catcher recess, No 20031 was photographed at Derby stabling point on 14 September 1977. *Norman Preedy*

Class 20 No 20031 was at work on the Keighley & Worth Valley Railway within days of arrival in the autumn of 1991, and is already a key member of the fleet, taking charge of works trains and, like all diesels, a saviour when a rescue is suddenly needed. This role is purely an extension of its final BR role, when it was part of the London Midland Region Civil Engineer's pool which required its use at weekends only until rendered redundant with several others of the same type at the end of 1990. No 20031's new owners, a group of Worth Valley line members, have chosen to repaint the locomotive into present-day BR blue livery with full yellow ends. When new in the first month of 1960, it would have been painted in all-over green with red buffer beams and light grey roof.

The English Electric Type 1 has given 30 years' sterling service all over the BR system, but the basics of the design can be traced back much further, especially the eight-cylinder 1,000hp 8SVT power unit, which shares many design characteristics with the K-type engine powering the 350hp shunter. Aberdeen's Kittybrewster depot acquired several of the type

at the beginning of 1960, but No D8031 was the only one which was brand new. It stayed in Scotland for another eight years working from Inverness, Polmadie and Haymarket before a transfer south to Toton in June 1968. Its transfers were then wide and varied, to Stratford three months later, on to York in October 1969, Gateshead (June 1970), Immingham (October 1970), Tinsley (July 1971), and Immingham again in October 1982. It was then consigned to store at Stourton and Healey Mills awaiting a visit to Crewe for dual braking, returning to traffic at Tinsley in October 1983.

As a Scottish loco, No D8031 was originally set up with cab recesses to accommodate a tablet catcher for operation over the single-track Highland main line between Inverness and Perth, but this was plated over during a works overhaul when the tokenless block system gained favour. In its original livery, No D8031 would, however, also have differed from most Scottish examples by carrying the conventional BR emblem compared with later production examples from No D8070 upwards which carried carriage-style emblems.

Class 20 Bo-Bo No 20048

Built: English Electric, December 1959
Numbers carried: (1) D8048, (2) 20048
First allocation: Hornsey
Final allocation: Toton
Withdrawn: (1) 1 February 1981, (2) 9 November 1990
Preserved: Peak Railway, Darley Dale

Nos 20048 and 20176 drag electric loco No 86238 into Crewe with the 11.00 Glasgow-Brighton on 20 July 1989. *Norman Preedy*

The fleet of English Electric Type 1s for the Great Northern suburban system out of King's Cross was topped up to 13 locomotives with the delivery of the last six examples of the first production series at the end of 1959. The last two, Nos D8048/9, were officially accepted into traffic on the very last day of the old decade.

No D8048 can certainly claim to have a varied life which, while showing how volatile BR operations are, also demonstrates the type's versatility. New to Hornsey, it moved across to the purpose-built Finsbury Park diesel depot in April 1960, but the effects of the National Freight Plan and a plentiful supply of other motive power saw No D8048 moved off to Immingham in April 1966. It was loaned to Gateshead in September 1967, but found little favour and migrated to Toton, home of over a hundred of the same type, two months later.

Its transfers were far from complete: Tinsley (October 1970), Eastfield (October 1971), and Toton again (February 1976). Its poor mechanical condition at a time of severe recession, coupled to its lack of versatility because it only had vacuum brakes, meant its withdrawal as long ago as February 1981, and dispatch to Swindon Works for storage and possible breaking up. However, all but one of the Class 20s sent there were reprieved towards the end of 1982 (the prototype No D8000 was sent to the National Railway Museum), and No 20048, as it had by then become, was parked at Tinsley depot until November 1982 when a slot was found in the general overhaul programme at Crewe Works.

The loco was reinstated to traffic, dual-brake-fitted, on 8 May 1983, and was soon on its travels again, working out of Eastfield (May 1984), Tinsley (September 1986), Eastfield again (October 1986), Bescot (March 1987), and finally Toton as part of the Civil Engineer's departmental pool for the Manchester area.

The need for reliable motive power on the recently re-opened southern section of the Peak Railway from Darley Dale to Matlock has made the offer of the use of No 20048 a most useful one. Its owners are the Coventry-based Midland Class 20 Association, who secured their machine in June 1991.

Class 20 Bo-Bo No 20056

Built: English Electric, April
1961
Numbers carried: (1) D8056,
(2) 20056
First allocation: Tinsley
Final allocation: Toton
Withdrawn: 1 October 1990
Preserved: Caledonian Railway,
Brechin

Nos 20056 and 20208 approach
Tapton Junction, Chesterfield,
with southbound coal empties on
3 February 1983. *Brian Cuttell*

The sectorisation of the BR locomotive fleet from the mid-1980s often resulted in the withdrawal of serviceable machines simply because their duty ended and there was no other sponsor prepared to take them on. This happened to Class 20 No 20056, which ended its career as part of the Civil Engineer's Nottingham area fleet, disbanded at the end of 1990. Although almost 30 years old, No 20056 could not be considered totally life-expired as it had visited Crewe Works as recently as November 1984 for the fitting of dual-brake equipment and slow speed control gear.

The influence of the English Electric Type 1s spread to South Yorkshire from March 1961 onwards with the allocation of 20 locomotives, Nos D8050-69, to Tinsley depot, Sheffield. No D8056 was one of several reallocated to Immingham on South Humberside in September 1965, back to Tinsley in March 1967, back to Immingham (October 1967), Stratford (August 1968), Tinsley (October 1971), Immingham (February 1984), Toton

(September 1984), Bescot (September 1985), and finally Toton (January 1987).

The loco visited the works many times. Its first intermediate overhaul took place at Crewe from 31 August to 10 October 1964, and another intermediate repair was undertaken there between 19 February and 11 March 1969. It was fitted with power unit No IH5240 when new, replaced by No IH5239 from loco D8055 in 1964. Engine No IH5039 was installed in the 1969 overhaul. The final major works attention was at Glasgow in March 1981.

The year 1990 was a bad one for Class 20s as no fewer than 31 examples were withdrawn, mostly from Toton, replaced in the main by Class 60s on coal traffic, or, in the case of the departmental locos, by cascaded Class 31s. After inspection for asbestos contamination, No 20056 was moved to its new home on the Caledonian Railway in 1991. Class 20s were a common sight in East Scotland until 1990 on coal trains to Longannet Power Station.

Class 20 Bo-Bo No 20069

Built: English Electric, June 1961
Numbers carried: (1) D8069, (2) 20069
First allocation: Sheffield Darnall
Final allocation: Thornaby
Withdrawn: (1) February 1981, (2) 20 May 1991
Preserved: Mid-Norfolk Railway

No 20069 parked outside Crewe Works on 19 March 1975. *Norman Preedy*

The only Class 20 ever to have ever allocated to the Western Region is also the first ex-BR main-line locomotive to move to the Mid-Norfolk Railway, dedicated to restoring passenger services to the Wymondham-Dereham line.

No D8069, bought for preservation at the very end of 1991, was the last of a series of 20 new to Sheffield Darnall in June 1961, and moved over to nearby Tinsley when the new depot linked to the marshalling yard was opened in April 1964.

The loco seems to have been regarded as very much a crew-training loco during its early life, spending two weeks at Cardiff Canton on loan from June 1965. The decision to equip Toton with 1,000hp Type 1 Bo-Bos for the Nottinghamshire coal traffic saw large numbers transferred there from 1966 onwards. No D8069 was on official four-week loan from Tinsley in January of that year, and again in April, after which the allocation became permanent. It gained blue livery in the mid-1970s.

Despite their age, Class 20s were largely immune from the heavy cutbacks in the BR locomotive fleet during the 1981/82, although economies dictated the removal of several of the most run-down examples to Swindon for storage. No 20069, which had not been overhauled since May 1978, arrived there on 23 February 1981. It stayed in the yard until 15 June 1982, when it departed for Glasgow Works for general overhaul and dual braking. It was reinstated to traffic on 20 June 1982, allocated to Eastfield.

Its allocations in its final BR years were to Haymarket in November 1982, Tinsley in March 1985, Immingham in May 1987, and finally Thornaby where it became part of the Railfreight Metals pool which in 1991 yielded several Class 20s for preservation. The decision to run down the fleet in the North East came as a result of a nationwide motive power reshuffle that resulted in the availability of spare Class 37s, and better-condition Class 20s from a Bescot weekend-use departmental group.

Class 20 Bo-Bo No 20098

Built: English Electric, November 1961
Numbers carried: (1) D8098, (2) 20098
First allocation: Eastfield
Final allocation: Thornaby
Withdrawn: 24 June 1991
Preserved: Great Central Railway, Rothley

Tinsley-based No 20098 on railtour duty at Chepstow with the 'Tintern Totter' on 13 August 1978. *A.O.Wynn*

Pairs of Class 20s saw regular use on steel traffic in the North East into early 1992, although new Brush Class 60s were by then displacing them in some numbers. However, several Thornaby-based Railfreight Metals (FMTY pool) examples were laid up in full working order, and thus became obvious preservation material.

The scheme to return the Great Central Railway to double track made an approach from the Type 1 Locomotive Association to base its Class 20 on the line a welcome one. Based at Rothley, it would be ideal for permanent way duties, as well as useful standby motive power for passenger trains.

No 20098, built as No D8098, worked on three regions of BR. Originally intended for Scotland, it spent most of its first 15 years north of the border, working variously from Eastfield and Polmadie, broken only by a spell at Toton from March 1970 to October 1971. While in Scotland, it would have seen occasional use on weekend passenger excursions as far as Carlisle and Newcastle, and later on trains of Rootes car components from Linwood (Glasgow) to Coventry, and possibly even Rugby-Coventry-Birmingham passenger locals.

Fresh from an intermediate overhaul, No 20098 was transferred to Tinsley in July 1976, and worked from there for another six years before being put into store in December 1982 to await the call to Crewe for a general repair and fitting with a dual brake system. It was back in traffic the following August. Large numbers of Class 20s were transferred to Immingham in January 1987, including No 20098.

No 20098 is credited with one celebrated solo passenger working, hauling the 'Tintern Totter', a three-coach special from Birmingham over the remaining spur of the GWR Chepstow-Monmouth line, retained as far as Tidenham Quarry.

Class 20 Bo-Bo No 20107

Built: English Electric, December
1961
Numbers carried: (1) D8107,
(2) 20107
First allocation: Eastfield
Final allocation: Thornaby
Withdrawn: (1) 5 December
1982, (2) 21 January 1991
Preserved: East Lancashire
Railway, Bury

Nos 20107 and 20094 at
Doncaster on 16 June 1981.
Norman Preedy

The East Lancashire Railway acquired its third English Electric main-line locomotive at the end of 1991 (the others are 2,000hp Class 40s) when members purchased withdrawn but serviceable No 20107 from those laid up at Thornaby. The closest Class 20 to its Vulcan Foundry birthplace, it will be useful for permanent way duties as well as summer passenger workings when no steam is available.

Ex-works in December 1961 to the Scottish Region, No D8107 spent its first 17 years working from Eastfield depot, and is rare for the type in never actually having been based at Toton depot! Its original livery of green would have been adorned, as with the rest of the Scottish-based examples, with a carriage-style circular 'lion and wheel' BR emblem. A cabside recess was provided for a tablet catcher. No 20107, as it was renumbered in April 1974, was repainted blue in the early 1970s.

It was amongst four pairs transferred to Immingham in December 1978. Although overhauled in January 1976, it lacked air brakes and as such fell prey to the severe steel traffic recession of the early 1980s, and was laid aside for almost a year awaiting a visit to Crewe for a heavy general repair and re-equipment. It was reinstated to Tinsley at the end of 1983.

A reshuffle of South Yorkshire and Humberside motive power needs saw No 20107 despatched to Immingham again in January 1987, and finally to Thornaby to join the North Eastern steel fleet (FMYI pool) on 13 May 1990. At a time when Class 20 withdrawals were almost wholesale, No 20107 was surprisingly granted a visit to Doncaster Works in the middle of the year for minor attention. The arrival of two Class 37 replacements saw two pairs of the Thornaby Class 20 FMTY steel fleet condemned on 21 January 1991, the others being Nos 20061, 20112 and 20127.

Class 20 Bo-Bo No 20110

Built: English Electric, January
1962
Numbers carried: (1) D8110,
(2) 20110
First allocation: Eastfield
Final allocation: Toton
Withdrawn: 16 September 1990
Preserved: South Devon Railway

Headlight-fitted No 20110 heads
Nos 20092, 20146 and 20066 at
York stabling point on 4 June
1988. *Brian Cuttell*

It was Scotland that was the most affected by the influx of Class 20 motive power because the final 58 of the initial series, Nos D8070-D8127, were delivered between June 1961 and July 1962 to eradicate steam power from southern Scotland, much of it dating back to pre-Grouping designs of the Caledonian and North British Railways. After successful trials with No D8006 at the end of 1958, a small number had already been allocated to Inverness and Aberdeen.

When new to Eastfield depot, No D8110 would have been distinctive from the English series by the provision of a cabside recess for a tablet catcher, although it is unlikely that it was ever fitted because the tokenless block system was gaining favour, and during the 1970s the gap was plated over. The original livery was standard Brunswick green, but on the Scottish series the circular BR emblem applied to coaching stock was preferred to the standard type.

Although of course intended for freight working, particularly coal, No D8110 would have also been seen regularly on summer passenger work to Wemyss Bay, Gourock,

Largs, Ardrossan, Ayr and Stranraer. By the late 1960s, however, changing traffic patterns saw the Type 1s grouped into their familiar pairs for merry-go-round coal workings into Ayrshire and Fife. Large numbers of redundant Scottish Type 1s were sent south to Nottinghamshire from 1969, but No D8110 stuck it out.

New in January 1962, No D8110's allocation history is as follows: Thornton Junction (December 1966), Polmadie (February 1967), and Eastfield (March 1972). It then spent long periods out of use, being laid up at Glasgow Works from January to August 1979, and similarly from April 1981 to January 1983 awaiting dual braking, apart from three months working out of Haymarket in mid-1981, variously parked up at Eastfield, Dundee, Haymarket, Aberdeen and Dunfermline. Returned ex-works to Eastfield, it was moved on to Motherwell in July 1986, Tinsley in September 1986, Immingham in January 1987, and finally Toton as a civil engineer's loco.

No 20110's first public outing since purchase was to the Laira Depot Open Day on 15 September 1991.

Class 20 Bo-Bo No 20166

Built: English Electric, October 1966
Numbers carried: (1) D8166, (2) 20166
First allocation: Toton
Final allocation: Toton
Withdrawn: 17 May 1991
Preserved: Bodmin Steam Railway

Nos 20166 and 20161 at Derby on the 13.02 Saturdays-only Skegness to Derby train on 29 August 1981. *Norman Preedy*

A Class 20 locomotive that will always be associated with the East Midlands coalfields was bought at the end of 1991 for preservation – in Cornwall.

No 20166 forms part of the second series of 100 English Electric Type 1s delivered from the beginning of 1966, an event that would also provide a replacement for the hopeless Class 17 Clayton Type 1s and the last steam survivors. Their distinguishing feature was the fitting of four-character headcode boxes at the front and rear in place of discs and lights. Nos D8144-99 inclusive were destined for Toton depot. Up to No D8179 were outshopped in green livery with small yellow warning panel, although very soon all would be coated with such a deep grime that the colour was often only noticeable by a clean patch around the cabside number.

For the next 17 years No D8166 would be seen paired to another Class 20 on various freight duties all over the East Midlands, also venturing to Skegness on occasional summer Saturday passenger turns. It was renumbered to No 20166 in April 1974, and given an intermediate overhaul in November 1978. Its lack of air brakes became an increasing handicap, and it was parked up in February 1983 awaiting a visit to Crewe Works for overhaul and re-equipment. It was originally moved to Leicester for safe-keeping, and after being fitted with slow-speed control for power station coal trains was back in traffic at Toton by July 1984.

No 20166's only reallocation in its long career was to Bescot in September 1985, and it returned to Toton for the last time in January 1987. On 8 August 1990, Nos 20166 and 20067 worked the 17.07 Liverpool to Preston service and 18.18 return because of a lack of other motive power.

As a Nottinghamshire power station coal train loco, its final partner before withdrawal was No 20023, which was the first to receive Railfreight grey livery back in 1985.

Class 15 Bo-Bo No D8233

Built: Clayton Equipment Co,
   August 1960
Numbers carried: (1) D8233,
   (2) DB968001,
   (3) ADB968001
First allocation: Stratford
Final allocation: Finsbury Park
Withdrawn: (1) 16 February
   1969, (2) December 1982
Preserved: Mangapps Farm,
   Burnham-on-Crouch

Newly restored to working order
and repainted green, No
ADB968001 is seen at
Colchester depot on 18 April
1980. *Howard Johnston*

A branch line in deepest Essex is the resting place for the sole surviving and enigmatic centre-cab Class 15 Bo-Bo No D8233, which has remained consistently popular with enthusiasts. The design had disappeared from BR main lines by 1971, but lingered on in four static vehicles for electric train heating.

It was the LMS that first contemplated the 800hp mixed traffic loco which was eventually built by North British at Glasgow as No 10800. BR updated the design into the Class 16s Nos D8400-9 (long extinct), while British Thomson Houston/Clayton came up with the Class 15 version. A succession of engine and radiator problems, plus the effects of the National Traction Plan at the end of the 1960s, meant the end for such types.

Great Eastern Lines took most of the Class 15s, and No D8233 will long be remembered for having caught fire between St Margarets and Buntingford on New Year's Day 1963. It was transferred to Finsbury Park later that year and was sometimes seen as King's Cross station pilot. Cutbacks in cross-London freights caused a sizeable surplus of locomotives, and No D8233's overhaul at Doncaster in February 1968 was its last. Its final workings before withdrawal with a badly smoking engine were

on Ashburton Grove-Blackbridge Sidings domestic rubbish trains.

Conversion to a mobile generator took place at Doncaster, involving removal of traction motors and control equipment, and rewiring. Renumbered to No DB968001, it was employed at Neville Hill, Haymarket and Finsbury Park before a requirement on the Great Eastern saw all four survivors taken to Colchester in late 1978 for three to be refurbished. Interestingly, No D8233 was repainted in authentic mid-1960s green, and not finally condemned until the end of 1982.

The Class 15 Preservation Society moved it from Healey Mills to Sheffield on 4 November 1984, and repainted it in false Railfreight grey livery to show what it might have looked like had it survived in traffic that long. A new home was found at Bury on 26 September 1986, but little mechanical work was carried out there. It moved to Essex in late 1988, thankfully repainted back into the green livery with small yellow warning panels in the spring of 1989. The search for replacement traction motors was more difficult than expected. Tracing all electrical circuitry has been undertaken by a local engineer, and bodywork restoration continues.

Class 20 Bo-Bo No 20227

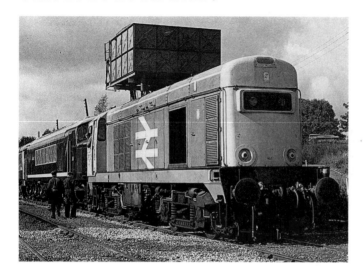

Built: English Electric, February
1968
Numbers carried: (1) D8327,
(2) 20227
First allocation: Polmadie
Final allocation: Toton
Withdrawn: 1 October 1990
Preserved: Midland Railway
Centre, Butterley

Railfreight-liveried No 20227
shunts at Swanwick on
22 September 1991. *John
Eggleshaw*

It was the abysmal failure of the 900hp Class 17 centre-cab Clayton Bo-Bo that caused a complete rethink of Type 1 motive power policy in 1966, and the placing of an order for an additional 100 English Electric locomotives. Thus it was that a design that might already have been described as old-fashioned began to re-appear from the Vulcan Foundry production line after a gap of $3^1/2$ years.

The last of the total build of 228 is now preserved by the Class 20 Society at the Midland Railway Centre, although it is one of the series that was intended for Scotland. Mechanically No D8327 differs very little from the original No D8000, although updated in minor mechanical and electrical ways. Cosmetically the front end was smartened up considerably by the replacement of the marker lights with a moulded-in headcode panel at the front, while the cab-end also supported a four-character box that looked very much like the afterthought it was. Blue livery with full yellow nose-ends and black buffer-beams was carried from new, and it took a total of 11 years for the rest of the class to adopt the style, via works overhauls. Its running number, a hundred higher than perhaps might have been expected,

was because of the D8200-99 gap left to allow for the BTH Type 1 series.

No D8327 started its career at Polmadie in February 1968. It was equipped with an electronic slow speed control device from new for use in tandem on 'merry-go-round' coal workings between the Fife coalfields and power stations such as Longannet, working from Edinburgh Haymarket depot from February 1969. Renumbering to No 20227 in December 1973 under the TOPS system saw the loco lose its status as the highest-numbered Class 20, that honour passing to the former No D8128, which became No 20228 in a complex but logical renumbering of two locomotives, Nos D8050 and D8128, to provide a place for No D8000 (qv).

Changing traffic patterns from April 1984 saw No 20227 moved back and forth at frequent intervals. After a short spell at Toton, it returned to Haymarket in March 1985, then to Motherwell and Eastfield, both in March 1985, Haymarket again the following month, Eastfield in June, Motherwell in September, and Bescot in March 1987. It was one of almost 20 to carry Railfreight grey livery.

Class 17 Bo-Bo No D8568

Built: Clayton Equipment Co,
  January 1964
Number carried: D8568
First allocation: Haymarket
Final allocation: Polmadie
Withdrawn: 6 October 1971
Preserved: Chinnor & Princes
  Risborough Railway

Its first home after sale by BR,
No D8568 is seen at Hemel
Hempstead on 8 April 1976. It
saw little use there. *Kevin Lane*

The good-looking centre-cab Clayton Class 17 rates as one of BR's least successful designs and, at a cost of around £60,000 apiece, they can hardly be considered to have been good value. One example only ran for three years before being sold for scrap.

No D8568, the only survivor of 119 locos, was a common sight in southern Scotland on coal traffic and Waverley Route duties before a drop in coal business, appalling reliability through cylinder head defects in its twin 450hp Paxman engines, and an excess of more reliable English Electric Class 20s resulted in its early demise. No D8568 only had one depot transfer, to Polmadie in September 1968, before withdrawal. It was stored there from October 1971 until a sale was agreed with the Hemel Hempstead Lightweight Concrete Company – certainly the first time the type had ever been seen in Hertfordshire! It worked south to Harpenden under its own power.

More new ground was broken when it was resold to the Ribblesdale Cement Company at Clitheroe, Lancashire, visiting Cricklewood depot in North London for attention on 24 June 1977 prior to despatch. It was repainted in the company's house livery of white, to perhaps match its surroundings. The firm rapidly found No D8568 too large for proper use in the works complex, but happily recognised its historical significance and offered it to the members of the Diesel Traction Group in December 1982 for preservation on the North Yorkshire Moors Railway. The deal included a third power unit.

The loco was moved by road and delivered to Pickering on 11 February 1983. NYMR Diesel Days saw its use on passenger trains, still in white livery, but 1985 saw it dismantled for heavy repair. Other priorities for the DTG meant it was four years before No D8568 returned to traffic. An important modification was to move the fuel pump below solebar level, hoping to put an end to fuel supply difficulties which bedevilled the entire class in BR service. A repaint in green with small yellow warning panels was also completed early in 1989, and after display at the September 1991 Old Oak Common Open Day, a new home was found on the fledgling Chinnor & Princes Risborough line in the Home Counties.

Class 55 Co-Co No D9000 *Royal Scots Grey*

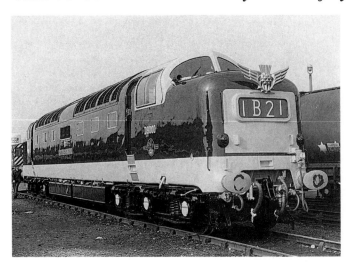

Built: English Electric, February
  1961
Numbers carried: (1) D9000,
  (2) 55022
First allocation: Haymarket
Final allocation: York
Withdrawn: 2 January 1982
Preserved: Old Oak Common

No D9000 at Doncaster Works
after its two-tone green repaint,
February 1986. *Howard Johnston*

Pioneer 'Deltic' No D9000 *Royal Scots Grey* has surely chalked up more exhibition appearances than any other preserved locomotive, but the true target of its owners – running it on BR main lines – has so far proved elusive.

Nevertheless, the high level of mechanical and external restoration has made it a recognised crowd-puller at depot open days and a reliable performer at diesel days on private lines. It is a far cry from March 1982, when it was bought from the Doncaster Works scrap-line on which it had stood for 15 months after hauling the final Edinburgh-King's Cross leg of the 'Deltic Scotsman' railtour that ended Class 55 operation on 2 January 1982.

No D9000 was new to Haymarket depot at the end of February 1961, and spent its entire career there apart from six months at Finsbury Park (fresh from overhaul and blue repaint) from November 1967 to June 1968 while others were being dual braked, and transfer to York with the rest of the survivors in May 1979. It was named at Edinburgh Waverley station on 18 June 1962, and ran over three million miles

in normal service on the East Coast Main Line. Renumbered to No 55022 in April 1974, it is credited with hauling the return inaugural 'Silver Jubilee' 15.00 King's Cross-Edinburgh service on 6 June 1977, the 50th anniversary of the 'Flying Scotsman' non-stop run on 1 May 1978, and a York-Paddington-Birmingham farewell excursion on 28 November 1981.

It was given minor attention and a repaint prior to hand-over to its new owners at Doncaster on 7 September 1983, and within four days was in action at its first home, the Nene Valley Railway at Peterborough. It returned to Doncaster for the winter of 1985/86 when two-tone livery was reapplied. Since then its open day appearances have been as diverse as Inverness, Bournemouth, Crewe and Birmingham.

When not on display it has normally been stabled at BR's Old Oak Common depot, London, along with sister 'Deltic' No D9016 *Gordon Highlander* (qv), also recently restored to matching Brunswick green livery. There is no public access to this location.

Class 55 Co-Co No 55002 *The King's Own Yorkshire Light Infantry*

Built: English Electric, March
1961
Numbers carried: (1) D9002,
(2) 55002
First allocation: Gateshead
Final allocation: York
Withdrawn: 2 January 1982
Preserved: National Railway
Museum, York

No 55002 *The King's Own
Yorkshire Light Infantry* at
Stalybridge with the 13.05
Liverpool-York on 5 August
1981. *Norman Preedy*

The officially preserved 'Deltic' is certainly the least celebrated, possibly because the NRM is less able to capture the enthusiasm of the groups that have saved five other examples of this famous class which revolutionised King's Cross-Edinburgh services when they replaced 2¹/₂ times the number of steam locomotives from 1961 onwards.

A contributory reason for No 55002's selection for preservation was that it was one of five Class 55s to receive major refurbishment at Doncaster Works during 1976, and as a North Eastern locomotive it continued the tradition of saving an example of the latest East Coast motive power. A final works visit in October 1980 provided the opportunity to repaint it in its original two-tone green livery for its final months in service, and its use on railtours. The bill was paid by the Friends of the National Railway Museum, and for the sake of modern operating methods more than authenticity the full yellow ends and sealed-in marker lights were retained.

No D9002 was named in a ceremony at York station on 4 April 1963. Unlike many other 'Deltics', it was allocated continuously to Gateshead until the final run-down saw survivors concentrated at York from May 1979. It is well remembered by enthusiasts for being the first to carry blue livery from 1966 onwards, always considered to be a retrograde step because the plain colour seemed to accentuate all the awkward features of the box-like design. Its most celebrated working, as No 55002, was the last southbound 'Liverpool Pullman' in May 1978.

The loco unfortunately failed to make it to the now legendary final series of 'Deltic' workings by just three days. A power unit defect made the 08.50 York-Liverpool and 13.05 return working on 30 December 1981 its last diagram. Although on regular display at the NRM since preservation, it has had few open day outings. Apart from an illicit run back to York from a Doncaster exhibition in February 1982, it did not work again until June 1989 when it was loaned to the Deltic Preservation Society for the annual diesel spectacular at the Midland Railway, Butterley. It also teamed up with old shedmate No 55015 (qv) for a celebrated double-headed working.

Class 55 Co-Co No D9009 *Alycidon*

Built: English Electric, July 1961
Numbers carried: (1) D9009,
(2) 55009
First allocation: Finsbury Park
Final allocation: York
Withdrawn: 2 January 1982
Preserved: North Yorkshire
Moors Railway

No 55009 at Grosmont on
3 August 1982. *Howard Johnston*

The prospect of a green-liveried Class 55 'racehorse' moved closer at the end of 1990 when *Alycidon* was scheduled to be moved from the North Yorkshire Moors Railway to ICI Wilton for heavy overhaul and bodywork repairs, involving replacement of much of the inner and outer bodyskins.

When it came to choosing its pair for preservation, the Deltic Preservation Society felt obliged to bid for one of the Finsbury Park 'racehorses', and No D9009 was regarded as being in the best overall condition. Apart from six months from December 1967 to June 1968 at Haymarket to balance the ETH conversion programme, it had worked out of London for 20 years. It was renumbered No 55009 in January 1974, and was the first BR loco to have its headcode blinds replaced by marker light dots in November 1972.

Apart from its usual East Coast activities, No 55009 had two notable forays during the 1970s – on a York-Aberystwyth service as far as Stockport on 18 March 1974, and the 12.10 Edinburgh-Euston diverted via the G&SW

route on 12 August 1979. *Alycidon* was the last 'Deltic' to receive a major works overhaul at Doncaster, and its last official duty on BR was to run between Peterborough and Newcastle and return in front of the 'Deltic Scotsman Farewell' railtour on 2 January 1982 as standby locomotive.

Nos 55009 and 55019 were sold for £6,550 each, but the DPS elected to pay an additional £10,000 each to keep the dual brake equipment intact. The locos were moved to the North Yorkshire Moors Railway on 20 August 1982 prior to operation the following day. In 1985 No 55009 established a 'Deltic' preservation first by undergoing a successful change of a defective power unit. Insuring against further problems, the DPS has five spare engines.

Although No 55019 has moved away from the line, *Alycidon* has been a consistent performer for some nine years. It was towed to ICI Wilton on 24 November 1990 by Class 37 No 37514. It will be the first Class 55 to be given such lavish treatment.

Class 55 Co-Co No 55015 *Tulyar*

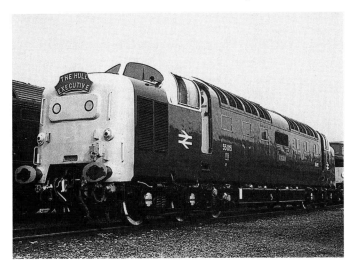

Built: English Electric, October
1961
Numbers carried: (1) D9015,
(2) 55015
First allocation: Finsbury Park
Final allocation: York
Withdrawn: 2 January 1982
Preserved: Midland Railway
Trust, Butterley

No 55015 *Tulyar* at Coalville
Open Day, 1 June 1986. *Philip
Sutton*

Buying a locomotive is one thing, maintaining it is another, as the Deltic Preservation Society has demonstrated with No 55015 *Tulyar*. Engineers not only renovated the locomotive from poor mechanical condition, but also undertook a complex traction motor change and boiler replacement.

With three million miles of East Coast travel to its credit over a 20-year BR lifespan, No 55015 had been on the Doncaster Works scrap-line for over two years when BR decided to auction it (on paper at least) at Christie's London saleroom. It failed to meet the reserve price, but enthusiast Peter Sansom stepped in to arrange purchase and a move to the Midland Railway at Butterley.

Tulyar's achievements are many, but it is perhaps best remembered for representing the class in the 24 May 1980 cavalcade at Rainhill to mark the 150th anniversary of the opening of the Liverpool & Manchester Railway, in recognition of which it often carries plaques on its nose-ends. As well as hauling railtours to Lowestoft (3 September 1978) and Bournemouth (17 October 1981), No 55015

also worked the prestigious northbound leg of the BR sponsored 'Deltic Scotsman Farewell' railtour on the last day of Class 55 activity on BR, 2 January 1982.

Arriving at Butterley on 6 February 1984, No 55015 was later sold to the DPS, and the power units were started on 28 August and 19 October respectively. It became the first preserved 'Deltic' to have its steam-heat boiler returned to working order, and hauled a heated passenger train on 2 January 1988. The Spanner Mark 2 boiler had been removed the previous July and despatched to BREL's No 2 Training School at Derby as an apprentice training exercise. While it was away, DPS members were able to effect further internal renovation.

Tulyar suffered a traction motor flashover at Bewdley during the Severn Valley Railway's Diesel Weekend on 7 May 1988. So, another first in preservation took place on 21 September when a motor change was undertaken at Butterley. Two substantial cranes were required to stabilise the locomotive, amid fear of No 55015 losing its balance and falling over!

Class 55 Co-Co No D9016 *Gordon Highlander*

Built: English Electric, October
  1961
Numbers carried: (1) D9016,
  (2) 55016
First allocation: Haymarket
Final allocation: York
Withdrawn: 30 December 1981
Preserved: Old Oak Common

A mighty restoration task ahead,
No 55016 *Gordon Highlander*
props up the Doncaster 'Deltic'
scrap-line on 7 September 1983.
Howard Johnston

No 55016, one of only five Class 55s to be given a heavy general overhaul involving an extensive rebuild, was nominally the 'Deltic' everyone thought would be preserved, but it was passed over because of fire damage in the last few days in service. An 11th-hour bid by the D9000 Group to buy it as 'spares on wheels' was successful, but the temptation to get it back into running order was too great to resist.

The second loco of that name to be preserved (GNSR 4-4-0 No 49 *Gordon Highlander* is in Glasgow Transport Museum), No D9016 was new to Haymarket depot in October 1961, and was named alongside No 49 at Aberdeen on 28 July 1964. Apart from a seven-month balancing swap-round of Class 55s with Finsbury Park between November 1967 and June 1968, No 55016 stayed north of the border until the final run-down in May 1979. Its principal achievement on the rails was to deputise for No 55002 on the 'Deltic Devonian' railtour from Liverpool Street to Exeter on 28 November 1981.

Off the main lines, No 55016 was certainly more newsworthy. Selected in the late-1970s for extensive rebuilding, with replacement of the inner body skin and rewiring, the cost ruled out repeat work on other 'Deltics' and helped convince BR that early withdrawal was inevitable. Although its power units Nos 406 and 418 had only run 1,000 hours, No 55016 suffered an engine room blaze while working the 08.07 York-King's Cross on 21 December 1981 and was promptly withdrawn and despatched to Doncaster for breaking up. Dumped there for $2^1/_2$ years, it was eventually sold for preservation, and arrived at the Nene Valley Railway on 23 July 1984 in a heavily cannibalised state. The first engine was restarted by the following 15 March, and the second on 23 December. HRH Prince Edward made a cab inspection on his visit to the NVR on 20 June 1986.

A significant double-heading took place on the Keighley & Worth Valley Railway on 6 November when No 55016 partnered blue-liveried sister No 55015 *Tulyar* (qv) during the line's diesel weekend, the first time they had been together since BR days. Repainted two-tone green at Selhurst during the winter of 1988/89 to match No D9000 (qv), it revisited Aberdeen in 1990 for a rededication ceremony with its namesake regiment.

Class 55 Co-Co No 9019 *Royal Highland Fusilier*

Built: English Electric, December 1961
Numbers carried: (1) D9019, (2) 55019
First allocation: Haymarket
Final allocation: York
Withdrawn: 31 December 1981
Preserved: Great Central Railway, Loughborough

No 9019 breaks the 'Welcome 9019' banner on entering Loughborough station on the Great Central Railway, 28 April 1989. *John B.Gosling*

'Deltic' No 9019 has been landlocked since 19 October 1988 when it was moved to the Great Central Railway at Loughborough. There it has benefited from much-needed covered accommodation as well as a whole new audience for this fine Class 55. *Royal Highland Fusilier* was always considered a superior example because it was one of only two to get a general overhaul and bodywork refurbishment late in its working career.

Delivered new to Haymarket depot on 29 December 1961, it was part of the depot's allocation until survivors were concentrated at York in May 1979. It ran exactly 20 years and two days in service on East Coast duties, covering three million miles in the process. The last of the class to be named, at Glasgow Central on 11 September 1965, it never could claim to have been one of the headline-makers during regular service. It took part in the Barrow Hill (Sheffield) Open Day on 5 October 1980.

Its greatest honour in BR service was to haul the final 'Deltic'-hauled service train, the 16.30 Aberdeen-York, from Edinburgh on 31 December 1981, and with No 55009 (qv) was selected for purchase by the Deltic Preservation Society as the best of the entire class left in service on withdrawal day. Part of the deal was that the then valuable dual brake equipment would be left in situ.

After attention at Doncaster Works, it was towed to the NYMR on 21 August 1982 prior to re-entry into service between Grosmont and Pickering the following day. Although still in BR blue livery in 1986, it has undergone considerable mechanical attention, and has made brief returns to its old BR haunts for exhibition at the 1982 Carlisle and 1985 Haymarket Open Days. Moved to the Midland Railway Centre at Butterley in 1987, it was moved again after exhibition at Bescot Open Day on 9 October 1988, this time to Loughborough; it was loaded on to a road vehicle at Mountsorrel freight depot, courtesy of Redland Aggregates.

The debut run from Loughborough to Rothley took place on 29 April 1989. No 9019 is currently shedded at Quorn, and in the spring of 1991 double-headed 'Merchant Navy' 4-6-2 No 35005 *Canadian Pacific* in one of the most powerful steam-diesel partnerships ever. A ballot of DPS members has voted to keep the loco in BR blue livery.

Class 14 0-6-0 No D9500

Built: BR Swindon, July 1964
Numbers carried: (1) D9500,
  (2) NCB No 1
First allocation: Bristol Bath
  Road
Final allocation: Cardiff Canton
Withdrawn: 26 April 1969
Preserved: West Somerset
  Railway, Williton

Before restoration, No D9500 is
'back home' at Swindon in 1989.
Mike Goodfield

Swindon's final diesel locomotive design was much-scorned, but in the event proved the longest-lived of all. Redundant on BR before they were barely run-in, the 650hp Class 14s performed an important role in private industry that was only ended by a new wave of rationalisation in the coal and steel industries.

The rigid-framed 0-6-0 diesel-hydraulic design on a 15 ft 6 in wheelbase owes a good deal to the Great Western three-axle pannier tank steam locomotive it largely replaced, but the Class 14 was inherently more efficient with a flexibly-mounted, six-cylinder Paxman Ventura 6YJXL power unit coupled to Voith/North British turbo-transmission and Hunslet final drive. When plans were formulated in the early 1960s, a fleet of 200 locomotives was anticipated, but by the time they appeared there was barely a need for them at all.

The pioneer, No D9500, officially commissioned on 24 July 1964, is a remarkable survivor into preservation. Although built for handling valuable but fragmented South Wales valleys coal traffic, the 50-ton machine led an embarrassingly quiet life, and lay out of use at Bristol and Cardiff for at least four months of its five-year BR career. It was after withdrawal in April 1969 that it was actually put to worthwhile use. Sold to the then National Coal Board, it was run long and hard on the Northumberland domestic system centred around Ashington until the network was closed down in its entirety as part of the national colliery cutbacks.

No D9500 was moved to Llangollen on 15 September 1987, supposedly in working order, but suffering oil leaks and lacking vacuum brake gear and radiator elements. It was, however, started up over the Christmas period, making it clear to its owner that a major top-end overhaul of the engine would be required. No D9500 was moved to its birthplace, Swindon Works, in early 1988 for a start to be made on restoration. No D9500 was then moved on to the West Somerset Railway to join operational sisters Nos D9526/53 (both qv). Restoration, although slow, will be a considerable task, involving the removal of the power unit for overhaul, the despatch of the wheels to Swindon for reprofiling, and attention to years of NCB coal, oil and grime.

Class 14 0-6-0 No D9502

Built: BR Swindon, July 1964
Numbers carried: (1) D9502,
  (2) 9311/97
First allocation: Bristol Bath
  Road
Final allocation: Cardiff Canton
Withdrawn: 26 April 1969
Preserved: Llangollen Railway

Still in BR ownership, No D9502
stands at Gloucester Horton
Road depot on 3 July 1969.
Norman Preedy

Orders for 56 new 0-6-0 diesel-hydraulic locomotives for the Western Region unfortunately coincided with the aftermath of the Beeching Report, which demanded increasing self-sufficiency for both the passenger and freight businesses. That inevitably meant closures and cutbacks, and much of the short-haul coal traffic for which the Class 14 was intended virtually disappeared overnight.

In its original plan to replace steam traction in the South West, the braking capacity of a 50-ton locomotive was considered insufficient for line service work on BR, but the increasing number of fitted wagons meant that trains could be more easily stopped by the use of train brakes, thus avoiding the need for construction of more expensive diesel-electric Type 1 Bo-Bos which would clearly be under-used.

No D9502, the third of the class, was the first delivered to Bristol Bath Road depot in July 1964, where it stayed for just over three years.

Like No D9500 on the previous page, it also endured spells of disuse, at Worcester and Cardiff, but still survived until the end of Class 14 operation on BR in April 1969. Two months later, it was on its way to Ashington in Northumberland by rail, but the beginning of 1987 saw the total closure of the Ashington system. It is interesting to consider that No D9502 lasted 18 years without a major overhaul, although some general maintenance was carried out at Ashington. It was withdrawn in working order, although extremely mechanically run-down, but an obvious interest in preservation prompted British Coal to offer all seven surviving Class 14s, Nos D9500/2/4/18/21/5/55, for sale in August, with a closing date of 2 September for sealed bids.

No D9502 was moved to Llangollen in 1987, primarily as a second priority project to sister Class 14 No D9500.

Class 14 0-6-0 No D9504

Built: BR Swindon, July 1964
Numbers carried: (1) D9502,
 (2) NCB No 506, (3) KESR
 No 48
First allocation: Bristol Bath
 Road
Final allocation: Hull Dairycoates
Withdrawn: 1 April 1968
Preserved: Kent & East Sussex
 Railway, Tenterden

No D9504 awaiting restoration at
Rolvenden on 14 August 1991.
Philip Sutton

The branch-line byways of South East England are amongst the most unlikely locations that you can find a Class 14 nowadays, thanks to the Kent & East Sussex Railway. The two locomotives on the line have, however, not so far been regarded as an unqualified operational success.

No D9504's diverse career started with delivery brand new from Swindon Works to the motive power depot next door in July 1964, and unlike most of the type it was never actually allocated in South Wales. One of many Class 14s consigned to temporary store at Worcester in December 1966, it was reallocated and transferred direct to Hull Dairycoates. On Humberside the locos were used in pairs, and No D9504 was often seen in partnership with No D9540, a loco scrapped in industrial service at the beginning of 1984.

The problem of so many virtually new machines standing idle was resolved by the end of the year with the dispersal of the North

Eastern fleet to private buyers and, on occasions, scrap merchants. The fate of No D9504 was against the trend as its new owner was to be the National Coal Board at Philadelphia, County Durham, doubtless a prelude to large-scale acquisitions of the type from Cardiff and Swansea the following year.

A series of transfers within the NCB's domestic system saw D9504, by now No 506, end up at Ashington, Northumberland, in the summer of 1983, where it was to see out all activity at the system four years later. Sale to the Kent & East Sussex Railway at the end of 1987 was not before some valuable components, including radiator elements, had gone missing, and considerable effort was required before it could be successfully started on 20 January 1988. It now carries the KESR fleet number 48 and has been used on permanent way and construction trains, and the occasional passenger working.

Class 14 0-6-0 No D9513

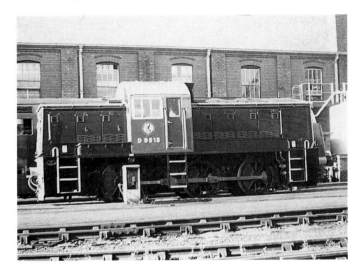

Built: BR Swindon, October
   1964
Numbers carried: (1) D9513,
   (2) D1
First allocation: Cardiff Canton
Final allocation: Cardiff Canton
Withdrawn: 10 March 1968
Preserved: Yorkshire Dales
   Railway, Embsay

Before acceptance by BR, a brand
new No D9513 at Swindon
Works, 27 September 1964.
Norman Preedy

There were fears for the future of the National Coal Board's Class 14 fleet when it became known that scrap merchants had joined preservationists in the bidding for the ten locomotives available. Three, Nos D9513/21/31, were actually sold to railway scrap dealer C.F. Booth of Rotherham for breaking up, but all three were resold for further use, bringing the grand total on private lines to 19, over one-third of the original class.

No D9513, new to Cardiff in the first week of October 1964, was one of the earliest casualties, being retired and consigned to store at Worcester as early as February 1968. It was condemned the following month, and consigned to Arnott Young at Parkgate, Rotherham, for scrapping. The firm, however, recognised that it was far from life-expired, and sold it on to British Coal for re-use in the North East. No D9513 worked the Lynemouth and Ashington systems in its latter days.

D9513 was sold for scrap a second time in 1987, and Yorkshire Dales Railway members who clubbed together to raise the finance to buy the locomotive for Embsay heard on 1 October that their bid had been successful. D9513 was actually bought in situ at Ashington, where the theft of its copper radiators actually helped reduce the asking price to an affordable level.

The immediate plan was to leave No D9513 in its dark blue National Coal Board livery to recognise the fact that it had been in industrial service far longer than in BR ownership. This is in contrast to most other Class 14 groups who have been quick to restore theirs to the original two-tone BR green with yellow and black nose-end 'wasp' stripes.

Class 14 0-6-0 No D9516

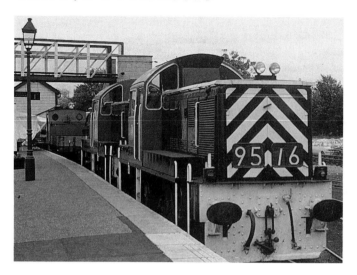

Built: BR Swindon, October
   1964
Numbers carried: (1) D9516,
   (2) BSC No 36, (3) BSC
   No 56
First allocation: Cardiff Canton
Final allocation: Hull Dairycoates
Withdrawn: 1 April 1968
Preserved: Nene Valley Railway,
   Wansford

No D9516 at Wansford on
6 November 1990. *Howard
Johnston*

The versatile BR Class 14 0-6-0 diesel-hydraulic is now a feature of preserved lines across the whole of Britain, and the Nene Valley Railway has three of them.

No D9516, together with sisters Nos D9523 and 14029 (both qv), moved to Cambridgeshire in 1988 after seven years on the Great Central Railway at Loughborough, and is in regular use on a variety of duties from permanent way trains to passenger services. It is also special in having been equipped with dual vacuum/air brake equipment to haul any train on the NVR, including continental passenger stock.

After trials with No D9501 in July 1964, South Wales depots took delivery of new Nos D9510-20 between the following September and November. Whether they wanted them or not, Cardiff and Landore depots took delivery of another 24, Nos D9529-52, between January and September 1965. No D9516 itself started work at Cardiff Canton, and after a short spell at Landore from May 1965 departed to Hull in December 1966, ironically coinciding with the drastic reduction in East Yorkshire dock rail

traffic; thus, with many others of the same type it was soon withdrawn as surplus.

Sold on to Stewarts & Lloyds in November 1968 for re-use at the firm's Corby steelworks, No D9516 was renumbered 8311/26 in the local fleet, later No 56. Redundant for a third time at the end of 1980, it moved to the Great Central on 19 October 1981, intended as a source of spare parts for sister No D9523 (qv), but was returned to traffic instead. It sports non-standard Great Western-style cast numberplates similar to those carried in BR service by the Class 52 'Western' diesel-hydraulics. In service, the D9500s' cabside numbers were applied in a distinctive non-standard style beneath carriage-style emblems.

A diminishing amount of use at Loughborough prompted the decision to move No D9516 and its two Class 14 shedmates to the Nene Valley Railway at Peterborough, where it arrived by low-loader on 8 December 1988. Since then it has been fitted with air brakes to enable it to haul continental stock.

Class 14 0-6-0 No D9518

Built: BR Swindon, October
  1964
Numbers carried: (1) D9518,
  (2) NCB No 7
First allocation: Cardiff Canton
Final allocation: Cardiff Canton
Withdrawn: 26 April 1969
Preserved: Rutland Railway
  Museum, Cottesmore

NCB 7, alias No D9518, at
Cottesmore on 19 January 1992.
Howard Johnston

Where Swindon-built BR Class 14s have been during their careers, they will always be remembered for accumulating in large numbers, not least at Hull Dairycoates depot in 1968, where more than half the fleet filled the former steam locomotive roundhouse awaiting their fates, either with a new user or the scrap merchant.

The arrival of a fourth member of the class to the Rutland Railway Museum at Cottesmore in Leicestershire at the beginning of 1988 continued the run of success for Class 14s which was to continue until no fewer than 19 had been secured for British preservation – the only hope of increasing this number is if any of those sold to the continent are purchased and repatriated. It is also interesting to note that every single member of the fleet left at the end of coal workings out of Ashington in Northumberland has survived.

No D9518, new to Cardiff Canton at the end of October 1964, remained a Western Region locomotive throughout its short BR career, working in South Wales. It was noted out of use at the depot in April 1969, when sale to the National Coal Board took place. The next four months saw it towed to its new home in a protracted journey with stop-offs at Gloucester and Birmingham Washwood Heath yard.

No D9518 was considered the best Class 14 left at the time closure was announced, although a fault necessitating the removal of the power unit was in the event never rectified. It therefore arrived at Cottesmore needing considerable work, which will take place when time and funds permit. To maintain variety, the plan is to leave it in the light blue Ashington Colliery Railway livery with its industrial number 7 on the cabside. In recent times, No D9518 has been part cannibalised for spares for the other Cottesmore Class 14s and the trio on the Nene Valley Railway at Peterborough.

Class 14 0-6-0 No D9520

Built: BR Swindon, November
   1964
Numbers carried: (1) D9520,
   (2) BSC No 24, (3) BSC
   No 45
First allocation: Cardiff Canton
Final allocation: Hull Dairycoates
Withdrawn: 1 April 1968
Preserved: Rutland Railway
   Museum, Cottesmore

No D9520 on a demonstration
run at Cottesmore, 11 November
1989. *Howard Johnston*

One of the first firms to realise that BR's loss of business could be its gain was the Stewarts & Lloyds division of the British Steel Corporation. The decision to buy 23 redundant BR Class 14 diesel-hydraulics was based on cheapness, relative newness, and the chance to eliminate the last steam locomotives from Leicestershire, Northamptonshire and Lincolnshire.

No D9520 was delivered new to Cardiff Canton on 11 November 1964, but saw relatively little use on the local trip workings for which it was intended. January 1967 saw it sent to Hull with many others of its class, but again declining traffic levels, problems with double-manning, and a non-standard diesel-hydraulic transmission saw the entire North Eastern Region fleet written off in April 1968.

No D9520 was sold on to S&L the same December for work at Glendon Quarries near Kettering. It retained full BR livery apart from renumbering as No 24, plant number 8311/24, and acquired headlights on its nose-ends. It moved to Corby's Gretton Brook depot in January 1970, where it was renumbered No 45.

Upon closure of the Corby steelworks complex, No D9520 was sold together with No D9529 (qv 14029) to the North Yorkshire Moors Railway, moving there in convoy by rail on 16 March 1981. Both were used on permanent way trains as well as passenger services, but a change in policy saw them put up for sale again after just three years because the NYMR wanted bigger locomotives.

The growth of the Cottesmore industrial ironstone museum was a natural home considering that the locomotive had spent most of its working life in the East Midlands, and it became a member's property on 24 February 1984. No D9520 visited the Great Central Railway at Loughborough in late 1985 for a Class 14 reunion, and has been a consistent and reliable performer.

1991 saw the loco taken out of service for a complete overhaul, and it is planned to repaint it in BR colours with British Steel Corporation number 45 – although a clean Corby locomotive was never actually witnessed!

Class 14 0-6-0 No D9521

Built: BR Swindon, November
  1964
Numbers carried: (1) D9521,
  (2) 9312/90
First allocation: Old Oak
  Common
Final allocation: Landore
Withdrawn: 26 April 1969
Preserved: Swanage Railway

NCB No 3 (D9521) at
Cottesmore on 17 October 1987.
Gordon Kobish

The 19th and perhaps final Class 14 to be preserved arrived at its new home in October 1987, completing the successful evacuation of every single example surviving at the time of the closure of the National Coal Board's complex at Ashington, Northumberland. It is also interesting that No D9521 shares the same depot yard as sister No D9520 (qv), produced before it at Swindon Works at the end of 1964, considering that they have had such diverse working careers.

D9521 was the first of a series of five allocated from new to Old Oak Common for London area trip freight workings, and was used for several weeks on crew-training duties between Paddington and Acton Yard. It was transferred to Swindon in October 1965 and then Landore in July 1967, a move which allowed it to survive in BR service for longer than most of the class.

Withdrawal saw it sold to the National Coal Board, where a long career beckoned in Northumberland from March 1970. It was still in use there at the end of 1987, in the blue livery of its owners and numbered NCB No 3, plant number 9312/20. No D9521's first preservation owner, the Rutland Railway Museum at Cottesmore on the Lincolnshire/Leicestershire border, maintained the loco in ex-BSC condition, but also considered an elaborate rebuilding scheme to reflect what might have happened to the nearby Corby steelworks Class 14 fleet had they not been made redundant by the cutbacks and eventual total closure in 1981. This included replacement of the six-cylinder Paxman 650hp 6YJXL power unit with a different type and, most controversial of all, altering the body outline more to the Hunslet shape. No D9521 was transferred to the Swanage Railway at the end of January 1992, the first of the type ever to be used in Dorset.

Class 14 0-6-0 No D9523

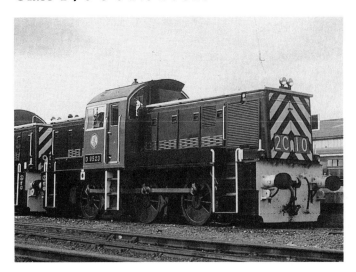

Built: BR Swindon, December
   1964
Numbers carried: (1) D9523,
   (2) BSC No 25, (3) BSC
   No 46
First allocation: Old Oak
   Common
Final allocation: Hull Dairycoates
Withdrawn: 1 April 1968
Preserved: Nene Valley Railway,
   Wansford

No D9523 at Wansford on
6 November 1990. *Howard
Johnston*

All preserved lines nowadays see the attraction of diesel locomotives for their ability to haul trains at a fraction of the cost of firing up steam traction, which mirrors the philosophy of both British Railways and the industrial concerns who readily accepted the Class 14 diesel-hydraulics back in the 1960s.

Unlike on BR, the increasing demands of preservation centres has made these 0-6-0 diesel-hydraulics an attractive commodity, and large numbers have had more than one home. No D9523, bought from Stewarts & Lloyds at the end of 1981, moved first to the Great Central Railway, and then to Peterborough in 1989.

No D9523 led an easier life than most of the class in the closed environment of Glendon Quarries for many years. One of a batch of four delivered to Old Oak Common at the end of 1964 for London trip workings, within a year it was transferred west to join the rest of the fleet at Bristol or in South Wales. Even that move was short-lived as nearly half the fleet were sent up to Hull Dairycoates for local duties until the axe fell on the entire Humberside contingent on 1 April 1968.

Sale to the British Steel Corporation took place in December 1968, then over a decade of work at Glendon ceased in May 1980, and D9523 was moved to the general BSC disposal point at Gretton Brook the following December. It moved on to Loughborough on 16 October 1981, and worked its first passenger train on 14 February 1982. Although it saw extensive use, the late 1980s saw it sidelined for installation of a complete new power unit, work which continued after its transfer during 1988, and further after its move to the Nene Valley Railway motive power depot at the beginning of 1989. After successful running-in trips, the most recent activity has been to install dual brake equipment.

External restoration has been to as-built condition with the exception of cast cabside numberplates. It was lifted off its wheels at the end of 1991 for new tyres and replacement of the crank pins.

Class 14 0-6-0 No D9524

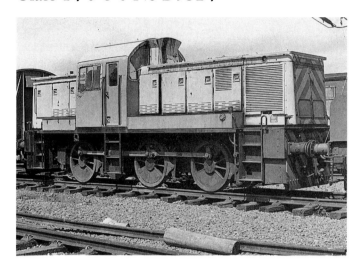

Built: BR Swindon, December
    1964
Numbers carried: (1) D9524,
    (2) BP Chemicals No 8
First allocation: Old Oak
    Common
Final allocation: Landore
Withdrawn: 24 April 1969
Preserved: Scottish Railway
    Preservation Society, Bo'ness

No D9524 at Bo'ness on 22 July
1990. *Brian Cuttell*

The most modified Swindon-built Class 14 is also the furthest away from the Western Region, discounting of course the five which are understood still to be working since export to Spain and Belgium.

No D9524 is on its third different design of power unit, its original six-cylinder Paxman 650hp engine having been replaced first by a 500 Dorman 8QT unit, then, after seizure, by a Rolls-Royce version. It has also lost its vacuum brakes in favour of an air-only system.

No D9524, new to Old Oak Common in December 1964, was one of four, Nos D9521-4, based at Reading to cover three diagrams covering freight and parcels turns to Newbury, Didcot, Southall and Basingstoke, plus a specific parcels turn to Paddington. It was transferred to Bristol in October 1965, yet unlike so many of its contemporaries it was not sent north to Hull, but was retained at Landore (its home from August 1967) until withdrawal in April 1969.

Further storage at Cardiff Canton from March to July 1970 preceded No D9524's sale to BP Chemicals at Grangemouth, Scotland, where it was repainted blue and acquired the fleet number 8. It continued in service there until January 1980, and even made a visit to the Andrew Barclay works at Kilmarnock for engine attention during this time.

After a long period out of use, No 8 passed into the custody of the Scottish Railway Preservation Society at Falkirk, and later transferred to the group's new site at Bo'ness. Although some maintenance has been undertaken, there is still considerable work to be carried out before it can haul works or passenger trains to Manuel.

Class 14 0-6-0 No D9525

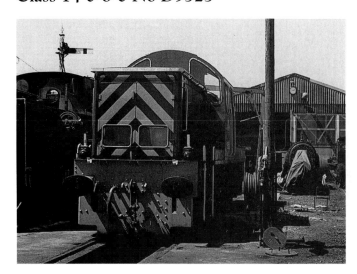

Built: BR Swindon, January
    1965
Numbers carried: (1) D9525,
    (2) NCB No 507, (3) KESR
    No 49
First allocation: Bristol Bath
    Road
Final allocation: Hull Dairycoates
Withdrawn: 1 April 1968
Preserved: Kent & East Sussex
    Railway, Tenterden

No D9525 after restoration at
Rolvenden on 14 August 1991.
Philip Sutton

The second Class 14 on the Kent & East Sussex Railway is also intended, after making up for 20 years of generally inferior maintenance, to run on both permanent way and passenger trains. In line with Colonel Stephens practice of sequential numbering for all the line's locos, it has the running number 49.

When built, the loco design represented a major departure from the practice of building twin-bogie units for main-line work. The 15 ft 6 in wheelbase enabled it to traverse all but the most sharply curved dock lines, and an axle-loading of less than 17 tons compared favourably with the six-coupled steam loco it was intended to replace. The decision to locate the locomotive's jackshaft arrangement between the intermediate and trailing axles followed common continental practice, but was new to Britain.

After taking the initial series D9500-5, No D9525 was the first of a second batch of four

Class 14s delivered new to Swindon depot from January 1965 onwards. Despatched direct from storage at Worcester to Hull Dairycoates in December 1966, it closely followed the career of KESR partner No D9504 (qv) with sale after withdrawal to the National Coal Board to replace steam at Philadelphia at the end of 1968. The locomotive saw extensive use at Backworth at the end of the 1970s.

No D9525 was out of use at Ashington shed in Northumberland by May 1985 awaiting scrap, but the execution was not carried out before closure of the system, after which it was stored pending sale. Again, sale by tender resulted in preservation. After transfer to Kent, it was in service on engineers trains by May 1988, and the Autumn 1990 passenger timetable advertised No D9525 as available for use every weekend during October and November.

Class 14 0-6-0 No D9526

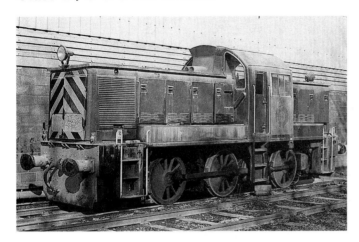

Built: BR Swindon, January
 1965
Number carried: D9526
First allocation: Bristol Bath
 Road
Final allocation: Cardiff Canton
Withdrawn: 30 November 1968
Preserved: West Somerset
 Railway, Williton

D9526 during its Associated
Portland Cement days at
Westbury, 26 February 1977.
A. J. Booth

Although preservation of ex-BR Class 14 diesel-hydraulics became a highly fashionable feature of the 1980s, No D9526 had the distinction of being the first of its type to be saved for preservation as early as April 1980, when it could not have been imagined that so many of its sisters would survive or be so highly regarded.

Delivered to Bristol Bath Road depot in the first week of 1965, No D9526 had a longer working life than most of its sisters, and was exclusively a Western Region engine until withdrawal. It was stored under tarpaulins at Cardiff Canton depot until the end of 1969 when Associated Portland Cement bought it for general shunting duties on block trains of up to 1,000 tons at their Westbury terminal, starting work there in February 1970.

No D9526 performed there quite happily until a relatively small power unit defect saw it laid aside. When the Diesel & Electric Group stepped in during 1978 to save it, they discovered that it had worked only 20,800 miles from new. APC responded by making an outright gift of the loco, provided that the society bought the spares. Thus it was that No D9526 was loaded on to a lorry for its journey to the West Somerset Railway.

Extensive restoration to its original condition was finally completed on 16 March 1984, when No D9526 was successfully started for the first time in preservation, and a rededication ceremony took place in the presence of Blue Circle management prior to the loco working its first passenger train on 15 July. It has since seen regular use on the WSR, often double heading the line's other Class 14, No D9551 (qv).

Persistent power unit problems, however, prompted the replacement of the Paxman engine by a 715hp version on 12 January 1988. It was honoured with the task of hauling BR Class 9F 2-10-0 No 92220 *Evening Star* from Bishop's Lydeard to Minehead on 13 March 1989 on the occasion of the locomotive's visit to the West Somerset Railway for a working season. It was repainted a second time at Williton depot during that year.

Class 14 0-6-0 No 14029

Built: BR Swindon, January
   1965
Numbers carried: (1) D9529,
   (2) BSC No 20, (3) BSC
   No 61, (4) 14029
First allocation: Cardiff Canton
Final allocation: Hull Dairycoates
Withdrawn: 1 April 1968
Preserved: Nene Valley Railway,
   Wansford

No 14029 in pseudo-BR blue at
Wansford, 15 February 1990.
Howard Johnston

The non-authentic livery of one of the diesel-hydraulic 0-6-0s on the Nene Valley Railway demonstrates what the Class 14s would have looked like had any of them survived long enough for major overhaul at Swindon Works when standard green was replaced by corporate blue from the end of 1967.

No D9529, new to Cardiff Canton depot in the opening weeks of 1965, moved to Landore (Swansea) in the May for short-haul freight services into West Wales. It was unique in actually visiting Swindon Works for attention in July 1965 after being involved in a severe collision which damaged the frames and scored the bodywork and cabside sheets. It was stripped down to the running plate and rebuilt. Across the Works, construction work was almost complete on the last examples of the class, Nos D9549-55.

No D9529 was rendered redundant as early as May 1967, and was one of the first of many to be sent to Hull. Condemned with the rest in April 1968, it was regarded as the best example to run trials with the British Steel Corporation,

resulting in its sale in August for use in the rural confines of Buckminster quarry in Leicestershire, and as No 61 (plant number 8411/20) was sent on to the Stewarts & Lloyds site at Gretton Brook in September 1972.

Closure of that site saw it sold with sister No D9520 (qv) to the North Yorkshire Moors Railway on 16 March 1981 via Toton yard, and considerable renovation was carried out before a change in the line's motive power policy saw it re-sold and moved to the Great Central Railway early in 1984. Delivery to the Nene Valley Railway took place on 8 December 1988. Its present number, 14029, applied at Loughborough in September 1985, is what it could have carried had it survived to be renumbered under the 1973 TOPS scheme.

No 14029 earned a place in the record books on 21 February 1990 when it was part of the heaviest train ever to be pulled by one man. From a standing start, Lincolnshire strongman Jon Maddock dragged the locomotive and three coaches – total weight 157 tons – 20 feet with his teeth.

Class 14 0-6-0 No D9531

Built: BR Swindon, February
  1965
Numbers carried: (1) D9531,
  (2) BSC No 523
First allocation: Cardiff Canton
Final allocation: Cardiff Canton
Withdrawn: 30 December 1967
Preserved: East Lancashire
  Railway, Bury

Newly restored, No D9531
stands outside Bury running shed
on 7 June 1989. *Howard
Johnston*

No D9531 had the shortest working life of any British Railways diesel locomotive, lasting just 34 months from delivery to condemnation. It was also, remarkably, sold for scrap twice, but reprieved both times.

The utter waste of resources at that time was emphasised most strongly with No D9531, which was clearly unwanted for most of its BR career. It was based at four depots in its short life: Cardiff in February 1965, Landore in May of that year, Bristol Bath Road in December, and back to Cardiff in December 1966, to be condemned a month later. Withdrawn sisters Nos D9522 and D9531 were despatched from Worcester to the yard of Arnott Young at Parkgate, Rotherham, in July 1968, the former being quickly cut up. No D9531, however, was sold on to the NCB at Ashington, Northumberland, for another 20 years' working life to be extracted from it.

East Lancashire Railway members had earmarked No D9521 (qv) as their loco, but the bid was not successful. They then had to make an emergency call to the scrapyard of C.F.Booth of Rotherham after learning that the last three had been sold for breaking up. They had just one last chance to buy a Class 14, and the offer for No D9531, one of three not immediately sold to preservationists, was fortunately successful.

No D9531 is now a key part of the East Lancashire Railway's fleet, which is a diesel-hydraulic 'full house' with examples of an ex-Western Region Class 14, Class 35 'Hymek', Class 42 'Warship' and Class 52 'Western' amongst its operational diesel fleet.

After a thorough rebuild at Bury during 1988, No D9531 made its maiden passenger run in preservation on 1 October of that year. In the space of only six months, a small team of engineers had lifted the power unit out from the frames for top-end overhaul, removed and reprofiled the wheelsets (twice), overhauled electrical and minor components, replaced stolen radiator elements (spares from a Class 52 'Western'), fixed the brakes, fitted new vacuum exhausters, put in new front-end headcode glasses, and effected a complete repaint from NCB to British Railways two-tone green livery with 'wasp' stripes. The locomotive returned to traffic on 18 August 1991 after suffering an engine compartment fire.

Class 14 0-6-0 No D9537

Built: BR Swindon, March 1965
Numbers carried: (1) D9537,
   (2) BSC No 32, (3) BSC
   No 52
First allocation: Cardiff Canton
Final allocation: Hull Dairycoates
Withdrawn: 1 April 1968
Preserved: Gloucestershire
   Warwickshire Railway,
   Toddington

No D9537 at Toddington on
20 February 1987. *Hugh
Ballantyne*

The lines of rusting Class 14s at the British Steel complex at Corby, Northamptonshire, in 1980 proved a morbid sight as the contractors dismantling the acres of foundry were also charged with the breaking up of 24 redundant ex-BR locomotives lined up inside.

Ex-works from Swindon in March 1965, No D9537 ran out of work after just two years and two months. Put into store, it was reinstated and transferred to Hull Dairycoates in May 1967. Lack of docks work meant that it ended up on less suitable main-line tasks, and was finally withdrawn by BR after just another 12 months, but in full working order.

No D9537 became part of the Corby fleet in December 1968. The fact that eight Corby engines survived into British preservation is

remarkable, but it is also worth reporting that three more, Nos D9515/48/9, were overhauled and regauged for export to Spain. The other 13, Nos D9503/7/10/2/32/3/8/41/2/4/7/52/4, were robbed for spare parts and then broken up where they stood.

No D9537 was one of the last to be inspected and found fit for re-use; it had in fact been in service right to the end of Corby operations in December 1980, and had a spell at the nearby tube works the following year. It moved to the Gloucestershire Warwickshire Railway site during November 1982, and since restoration to original two-tone green livery has been in regular use on passenger and freight trains. The headlights on the bonnet ends have, however, been retained.

Class 14 0-6-0 No D9539

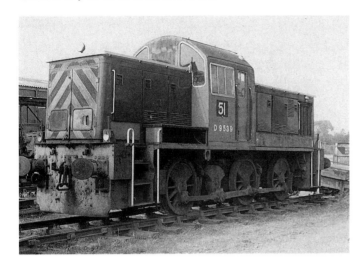

Built: BR Swindon, April 1965
Numbers carried: (1) D9539,
    (2) BSC No 51
First allocation: Cardiff Canton
Final allocation: Hull Dairycoates
Withdrawn: 1 April 1968
Preserved: Gloucestershire
    Warwickshire Railway,
    Toddington

Still carrying its former BSC
Corby ironstone number,
No D9539 at Toddington on
4 October 1986. *Brian Cuttell*

Although happily now preserved, No D9539 only worked for 26 months in its intended sphere of operation, South Wales. New to Cardiff Canton depot in April 1965, it was officially in store as early as May 1967, but quickly transferred to Hull, where it was often seen double-heading with No D9503, one of those unlucky not to survive its industrial career.

Criticism of the D9500s in their early days for a miscellany of faults was perhaps unfair, because many would have been solved either at the first Swindon Works overhaul or by a programme carried out at depots, as is the case nowadays. In this instance it was left to the private operators to do this work. In the case of Class 14s, one major fault centred on cylinder-head leaks, cured when aluminium heads were replaced by a modified design in cast iron.

Transmission faults were many, but poor working conditions and lack of staff skills were often to blame.

No D9539 was one of the first to arrive at the Corby steelworks site in October 1968, and was put to work on payloads of up to 500 tons of raw minerals on indifferent track and punishing gradients. It performed loyal service at Corby until December 1980 and, with No D9553 (qv), was the last loco in the complex awaiting export to Turkey. The deal fortunately fell through, and both were sold on to members of the Gloucestershire Warwickshire Railway in December 1982, and moved to Toddington the following March. Although the power unit was successfully started up at the end of 1987, No D9539 was then regarded as an immediate source of spare parts for Nos D9537 and D9553 until resources allowed it to be restored itself.

Class 14 0-6-0 No D9551

Built: BR Swindon, September
   1965
Numbers carried: (1) D9551,
   (2) BSC No 29, (3) BSC
   No 50
First allocation: Cardiff Canton
Final allocation: Hull Dairycoates
Withdrawn: 1 April 1968
Preserved: West Somerset
   Railway, Williton

No D9551 parked at Williton on
8 July 1984. *Brian Cuttell*

The West Somerset Railway partly owes its survival and revival to the efforts of Class 14 No D9551, which was available to haul passenger trains during the difficult early and mid-1980s when steam power was in desperately short supply. It was therefore appropriate that when the locomotive became available for sale during early 1990, the railway company effected purchase for domestic use.

As one of the last handful of Class 14s delivered from Swindon in the first week of September 1965, No D9551's BR career was inevitably short, and represented the penultimate delivery to the already overstocked Cardiff Canton depot. As road transport mopped up wagonload business and small collieries became uneconomic, there was scope for using a trip locomotive with a 40 mph top speed. No D9551 finished work and with the

rest of the class was transferred to Hull, and was one of the large number despatched to Corby to replace steam at the steelworks there.

No D9551 was in generally good order when it arrived in Somerset from Corby on 6 June 1981, having been virtually the pick of the bunch. Minor technical problems associated with a year's disuse were quickly sorted out in order for it to carry out fill-in turns for the line's steam and DMUs, and it provided excellent training and inspiration for the more complex Diesel & Electric Preservation Group's No D9526 (qv), also on the WSR.

In common with many other preserved Class 14s, a positive link with No D9551's industrial past has been the retention of the two large spotlights on the bonnet front, and a pair of flashing lights on the cab roof. Major engine repairs were completed during early 1990.

Class 14 0-6-0 No D9553

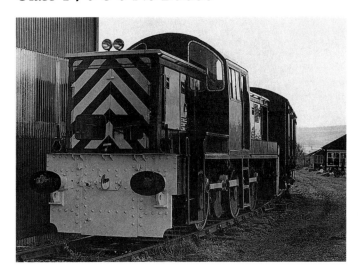

Built: BR Swindon, September
 1965
Numbers carried: (1) D9553,
 (2) BSC No 34, (3) BSC
 No 54
First allocation: Bristol Bath
 Road
Final allocation: Hull Dairycoates
Withdrawn: 1 April 1968
Preserved: Gloucestershire
 Warwickshire Railway,
 Toddington

No D9553, externally restored,
at Toddington on 22 March
1990. *Mike Goodfield*

Modern traction preservation was still in its relative infancy in 1980, although the usefulness of Class 14s was already recognised when the tenth was saved from export to Turkey for re-use on the Gloucestershire Warwickshire Railway which is aiming to restore as much as possible of the former Great Western route between Stratford-upon-Avon and Cheltenham.

The final three of the 56-strong class were delivered to Bristol Bath Road depot, and No D9553 worked on local trip freights for a short time before the move to Hull in December 1966 with 30 others of the same class. Sold in November 1968, its next 12 years were spent working ironstone trains, and when that ended in December 1980 it was stored first at Pen Green depot, Corby, and then the main works site, awaiting resale or scrap.

Although the BSC numbering scheme appears complex, the 23 locos in the pool were originally allocated Nos 20-3 for Buckminster Quarry, Nos 24/5 for Glendon, Nos 25-7 for Harlaxton, and Nos 26-38 for Corby. Prefixes of 8311 were also added for Glendon/Corby locos, and 8411 for Buckminster/Harlaxton. Concentration of the fleet in 1974 put them into one series, Nos 45/6 (ex-Glendon), Nos 47-58 (ex-Corby), Nos 59-63 (ex-Buckminster), No 64 (Corby), and Nos 65-7 (Harlaxton).

Never a popular individual at Corby, No D9553 shows evidence of rebuilding after collision damage in that the frames are fully 1 foot shorter than Toddington's other Class 14s, with modified headstocks moved inside the frames. Although in good basic condition, vandalism prior to sale has slowed down restoration to working order, though it remains second in line for renovation after No D9537 (qv).

Class 14 0-6-0 No D9555

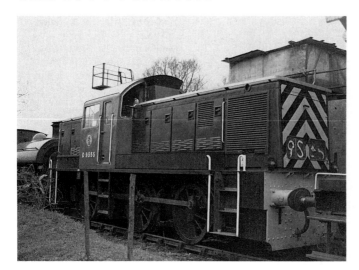

Built: BR Swindon, October
  1965
Number carried: D9555
First allocation: Bristol Bath
  Road
Final allocation: Landore
Withdrawn: 26 April 1969
Preserved: Rutland Railway
  Museum, Cottesmore

No D9555 restored to BR livery
at Cottesmore on 19 January
1992. *Howard Johnston*

Amidst all the euphoria of Class 14 preservation in the mid-1980s, there was always the danger that one of the most important celebrities, last-built No D9555, might not escape the scrap-man. The reason was a minor collision sustained at Lynemouth, which damaged the brake gear and prematurely ended its career.

Although partly robbed for spares, it was, however, secured by a member of the Cottesmore Railway, where it arrived at the end of 1987 to join three others of the same class, Nos D9518/20/1 (all qv).

By definition, No D9555 marked the completion of Swindon Works's final contract for locomotives for British Railways, a tradition initiated with the construction of a broad gauge steam locomotive for the Great Western Railway in April 1846.

New to Bristol Bath Road depot in October 1965, No D9555 also worked from Cardiff Canton (May 1967), and Swansea Landore (July 1967). Crews disliked the locos' handling characteristics, particularly on steep gradients, where their braking power was often inadequate.

It is unlikely that No D9555 ever visited a works for repair. It was consigned to store on 21 April 1969, and was withdrawn five days later along with the other nine survivors, Nos D9500/2/14/8/21/4/7/36/8. It had taken just 45 months from the delivery of the first to the end of the class.

No D9555 was originally reported sold to Gulf Petroleum at Milford Haven, but turned up at Burradon Colliery, Tyne & Wear, at the beginning of 1970. It had reached Ashington Colliery by August, joining the large numbers of Class 14s already there. The damage incurred at Lynemouth was nowhere near as severe as first imagined, and the loco was back in running order at Cottesmore by the summer of 1989. It has been restored to original BR livery as new in 1965 with the intention of making it available for display at BR open days and exhibitions.

Unclassed 0-6-0 No 7069

Built: Hawthorn Leslie, January
   1936
Number carried: 7069
First allocation: Crewe
Final allocation: Swansea East
   Dock
Withdrawn: December 1940
Preserved: Poole

No 7069 arrives at Swanage
station in 1987. *Andrew Wright*

A significant gap in British diesel locomotive preservation was filled on 27 November 1987 when a war veteran returned home to the Swanage Railway after 48 precarious years of avoiding either destruction by German bombing or scrapping by the French on the grounds of its venerable state. It still carries bullet holes in its cab as a permanent reminder of troubled times.

No 7069 is a direct forerunner of the English Electric 350hp shunter which was multiplied to over 1,400 examples before 1962. Built by Hawthorn Leslie (later part of Robert Stephenson & Hawthorn and English Electric) at Newcastle in 1936, it met the LMS criteria for experimentation with the then new EE 6K 350hp engine with two axle-hung nose-suspended traction motors set between six coupled wheels.

The original demonstrator loco was taken into LMS stock as No 7079, while ten more (Nos 7069-78) followed. Eight of these were sent out to France during December 1940 by the War Department, but all were destroyed apart from No 7069 which ended up on the minor Mamers-Saint Calais Railway until it closed in 1973. Paris loco dealer L. Patry bought it for yard duties and actually undertook some repairs in an abortive attempt to find a buyer.

BR scrapped the other three, Nos 12000-2, many years ago, but the design was perpetuated with single traction motor and jackshaft drive by the LMS (Nos 12003-32), and Class 11, 12, 09, 10, and 13 followed from 1948 onwards.

At Swanage, the repatriated No 7069 arrived still sporting the legend LMS on its engine compartment doors, although the doors were in the wrong order! Considerable mechanical and electrical attention will be required before it works again. The only external modifications visible are out-of-gauge battery boxes. No 7069 has been moved to a private site near Poole for restoration, and on 11 May 1991 the power unit was lifted out for overhaul.

Class 11 0-6-0 No 12052

Built: BR Derby, April 1949
Numbers carried: (1) 12052,
  (2) MP228
First allocation: Crewe South
Final allocation: Crewe
Withdrawn: 13 June 1971
Preserved: Ayrshire Railway
  Preservation Society,
  Dalmellington

In part-dismantled state,
No 12052 stands at Widdrington
on 4 November 1985. *A.J. Booth*

The oldest preserved ex-BR 350hp shunter is No 12052; it was actually allocated LMS number 7139, but it appeared too late to carry it. Its working career of just 30 years represented better value that most of the class, which were scrapped through no fault of their own, but due simply to a lack of work.

Showing its antecedents clearly, No 12052 was one of the designs evolved in 1948 from the pre-war LMS/English Electric types, and perpetuated until 1962 to the tune of almost 1,400 examples by BR's Class 08. The principal alteration from the early designs was the replacement of the cumbersome jackshaft to double reduction gear drive from two 135hp nose-suspended traction motors.

No 12052's first depot was Crewe South in April 1949, and in its 22-year BR life it also worked out of Rugby (September 1953), Willesden (November 1954), Nottingham (July 1957), Westhouses (March 1966), and finally back at Crewe (November 1966). It then became one of a pair sold in working order to the Derek Crouch opencast site at Widdrington, Northumberland, at the end of 1971, where it gained the plant number MP228.

Out of use for a number of years, No 12052 was sold again to the embryonic Ayrshire industrial preservation scheme, and was moved from Widdrington at the end of 1988. (An LMS/WD version is preserved on the Lakeside & Haverthwaite Railway.)

Class 11 0-6-0 No 12061

Built: BR Derby, November
  1949
Numbers carried: (1) 12049,
  (2) NCB No 4
First allocation: Saltley
Final allocation: Allerton
Withdrawn: 10 October 1971
Preserved: Gwili Railway

No 12061 stored at Aberdulais
awaiting movement to the Vale of
Neath Railway, 9 July 1989.
Brian Cuttell

The closure of Nantgarw Coking Plant (between Cardiff and Pontypridd) on 11 November 1986 yielded a further LMS-design Class 11 locomotive for preservation. No 12061 made passenger runs on the Gwili Railway in September 1991 after its transfer from the Vale of Neath steam centre project, which has fallen foul of BR plans to reopen the line for its own use.

The declining usefulness of the oldest production batch of English Electric 350hp shunters on BR did not mean the end of the class after the final withdrawals at the end of 1972. A total of 23 of the original 106 were sold to industrial users, and a handful are still earning their keep into the 1990s. The vast number of closures of smaller collieries and the installation of conveyor systems linked to merry-go-round traffic at others is, however, robbing them of further work.

The BR history of No 12061 can be politely described as unspectacular. Derby Works was turning out shunters at the rate of one every couple of weeks at the end of 1949, and this particular example (ordered by the LMS and intended to be No 7148 in its series) was outshopped during November, one of four required by Saltley depot, Birmingham. It stayed there for a full 18 years before transfer to Speke Junction, Liverpool, in October 1967. A final move to Allerton preceded its withdrawal on 10 October 1971, and movement to Wigan Springs Branch for storage and sale the following year.

It was bought by a Vale of Neath member in full working order, and was due to be repainted in green livery early in 1992. Electrical repairs have been carried out, and vacuum gear is also to be fitted. A large number of spares were obtained from sister loco No 12063 (Nantgarw No 5) which had been out of service for many years with a burned-out traction motor and was little more than a derelict shell when bought by a local scrap merchant and broken up on site during 1988.

Class 11 0-6-0 No 12071

Built: BR Derby, August 1950
Numbers carried: (1) 12071,
  (2) NCB No 6
First allocation: Toton
Final allocation: Wigan Springs
  Branch
Withdrawn: October 1971
To be preserved: South Yorkshire
  Railway, Meadowhall, Sheffield

Awaiting sale or scrap, No 12071
at C.F.Booth's, Rotherham,
28 October 1990. *A.J.Booth*

Although heavily robbed for spares, negotiations were in hand at the end of 1991 for LMS-design Class 11 shunter No 12071 to move to the South Yorkshire Railway Museum with the intention of eventually returning it to working condition. It had lain in the scrapyard of Booth Roe at Rotherham since purchase from British Coal's South Wales coalfield.

The Western Region was loaned an LMS-design Class 11 0-6-0 diesel-electric shunter in May 1951 to familiarise Tyseley depot staff before the arrival of the first BR standard Class 08s the following year. This was part of the systematic re-equipment of BR depots with diesel shunters, which had reached the Nottingham area in the summer of 1950, with five brand-new 11s from Derby Works; No 12071 was the second of them.

No 12071 was back at Nottingham from Tyseley in December 1952, but was soon on the move again. It was loaned to Newton Heath in May 1952, was back at Nottingham by July 1955, and loaned for a third time, to Saltley, in October 1955. Further transfers were to Rugby (December 1955), Chester (November 1956), Willesden (July 1957), Wigan Springs Branch (September 1958), Crewe South (January 1961), Monument Lane (September 1961), Bescot (April 1967), Tyseley (February 1968), Chester (January 1969), Allerton (October 1970), and finally Wigan (November 1970).

Withdrawn in October 1971, it was sold at the end of 1972 to the National Coal Board for use at Nantgarw smokeless fuels plant, Glamorgan, along with Nos 12061/3. Three visits were made to BR depots for maintenance, to Cardiff Canton in November 1974 and November 1976, and Newport Ebbw Junction in March 1977. It ventured to Swindon Works in July 1977 for a more protracted three-month overhaul.

The rapid reduction of coal-mining and associated product refinement after the 1985 national miners' strike resulted in the closure of the Nantgarw plant, and No 12071 was rendered surplus. Interestingly, few ex-BR locomotives that have survived beyond the mid-1980s have been scrapped.

Class 11 0-6-0 No 12074

Built: BR Derby, September
    1950
Number carried: 12074
First allocation: Saltley
Final allocation: Chester
Withdrawn: 1 January 1972
Preserved: South Yorkshire
    Railway, Meadowhall, Sheffield

No 12074 soon after arrival at
Meadowhall, 27 August 1989.
Brian Cuttell

The closure of the coal depot at Swalwell to the east of Newcastle for redevelopment in early 1989 provided a preservation opportunity for the two LMS-design Class 11 shunters there, and both were indeed secured for the South Yorkshire Railway's Meadowhall site in Sheffield (see also next page).

The BR career of No 12074 broadly follows the pattern of the early 0-6-0 diesel electric shunters. New to Saltley, it worked out of Willesden from July 1957, Bletchley from November 1960, Wigan Springs Branch from April 1968, and finally Chester from December 1971, where it was condemned just a month

later. It was moved to Crewe South for storage, and sold on to Johnsons Ltd of Chopwell for use at its coal disposal site.

By the time of the Swalwall site's closure, No 12074 was laid up with cylinder-head faults, and was being used as a source of spares for the other locomotive, No 12088. It is, however, intended to restore it to full working order again, carrying BR green livery. The terms of the preservation agreement include applying the name of the parent company, Bower Kirkland Group of Ripley, Derbyshire, to the toolboxes, and return on loan if the company needs a shunting locomotive in the future.

Class 11 0-6-0 No 12077

Built: BR Derby, October 1950
Number carried: 12077
First allocation: Saltley
Final allocation: Wigan Springs
  Branch
Withdrawn: October 1971
Preserved: Midland Railway
  Centre, Butterley

No 12077 stabled at Butterley,
9 April 1985. *Howard Johnston*

The Midland Railway Centre's preserved LMS-design Class 11 shunter No 12077 has the rare distinction of being occasionally used for revenue-earning freight trains, being borrowed for use on the adjoining Butterley Iron Works branch, where steel girders are manufactured for BR, and train movements are required to the main-line exchange sidings at Swanwick Junction.

No 12077, preserved only a few miles from its birthplace, is the only ex-BR locomotive to have entered the famous West Midlands scrapyard of Cashmore's at Great Bridge and emerge intact. Hundreds of steam locomotives, including many ex-LMS Pacific types, were broken up there in the mid-1960s.

No 12077 started life at Saltley, Birmingham, and surprisingly worked at many London Midland depots: Cricklewood (from January 1956), Derby (March 1957), Saltley (October 1957), Tyseley (September 1964), Bescot (October 1965), Walsall (April 1966), Chester (September 1966), Longsight (April 1971), and finally Wigan Springs Branch (May 1971) before withdrawal in October 1971.

Sold to Cashmore's, it was still in the yard five years later when spotted by an alert Midland Railway Trust member who arranged its purchase for preservation. It was the first of the type to be saved, and was moved by road to Butterley in December 1978. It made its first run on 13 January 1979, and is currently in post-1957 BR green livery with 'wasp' stripes. For those who enjoy visual authenticity, its somewhat weathered appearance makes it a pleasing sight.

Class 11 0-6-0 No 12082

Built: BR Derby, November
   1950
Number carried: 12082
First allocation: Carlisle
   Kingmoor
Final allocation: Llandudno
   Junction
Withdrawn: October 1971
Preserved: South Yorkshire
   Railway, Meadowhall, Sheffield

Still in BR livery, No 12082 is
seen at UKF Fertilisers, Ince, on
11 June 1986. *A.J. Booth*

The continued search for ex-BR industrial motive power for preservation at the South Yorkshire Railway site at Meadowhall mopped up one of the last remaining revenue-earning LMS-inspired 0-6-0 diesel-electric shunters at the beginning of 1992. It is in full working order.

No 12082, a Derby Works product, had spent almost exactly the same number of years in private hands as in nationalised ownership. Even so, it retained blue livery and BR markings throughout this time. The only major physical change was the addition of flashing warning lights.

When new in November 1950, No 12082 was one of four Class 11s formally allocated to the Scottish Region, although actually based in England at Carlisle Kingmoor depot. It also saw service at the nearby Upperby depot at various times until transfer south to Speke Junction, Liverpool, in November 1956. It was loaned to Chester for a short spell at the beginning of

1957, and moved away to Toton in July 1959. Never settled for long, No 12082 was reallocated to Crewe in December 1966. It seems strange that, in view of the obvious surfeit of shunters, the class was still considered for works overhaul at this time, and No 12082 was outshopped early in 1968 in the new corporate BR livery. It was noted at Chester in July 1969, and transferred to Llandudno Junction in August 1970. A surfeit of London Midland motive power saw it laid up at the end of 1971, and because of its good condition was parked at Chester depot to await a prospective buyer.

Shellstar UK employed No 12082 at its Ince Marshes fertiliser complex on the southern bank of the River Mersey from March 1983 onwards, although it is also reported to have worked over the Manchester Ship Canal Company's system at nearby Ellesmere Port between July and October 1974.

Class 11 0-6-0 No 12088

Built: BR Derby, June 1951
Number carried: 12088
First allocation: Aston
Final allocation: Allerton
Withdrawn: 11 May 1971
Preserved: South Yorkshire
   Railway, Meadowhall, Sheffield

After 16 years in industrial use,
No 12088 arrived at Meadowhall
in 1989, and is pictured there on
27 August. *Brian Cuttell*

One of the last LMS-design Class 11 diesel-electric shunters in industrial service, No 12088 retained its BR identity and livery and identity right through its career.

The closure of Swalwell coal disposal point in County Durham during 1989 paved the way for No 12088 and its companion, No 12074 (see previous page), to be preserved.

No 12088, new from Derby in June 1951, was sent with No 12089 to work from Aston depot, Birmingham, and stayed there until December 1964 when transfer was effected to Rugby. It moved on to Bletchley in January 1969, Wigan Springs Branch in November 1969, and Allerton in November 1970 for a final seven months before being laid up. It was sold to Swalwell from Springs Branch, and moved there in July 1972.

Although in working order right to the end, No 12088 was latterly only kept as standby for the firm's 1976 Hunslet 0-6-0 diesel-hydraulic shunter. Like No 12074 mentioned earlier, the plan is to repaint it in BR green livery with the company's name on the toolboxes. The acquisition remarkably left the Meadowhall site with just a Class 05 and Class 09 to obtain to complete the range of BR shunters between Classes 01 and 11.

Class 11 0-6-0 No 12093

Built: BR Derby, August 1951
Numbers carried: (1) 12093,
    (2) MP229
First allocation: Bushbury
Final allocation: Crewe
Withdrawn: 16 May 1971
Preserved: Ayrshire Railway
    Preservation Society,
    Dalmellington

MP229 (No 12093) at
Widdrington on 21 May 1977.
A.J.Booth

The pair of Class 11s which worked together for 17 years at a Northumberland opencast site have also moved to the same preservation site; they are also the first pair to reach Scotland.

The effect of the National Traction Plan, which advocated more intensive use of a small locomotive fleet, coupled to a substantial reduction in wagon-load freight business through road competition and the effect of the Beeching Report, meant that the non-standard Class 11s were early candidates for withdrawal. The early post-war examples went from 1967 onwards, and all had gone by the end of 1972. Some did survive, however, to carry BR blue livery and the 'double arrow' symbol.

No 12093 was new to the small shed at Bushbury, Wolverhampton, in August 1951, and when that depot closed it moved to nearby Bescot in April 1965. The next move was to Ryecroft, Walsall, in April 1966, and finally Crewe in September 1966. Withdrawn as surplus on 16 May 1971, it was parked up for some six months before sale for further use at the Derek Crouch opencast site disposal point at Widdrington coal disposal point, Northumberland.

When redundant in 1988, No 12093 was moved with No 12052 (qv) to the former British Coal locomotive shed at Dunaskin. Operating at the Scottish Industrial Railway Centre at Minninvey, Dalmellington and Waterside, the Dalmellington & District Conservation Trust is establishing a national industrial heritage centre at the former Dunaskin ironworks site.

Class 11 0-6-0 No 12098

Built: BR Derby, February 1952
Numbers carried: (1) 12098,
    (2) NCB 513
First allocation: Nottingham
Final allocation: Longsight
Withdrawn: February 1971
Preserved: Tyne & Wear
    Museum, North Tyneside

No 12098 outside the
Stephenson Railway Museum,
Percy Main, 1 April 1990.
Michael Whatmough

Although not one of the batch built in the North East, No 12098 is totally at home at the Tyne & Wear Museum as several others were built at nearby Darlington, and this particular example typified a type which saw many years' service beyond what BR expected of it.

The final Derby order for 15 of the standard LMS-design large shunter, Nos 12088-12101, was completed during 1952 before work began on the very similar BR standard design, although it was another year before Darlington completed the 120-strong class. The first 14 to LMS design, constructed from 1946 onwards, were built for the War Department and most saw service in the Netherlands, France and West Germany.

No 12098 was delivered new to Nottingham, and worked in local yards until a move to Newton Heath in November 1966; it then worked at Longsight from July 1968 until withdrawal, as the full force of the National Traction Plan took effect. Still in working order, No 12098 was one of seven sold to the National Coal Board as part of the North East area's dieselisation scheme. It was renumbered No 513 in the domestic fleet, and within a few weeks was in residence at Derwenthaugh, Blaydon, for duties including shunting wagons at Clockburn drift mine and the local coking plant. It was soon moved to the extensive network based at Philadelphia, and survived until the swingeing system cutbacks following the 1985 miners' strike.

Although the other Class 11s were sold for scrap, No 12098, by then in store at Lambton coke works near Sunderland, was bought privately for the Tyne & Wear Museum Services Land Transport Centre at Middle Engine Lane, North Tyneside. It was moved there by low-loader on 5 January 1987.

Class 11 0-6-0 No 12099

Built: BR Derby, March 1952
Number carried: 12099
First allocation: Nottingham
Final allocation: Bletchley
Withdrawn: 17 July 1971
Preserved: Severn Valley
    Railway, Kidderminster

No 12099 at Kidderminster on
the Severn Valley Railway,
31 March 1991. *A.J.Booth*

Class 11 No 12099 has had no fewer than four different owners since withdrawal from BR service in 1971, demonstrating the versatile nature of the standard LMS-inspired 350hp diesel-electric shunter. At the end it was sold for scrap, but was rescued from a South Yorkshire dealer increasingly known for passing on interesting vehicles for preservation.

No 12099 was outshopped from Derby Works in March 1952 and allocated to Nottingham. Subsequent transfers were to Willesden (July 1957), Wigan Springs Branch (September 1958), Crewe South (January 1961), Nuneaton (June 1961), Rugby (May 1962), and finally Bletchley (January 1969). Along with sister No 12122, the loco was sold on to Murphy Brothers for use at the National Coal Board's Lion coal disposal site at Blaenavon in South Wales in March 1972. Their new owners were Taylor Woodrow at Cwmbargoed coal disposal point in Mid-Glamorgan from October 1975, and although No 12122 was by now severely collision-damaged and therefore only fit for spares, both moved north in September 1981 to Hargreaves Industrial Services, opencast contractors for the National Coal Board at the British Oak disposal point near Wakefield. No 12122 was scrapped in 1985, but No 12099 soldiered on to move yet again to Bowers Row in January 1983.

Redundant for the last time early in 1989, No 12099 was sold to Booth Roe Metals of Rotherham, but survived breaking up and attracted interest from the Severn Valley Railway, already home of two broadly similar Class 08s. It travelled to its final home by road in April 1990, and is normally seen at Kidderminster, the southern end of the line. A repaint has taken place to all-over black livery as carried when the locomotive was new.

Class 11 0-6-0 No 12131

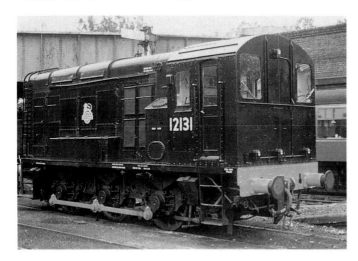

Built: BR Darlington, November
  1952
Number carried: 12131
First allocation: March
Final allocation: Stratford
Withdrawn: 2 March 1969
Preserved: North Norfolk
  Railway, Sheringham

Restored to black livery,
No 12131 is seen at Sheringham
on 7 August 1987. *Howard
Johnston*

When most preserved lines have attracted children with images of Thomas the Tank Engine, the North Norfolk Railway has chosen to take full advantage of another character in the Rev W.Awdry's books, Derek the Diesel. A scowling face is therefore often seen on the front of its LMS-design 350hp shunter.

Thirty-six of the class, later designated Class 11, were built for the Eastern Region in 1952-53 at the former North Eastern Railway workshops at Darlington, and production actually overlapped the first of the mechanically similar BR standard Class 08s.

Painted in unlined black livery, No 12131 entered traffic on 18 November 1952 at March, the Cambridgeshire depot which was one of the first on the former LNER system to gain experience with shunters of this type at the end of war; a substantial locomotive fleet was needed at the once vast Whitemoor hump marshalling yard.

No 12131 drifted away to King's Cross in March 1953, and stayed in the London area for the rest of its BR career, with spells at Hornsey from September 1955, Finsbury Park from April 1960, and finally moving to Stratford in September 1966. It was withdrawn there on 2 March 1969 as surplus, but was picked up for reuse by the National Coal Board at its Betteshanger colliery in Kent, working in a geographical area unused to this particular type. The final move was to Snowdown colliery in June 1976, by which time it had acquired a blue livery.

Members of the North Norfolk Railway secured No 12131, then unworkable, for preservation in April 1982, with the aim of fitting vacuum brake equipment and using it on works trains between Sheringham and Holt, as well as the occasional passenger duty. It has been restored and repainted in the 1950 black livery with red buffer-beams and steam-size cabside numerals. It was approved for proper operation on 10 August 1986 at Weybourne.

Class 12 0-6-0 No 15224

Built: BR Ashford, October 1949
Number carried: 15224
First allocation: Hither Green
Final allocation: Selhurst
Withdrawn: October 1971
Preserved: Isfield Railway,
    Lewes, Sussex

No 15224 at Snowdown Colliery,
Kent, on 13 September 1979.
A.J. Booth

This diesel shunter is unmistakably Southern, as the 4 ft 6 in Bulleid-Firth-Brown 'Boxpok' wheels testify. The Southern Railway conducted trials with three 350hp English Electric shunters (Nos 1-3, later 15201-3) from 1936, and was clearly impressed enough to order some more. The war intervened and it was not until 1949 that the first of a batch of 26 was delivered from Ashford Works, and by then the design had evolved to a virtual clone of the LMS design. Principal alterations were the wheel type and diameter, and a high top speed of 27.5 mph for trip work over the Southern's third-rail network (perpetuated today in the Class 09s).

No 15224, the 14th of the class, worked in the Hither Green area until transfer to Ashford in February 1958, Norwood Junction in May 1962, and finally Selhurst in September 1966.

It lasted to within two months of the end of the class, and three were sold for industrial use; the subsequent scrapping of sisters Nos 15222 and 15231 by 1984 left it the only survivor of its type.

No 15224 went to NCB Betteshanger in Kent in October 1972, and moved to nearby Snowdown on 27 May 1976 with Class 10 No D4067 (qv). Out of use by 1981, it was sold the following year for preservation. At first intended for the North Downs Railway and the Brighton Locomotive Works project, by June 1985 it had arrived for use on the Lavender Line as Isfield on the former Uckfield-Lewes line. It is restored to its original black livery. The proposed sale of the Isfield operation at the start of 1992 made a further move for No 15224 a possibility.

Class 76 Bo-Bo No 26020

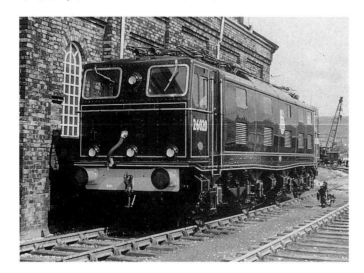

Built: BR Gorton, February 1951
Numbers carried: (1) 26020,
  (2) 76020
First allocation: Gorton
Final allocation: Reddish
Withdrawn: 11 August 1977
Preserved: National Railway
  Museum, York

No 26020 in restored condition
at Dinting, 3 June 1981. *Howard
Johnston*

LNER steam locomotive designer Sir Nigel Gresley is credited with much of the inspiration behind this design, which doubtless would have been working today but for the closure of the Manchester-Sheffield/Wath line via Woodhead Tunnel in July 1981, which robbed this 1,500v DC design of its only workable route.

Prototype Class EM1 locomotive No 6701 (later Nos 6000 and 26000) was completed at Doncaster in 1941, but wartime delay in completion of the Woodhead modernisation scheme saw it sent to the Netherlands from 1947-52, after which it was named *Tommy* as a mark of respect to the British soldier. The production examples with larger cabs and rheostatic brakes appeared between 1950-53, the first 11 working in East London for a time. No 26020, the preserved example, was given a special exhibition gloss finish for display at Willesden during the 1951 Festival of Britain, including chromed cab handrails. It was one of 13 production versions fitted with steam-heat boilers for passenger use, but the only one not to carry a name commemorating a Greek god.

The decision to concentrate on 25kV AC power for all future electrification schemes restricted the EM1 build to 58 locos, and they all became freight-only machines after the end of passenger services between Manchester Piccadilly and Sheffield Victoria in January 1970. At the same time, the EM2 Co-Co versions were sold to the Netherlands (see next page).

Although by no means worn out, a lack of traffic saw the Class 76s (as they had by then become) go into decline from the mid-1970s onwards. A handful were fitted with air brakes to haul merry-go-round coal hoppers, but all-original No 76020 was laid up at Reddish depot during 1977, four years before the final survivors. It was not officially withdrawn until August 1977, and was then towed to Doncaster for restoration to its original black livery. It arrived at York on 31 August 1978, and since then has had several outings, including a spell at Dinting Railway Centre (within a stone's throw of its old stamping ground), the 1980 Rainhill cavalcade, and the 1990 'NRM on Tour' exhibition at Swindon.

Unclassed Bo-Bo No 26500

Built: Brush, 1904
Numbers carried: (1) No 1,
   (2) 4075, (3) 6480, (4) 26500
First allocation: Heaton
Final allocation: South Gosforth
Withdrawn: 14 September 1964
Preserved: National Railway
   Museum, York

Restored No 26500 on display at
the National Railway Museum,
York, on 27 February 1983.
Howard Johnston

Although Brush's Falcon Works at Loughborough is now associated with diesel locomotive construction (the 1,000th machine was due for delivery to BR early in 1992), the firm built its early reputation on electric power, and one of its earliest products is on display at the National Railway Museum.

The North Eastern Railway's electrified suburban system around Newcastle opened in 1903, was turned over to diesel operation in 1967 when rolling-stock became due for renewal, but has happily been reborn since 1980 with the impressive Metro system. Two 640hp 'camel-back' profile Bo-Bo locomotives were taken into stock during 1904 for the Trafalgar Yard (Manors East)-Quayside freight branch. They had pantographs for yard working, and third rail pick-up for use in tunnels and movement to and from South Gosforth and Heaton depots. Power came from four BTH traction motors, on the 600/630 V dc system.

The pair were renumbered many times during their long careers. Designated London & North Eastern Railway Class ES1, No 1 swapped numbers with 4-4-0 steam loco No 4075 in 1944, and with its sister became 6480/1 in the electric series in 1946. Reportedly allocated Nos 26480/1 in the post-1948 BR series, they in fact became Nos 26500/1, and in 1961 were repainted from their drab black into NER livery with the old company's coat of arms next to the BR totem in their cabsides. No 26500 is credited with the last Quayside branch working on 29 February 1964 before diesel shunters took over.

Both locos were stored at Hellifield MPD in North Yorkshire along with other nationally important exhibits, but No 26501 was towed back to Choppington, Northumberland, during 1966 for scrap. Periods of storage at Rugby, and display at Leicester, preceded final movement of No 26500 to York, where it can frequently be viewed in the central display area.

Class 77 Co-Co No 27000 *Electra*

Built: BR Gorton, December
  1953
Numbers carried: (1) 27000,
  (2) NS 1502
First BR allocation: Wath
Final BR allocation: Reddish
Withdrawn: (BR) 5 October
  1968, (NS) 14 June 1986
Preserved: BR Ilford depot

No 27000 *Electra* at Ilford Depot
Open Day, 20 May 1989.
Howard Johnston

LNER-designed 1500v DC Class EM2 No 27000 has the distinction of being a celebrity in two countries, and has crossed the English Channel no fewer than four times, both as a working and preserved locomotive. It was a star at the Netherlands Railways' 150th anniversary celebrations in 1988, having returned to its old stamping ground after restoration on this side of the water.

A larger version of the Class EM1 (see previous page), No 27000 was conceived as the future BR standard express electric loco, but foundered when the decision was taken in 1958 not to proceed with 1500v electrification beyond the existing Manchester-Sheffield/Wath route. Orders were cut back from 27 to just seven examples and, like its sisters, No 27000 was declared redundant in October 1968 with the downgrading (and withdrawal 18 months later) of passenger services over that route.

Named *Electra* in August 1959 by its builders, Metropolitan Vickers, No 27000 was mothballed at Bury steam shed in April 1968 until sale and shipment to Holland in September 1969. Six were refurbished with electric train heating, air brakes, right-hand drive, and yellow and grey NS livery. The seventh, No 27005 *Minerva*, was scrapped for spares. *Electra* ran up 2.6 million miles in the

Netherlands, and received replica brass nameplates in July 1985 for its final year in traffic.

A remarkable 600-seat sell-out railtour over the Dutch network with all four surviving EM2s on 14 June 1986 proved a perfect swansong for the class, and No 27000 arrived back in England via the Harwich train ferry on 15 July. It was stored at Butterley for two years, and was then displayed at Basingstoke, Tyseley, Coalville, Worksop and even the Severn Valley Railway. It left for Bradford Hammerton Street on 27 June 1988, where in little over six weeks the locomotive was sandblasted to bare metal, platework replaced, and repainted in Brunswick green. The NS pantographs, headlights and buffers were retained for a return to the Netherlands in 1989. The BR bodyside emblems have been mounted on central bodyside plates as in the 1950s, and the locomotive was officially renamed at Basingstoke on 16 September 1988, partnered at the ceremony by NS-liveried No 1505 *Ariadne* (see next page) conveyed from Manchester Museum for the occasion. It left for Holland on 24 May 1989 via France and Belgium and was recommissioned to Dutch standards at Tilburg Works, covering practically the entire NS system on four railtours between June and July.

Class 77 Co-Co No 1505 *Ariadne*

Built: BR Gorton, March 1954
Numbers carried: (1) 27001,
  (2) NS 1505
First BR allocation: Wath
Final BR allocation: Reddish
Withdrawn: (BR) 5 October
  1968, (NS) 14 June 1986
Preserved: Greater Manchester
  Museum of Science &
  Technology

NS No 1505 at Boxtel yard,
Utrecht, Holland, on 14 June
1986. *Howard Johnston*

By no means overshadowed by the exploits of Class EM2 sister No 27000, second-built No 27001 *Ariadne* is preserved in its home city as a symbol of the goodwill between the Nederlandse Spoorwegen and the EM2 Locomotive Society, which successfully negotiated the donation back in 1980. The original intention was to preserve NS No 1506 (27002) *Aurora*, but this was unfortunately severely damaged by fire and No 1505 was substituted, as it had just undergone major overhaul.

New from Gorton in 1954, No 27001 was named after a Greek goddess without ceremony in October 1959, and went to Holland from store at Bury in 1969. It was withdrawn too early to receive a TOPS classification, although Class 77 was allocated and is now often used to describe the type.

Last overhauled at the NS Tilburg Works in June 1984, No 1505, as it was then numbered in the NS fleet, was repainted prior to the 14 June 1986 farewell railtour that included an incredible Class EM2 treble-header for the final

run into Hook of Holland. It was then fitting that doomed sister No 1503 (ex-No 27004 *Juno*) should be revived for a last time to tow Nos 27000/1 from Tilburg to Roosendaal, *en route* for Zeebrugge and the *Cambridge* ferry, which coincidentally had shipped the locos out from England 19 years earlier.

No 1505 was then hauled from Harwich on 15 July via the 6M88 Willesden Speedlink freight hauled by No 47121. *Ariadne* then had its first trip under BR 25kV wires behind No 85015 in the 6F86 Willesden-Warrington Speedlink. Successful trials were conducted on the Manchester museum's demonstration track in June 1987, when the loco ran under its own power on a special 750-volt supply.

It is intended to keep *Ariadne* in its yellow and grey NS colours, although the brass nameplates are a reminder of its days on the Manchester-Sheffield/Wath route. It is also promised a few outings, and was reunited with No 27000 *Electra* at Basingstoke on 16 September 1988 at the latter's formal renaming ceremony.

Class 77 Co-Co No 1501 *Diana*

Built: BR Gorton, August 1954
Numbers carried: (1) 27003,
  (2) NS 1501
First BR allocation: Reddish
Final BR allocation: Reddish
Withdrawn: (BR) 5 October
  1968, (NS) 14 June 1986
Preserved: Rotterdam Feyernoord

No 27003 after overhaul at
Crewe Works, 18 April 1964.
Peter Hogarth

Affection for the Manchester-Sheffield/Wath Class EM2s is such that a group of Dutch enthusiasts preserved their own after Nos 1502/5 (27000/1) were returned to their homeland after the final withdrawal of the class on Netherlands Railways in June 1986.

A small group of drivers rescued No 1501, alias No 27003, only hours before incisions were due to be made to remove parts. The sale deal was concluded in April 1987, and after minor repairs the locomotive was granted a running certificate for the Rotterdam area which was put to full use on 10 October 1987.

The original livery for the EM2s in Britain was standard all-over black, although this later gave way to lined green and, in one or two cases, a non-standard shade of light blue. Once overhauled and modernised by NS, No 1501, as it had by then become, carried a much more ambitious yellow and grey that eventually became the Dutch standard colour scheme.

The fleet of six Class 1500s were regularly employed from 1971 onwards from The Hague/Hook of Holland, plus nightly and weekend freight services and car sleeper services. At Venlo, the eastward national boundary with Germany where they had to be removed because the voltage changed, they could frequently be seen in the company of German locomotives, while the coaching stock would often be marshalled by another British exile, a 350hp Class 10-style diesel-electric shunter!

Diana was employed on the 14 June 1986 farewell railtour, and had the distinction of being the first of the four survivors to be taken out of passenger use, being driven into the centre road at Rotterdam Central and switched off. Restored to good external order, it was exhibited at the Dordrecht Open Day on 4 June 1986, and attention was also being turned to a mechanical refit. The locomotive was exhibited in the 1989 NS 150th anniversary celebrations, and moved from Rotterdam to the state workshops at Feyernoord on 18 January 1991 for minor attention. It was also due to feature in a two-day railtour during June 1991 to mark the last workings in the Netherlands of the NS 2400 Class.

Class 71 Bo-Bo No E5001

Built: Doncaster, January 1959
Numbers carried: (1) E5001,
    (2) 71001
First allocation: Stewarts Lane
Final allocation: Ashford
Withdrawn: November 1977
Preserved: National Railway
    Museum, York

Class 71 electric loco No E5001
at Faversham. *Norman Preedy*

A direct descendant of an earlier Bulleid/Raworth third rail/overhead electric locomotive for the Southern Railway, the 24 2,552hp Class 71s were introduced for the Kent electrification scheme to haul heavy freight and express passenger trains, including the famous 'Golden Arrow' and 'Night Ferry' services, at speeds of up to 90 mph. Dual-braked and ETH-fitted from new, they incorporated a heavy flywheel motor-generator to maintain traction over gaps in the third rail. In practice, the diamond-shaped pantograph for shunting in freight yards spent more time under repair than in use!

A change in traffic patterns prompted the conversion of 10 to electro-diesels (Class 74) for the Bournemouth line electrification, with a 650hp Paxman 6YJXL diesel engine installed after removal of the flywheel from the booster set and motor blower cells. The pantograph was removed and the body strengthened to carry a 310-gallon fuel tank. Buckeye couplers and multiple working equipment were fitted, and the Achilles' heel, the 'new technology' computerised control equipment.

The preserved No E5001 was in fact the second of the class to be delivered. The pioneer

No E5000 (later altered to No E5024 to conform with numbering practice) was not considered worth saving because it had been rebuilt as No 74004. No E5001 was renumbered No 71001 in January 1974 and had by then been repainted blue.

Lack of work saw all the 71s put into storage in the first week of October 1976, No 71001 at Ashford, and along with the surviving 74s they were all condemned at the end of the following year, but No 71001 left Ashford for Doncaster on 23 June 1978 via Stratford, Cambridge, Spalding and Lincoln. A full repaint to green livery with red and white lining was effected by 13 March 1979, and No E5001 was towed to York for display six days later as part of the electric centenary exhibition.

No E5001 returned to the Southern Region in September 1988 for the first time since preservation for display at the London & South Western Railway 150th anniversary celebrations at Winchfield. It was towed from the National Railway Museum by green-liveried Class 45 'Peak' No 45106 on 22 September bound for Bescot and Basingstoke. It was also on display at Waterloo station on 1 October 1988. It is in full working order.

Class 81 Bo-Bo No 81002

Built: Birmingham Rail Carriage
& Wagon Company, February
1960
Numbers carried: (1) E3003,
(2) 81002
First allocation: Longsight
Final allocation: Willesden
Withdrawn: 17 October 1990
Preserved: Crewe Heritage
Centre

No 81002 stabled at Wigan
Springs Branch depot, 9 February
1978. *Norman Preedy*

It is pleasing that the oldest surviving 25kV ac electric locomotive has been saved for preservation, almost at the last moment as the final survivors were being lined up for sale to a Sheffield scrap merchant.

The 3,200 hp AEI/BTH Class 81 Bo-Bo was the first of five designs introduced between 1959-64, totalling 100 locos, and certainly amongst the most successful. The third built, No E3003, was new to Longsight, Manchester, in early 1960 when only the short stretch of line to Liverpool was actually electrified. No E3003 was considered part of a general West Coast pool until May 1973, when it was formally allocated with the rest of the 81s to Crewe electric depot. It had been dual braked during a works overhaul at Crewe in 1972.

The extension of the electrification south to London in 1966 and north to Glasgow in 1974 inevitably saw E3003's sphere of operation extended, although the arrival of the more powerful Class 86s and 87s saw the 81s relegated to secondary work including freight haulage. The entire class was transferred en bloc to Scottish Region control at Glasgow

Shields Road in March 1975, and the older designs were progressively eliminated from 1977, although the Class 81s continued to receive works overhauls and were not phased out until 1989.

No 81002, as the preserved locomotive had become, was one of two reprieved by InterCity for hauling empty stock between Euston and Stonebridge Park carriage sidings, restricted to 40 mph operation to reduce maintenance costs and risk of failure. No 81002 was replaced by a Class 85 at the end of 1990, and taken to Crewe electric depot for storage and disposal.

When new, No E3003 carried a livery of all-over light blue, with the later addition of a yellow warning panel, and in 1968 the new standard blue with yellow ends. The four-character headcode panels were later replaced by sealed-beam marker lights. When preserved it was the oldest Class 81 still in existence, the pioneer No E3001 (81001) having been destroyed by fire while hauling a train through Carstairs in 1983, and No E3002 having also been lost by fire back in 1968.

Class 84 Bo-Bo No 84001

Built: North British Locomotive
  Co, March 1960
Numbers carried: (1) E3036,
  (2) 84001
First allocation: Longsight
Final allocation: Crewe
Withdrawn: 22 January 1979
Preserved: National Railway
  Museum, York

No 84001 in the National
Railway Museum yard,
September 1991. *Murray Brown*

The National Railway Museum took possession of No 84001 as a temporary measure pending the arrival of a 'more suitable electric locomotive' to place on display. Thirteen years later it is still at York. Although not the most successful of the 25kV AC prototype designs, there is hope that it will become officially claimed, considering that it is the sole example of a modern main-line locomotive built by the North British Locomotive Company at Glasgow to be in a British museum.

Within strict equipment guidelines, private firms were invited to tender for 3,100hp 100 mph locomotives with a 20-ton axle loading for the LMR's main-line electrification scheme which opened between Manchester and Liverpool in 1959, and was later extended to the entire Euston-Glasgow West Coast Main Line.

A high standard of body construction was achieved with the NB-assembled Nos E3036-45 in 1960-61, incorporating GEC Traction equipment. But within seven years they and the English Electric Class 83s were all laid up with rectifier faults, and No E3036 spent from October 1967 to May 1972 stored at the former Bury steam shed. It was refurbished (and renumbered No 84001) at Doncaster Works for re-entry into traffic on 5 December 1972, only to be laid up again within 12 months, the stay at Doncaster this time lasting until August 1976.

No 84001's career ended with a major failure in December 1978, and it was again stored out of use, this time at Crewe electric depot. The writing was on the wall for the 84s by this time, but the NRM's decision to build up an electric railway centenary display saw No 84001 (already cannibalised for vital components to keep other 84s running) towed to York via Healey Mills on 8 May 1979 for exhibition. It was repainted in corporate blue livery with yellow ends for the display at the entrance to the Great Railway Show exhibition at York which opened on 1 March 1990; it stood under a short length of overhead traction line sponsored by Balfour Beatty, main contractors for the East Coast Main Line electrification project.

Unclassed A1A-A1A No 18000

Built: February 1950
Number carried: 18000
First allocation: Swindon
Final allocation: Old Oak
    Common
Withdrawn: 16 December 1960
Preserved: Arsenal Testing
    Station, Vienna

No 18000 in A Shop at Swindon
Works, 7 June 1953. *Norman
Preedy*

Three experiments were conducted with gas turbine locomotives between 1950 and 1961, but without sufficient success to make them worthy of full-scale production runs. The first of them was No 18000, ordered by the Great Western Railway from the Swiss Federal Railways following a visit there by Chief Mechanical Engineer F.W.Hawksworth in 1945.

No 18000, assembled with a Brown Boveri 2,000hp unit, ran trials in Switzerland before being shipped via Harwich in February 1950, making its first run between Swindon and Badminton on the 13th. It worked its first revenue passenger train on 19 May of that year, but suffered a series of electrical, combustion chamber, traction motor and train heating boiler faults that required expensive and specialist attention.

It did, however, operate on a restricted route of Paddington-Plymouth until about 1955, and had accumulated 400,000 miles when a further failure precipitated its withdrawal. At first it was commandeered by Rugby Testing Station for use as a power supply generator. Returned to Swindon in the summer of 1960, it lingered in a semi-derelict condition in the yards until returned to Switzerland. There it was used for some time as a counter pressure locomotive at the UIC headquarters. At Bellinzona works, the gas turbine was later removed, and a replacement bogie fitted for Alsthom traction motor experiments. It later moved to Zurich and finally to the European testing station at Vienna Arsenal, where it still resided in 1991.

Now an almost forgotten piece of British railway history, No 18000 is preserved according to the common continental practice of plinthing historic machines outside depots on a seemingly arbitrary basis. No 18000, painted plain dark green with windows silvered over but the original cast number still in place, can be seen at the entrance of the Electro Technical Institution.

Class 43 Bo-Bo No 41001

Built: BR Derby, June 1972
Numbers carried: (1) 41001,
   (2) 43000, (3) ADB975812
Withdrawn: February 1977
Preserved: National Railway
   Museum, York

The prototype HST takes part in
the Rail 150 cavalcade at Shildon
on 31 August 1975. *Norman
Preedy*

Hardly revolutionary in its concept, the 125 mph High Speed Train has nevertheless been one of BR's greatest successes, transforming InterCity services into the fastest diesel-powered routes in the world. The production versions have been the backbone of East Coast services in the prelude to electrification, and are destined to be the mainstay of the Western Region, Midland Main Line, and North East-South West routes for many years to come.

The principal of a fixed formation of coaching stock with a diesel power car at each end dates back to the less than successful Metro-Cammell/North British 'Blue Pullman' sets of 1959. Work on the HST project was approved in February 1969, involving two power cars (then numbered 41001/2, later Class 252), and 12 redesigned Mark 3 trailers in a reversed livery of grey and blue. Power was provided by the 12-cylinder Paxman Valenta 12RP200L 2,250hp engine, and the bodies were assembled at BR Crewe Works. The aerodynamic glass fibre cab cost a year's delay in testing because it fell foul of the ASLEF union for having no place for a secondman.

The inaugural runs were made from Derby in January 1973, and 12 June witnessed the historic 143 mph speed record set up (and held for 12 years) between Thirsk and Northallerton on the East Coast Main Line. The unit carried fare-paying passengers for the first time between Paddington and Bristol on 5 May 1975, and later that year participated in the Stockton & Darlington 150th anniversary celebrations.

After the entry into service of the first of 95 production Class 253 and 254 sets, the Class 252 unit was taken out of traffic in February 1977. The intermediate trailers are still in use, either rebuilt into conventional sets, or in Departmental service. Nos 41001/2 (by then Nos 43000/1) were renumbered ADB975812/3 for trailing Advanced Passenger Train vehicles on test from Derby Technical Centre. After a long period dumped in a semi-derelict condition at the back of Derby Works, No 41001 was restored for exhibition at the NRM, with its power unit sectioned for educational purposes. It travelled to Swindon Works for the 'NRM on Tour' display from 10 April to 31 October 1990. No 41002 was scrapped at the end of that year.

Unclassed 0-4-0 No 7050

Built: English Electric/Drewry,
Preston, October 1934
Numbers carried: (1) 7050,
(2) Air Ministry No 25,
(3) 7050, (4) WD224,
(5) WD70224, (6) 846,
(7) 240
First allocation: Agecroft
Withdrawn: Sold by LMS to War
Department, March 1943
Preserved: Museum of Army
Transport, Beverley

LMS No 7050, named *Rorke's Drift*, at the Army Museum, Beverley, on 9 June 1990. *Robert Casselden*

The LMS experiments with diesel traction for shunting duties during the 1930s were based around the 0-6-0 design which developed into the BR Class 08, and No 7050 was the only four-wheel design accepted for trial. Typical of any demonstration loco, its sphere of operation has been vast, and to a large extent unrecorded.

It was assembled at Preston by English Electric for the Drewry Car Company with a 160 hp Allen 8RS18 power unit and Wilson four-speed gearbox, and after trials at Preston Docks became part of the LMS allocation at Agecroft, Manchester, from November 1934. It stayed there until August 1940 when it was loaned to the Air Ministry and used at its bases at Stafford and Leuchars. Then it was back to the LMS at Agecroft before sale to the War Department in 1943.

The War Department used it at many locations; it was the responsibility of the Royal Naval Depot at Botley in 1974 and later went to the Army base at Warminster. No 7050, the forerunner of many smaller shunting types, had by this time been re-equipped with a Gardner 6L3 power unit and Wilson-Drewry transmission.

Its historical significance was thankfully recognised, and it has been part of the National Collection since 1979. After a spell on display at York, No 7050 is now on display at the Museum of Army Transport, Beverley, North Humberside, along with a number of other standard and 60 cm gauge locomotives and other items of rolling-stock.

Unclassed 0-6-0 No 7051 *John Alcock*

Built: Hunslet Engine Co, 1932
Numbers carried: (1) 7401,
    (2) 7051, (3) Ministry of
    Works & Buildings No 27,
    (4) 7051, (5) Admiralty No 87
First allocation (LMS): Leeds
Withdrawn: Sold by LMS to War
    Department, March 1943
Preserved: Middleton Railway,
    Leeds

No 7401 at Middleton, Leeds, on
23 June 1990. *Howard Johnston*

The first diesel locomotive operated by a British main-line railway has had a long and eventful career, but was recognised as a worthy preservation candidate during the early 1960s, when many other equally significant modern traction items were discarded without a second thought.

Desperately searching for ways of cutting the cost of its shunting operations, the LMS showed great interest in offerings from private builders. One such item was 0-6-0 No 1697 from Hunslet of Leeds, developing ideas from the firm's recent acquisition of the Kerr Stuart operation.

Completed in record time at Hunslet for the British Industries Fair in Birmingham in February 1932, the loco featured a 150hp MAN engine, mechanical transmission and jackshaft drive, and weighed 21 tons 8 cwt. It ran trials at Waterloo Main Colliery, Leeds, as well as at an LMS depot, and was eventually bought by the LMS along with three other Hunslet prototypes for comparison trials.

No 7401 worked at Crewe and Chester before being loaned to the War Department for two spells in 1940-41 and 1944-45, after which the builders reclaimed it for their own use, employing it within the works confines; they loaned it to a Thames Haven, London, oil depot from 1949 to 1951. Back at Hunslet it saw regular employment until June 1960, when it became the pioneer locomotive of the Middleton Railway Trust, and where it carried the number 7051; it was named *John Alcock* on 21 January 1961 after the then chairman of the Hunslet Engine Co. No 7051 was exhibited at the National Railway Museum during January 1979, but has since returned to the Middleton where it now wears LMS livery and the number 7401.

Unclassed Bo No 75S

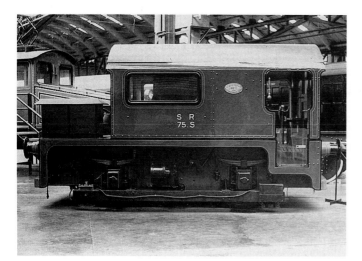

Built: Siemens, 1898
Numbers carried: (1) 75S
    (2) DS75
First allocation: Waterloo
Final allocation: Waterloo
Withdrawn: May 1968
Preserved: National Railway
    Museum, York

No 75S at the National Railway
Museum, York, on 29 July 1981.
Michael Whatmough

The isolated and enigmatic Waterloo & City underground line in London used to have its own electric locomotives for general shunting work, and the example preserved at the National Railway Museum represents by far the oldest modern traction exhibit from a British public railway.

Built by Siemens of London in 1898 for the London & South Western Railway's new tube-size line between Waterloo and Bank, it ran on DC current lifted from the 500 volts centre live rail to the two Siemens 60hp electric motors. The loco was converted to outside rail collection during he 1940s, and was further modified from 1954 when the line's voltage was increased to the Southern Railway's standard 750V.

The Southern attached its own departmental number 75S to the loco, and BR in turn altered it to DS75 in its own series. Its 1899-built sister (assembled at Nine Elms and later transferred to Wimbledon depot) was scrapped in 1965, but DS75 ran until a serious electrical fire in May 1968 made it uneconomic to repair. Removed to Brighton's former Preston Park Pullman Works with other relics for storage, it was removed to the National Railway Museum at the end of 1977 for restoration to its original livery of predominantly mid-green.

Class 97 0-6-0 No 97650

Built: Ruston & Hornsby, 1952
Numbers carried: (1) PWM650, (2) 97650
First allocation: Swindon
Final allocation: Reading
Withdrawn: April 1987
Preserved: Lincoln

Awaiting spares and a repaint, No 97650 stands at Gloucester Horton Road depot in May 1979. *John Chalcraft*

Aside from the Class 07 0-6-0 diesel-electric shunters for Southampton Docks, the Boultham, Lincoln, firm of Ruston & Hornsby made no progress as a volume supplier to BR.

A total of 127 examples of the Type 165DE, which as the product name suggests was fitted with a 165hp Ruston 6VPH power unit, were built between 1947 and 1962, of 0-4-0 and 0-6-0 configurations, and featuring electric transmission. In 1952 the Western Region, which had no experience with small shunters, bought this example for the civil engineer's department based at Swindon. Its identity, No PWM650, defines its role as specifically for permanent way maintenance. Its original livery was black, later replaced by mid-green. Four similar machines, Nos PWM651-4, were purchased from Ruston in 1959 and allocated to Cardiff, Taunton, Hayes and Worcester respectively.

As a departmental shunter it would see weekday use at a permanent way depot, and then at weekends would be towed out with other vehicles to a main-line location closed for heavy maintenance. No PWM650's longest continuous spell of active service was at Newlands CCE depot near Malvern, from at least 1964 until 1970.

No PWM650 was a late entry to the TOPs renumbering system, being amended to No 97650 in September 1979. It had by that time acquired blue livery, which on other Ruston locomotives gave way to pale yellow. PWM650 stickers later appeared on the loco's bonnet sides. It became spare at Reading during 1983, and at the time of its withdrawal in April 1987 was the oldest operational locomotive on the BR system, although it had been laid up for some time with serious mechanical faults.

Lincoln City Council, already the owner of a Class 08 shunter exhibited next to the station, wanted a Ruston-built locomotive to reflect the city's railway locomotive construction business, and took delivery of No 97650 on 27 February 1991. It rests on a short length of track next to the old steam depot.

Unclassed 4wBE No BEL2

Built: Thomas Bolton, 1917
Numbers carried: (1) No 2,
 (2) BEL 2
First allocation: Oakamoor
Withdrawn: June 1963
Preserved: National Railway
 Museum, York

No BEL2 at the National
Railway Museum, York, on
25 August 1986. *Michael
Whatmough*

A small but significant relic of the North Staffordshire Railway is this 17-ton battery-electric locomotive which saw 46 years continuous service within a very small sphere of operation.

Similar in design to a 1914 Midland Railway version built at Derby (No 1550, later BEL No 1 and scrapped in 1964), No 2 incorporated two 82hp BTH traction motors and was assembled as a joint project between the NSR and Thomas Bolton for shunting at the latter firm's copper works at Oakamoor, Staffs, on the Burton-on-Trent to Macclesfield line. Its final duties were at the local electrical engineer's depot.

Renumbered BEL No 2 (the reason is self-explanatory) during 1955, it never carried anything but a departmental number. It was finally retired in June 1963, and stored at Uttoxeter prior to restoration to North Staffordshire livery for exhibition at the Staffordshire Industrial Museum at Shugborough Hall. It was later transferred to the National Railway Museum, where it now resides.

Unclassed 0-6-0 D0226

Built: Vulcan Foundry, 1956
Numbers carried: (1) D226,
  (2) D0226
Withdrawn: October 1960
Preserved: Keighley & Worth
  Valley Railway, Haworth

No D226 next to Keighley
turntable, 4 November 1989.
Murray Brown

English Electric built two 500hp prototypes, Nos D226 and D227, in 1956 to compare the benefits of electric and hydraulic transmission. Their higher power and 40 mph top speed made them more suitable for transfer work than the Class 08 design, but no more were built because it was decided that the 1,000hp Type 1 Bo-Bo (Class 20) then emerging was better still.

No D226, weighing 48 tons, was fitted with a single EE traction motor and double reduction final drive gearbox. Renumbered No D0226 to avoid a clash with the Type 4 Class 40s then being produced, the loco chalked up 38,000 miles over three years in yards at Liverpool, Doncaster, Sheffield, Stratford, Bristol Barrow Road and Swindon, and clearly proved its superiority over its hydraulic twin sister which was eventually scrapped at Darlington.

No D0226 returned to the Vulcan Foundry in January 1961 and was works shunter there for a spell before being given to the K&WVR on permanent loan in March 1966. Used immediately on heavy works trains, it has also been known to deputise on passenger services where its capability of hauling a 450-ton train up a 1 in 57 gradient has been useful. The loco, now named *Vulcan*, travelled to Doncaster Works for wheel-turning during 1980, and was repainted in crimson lake livery in 1984.

Unclassed Co-Co 'Deltic'

Built: Vulcan Foundry, 1954
Number carried: None
First allocation: Speke
    (Liverpool)
Final allocation: Hornsey
Withdrawn: March 1961
Preserved: Science Museum,
    South Kensington, London

'Deltic' departs English Electric
for the Science Museum. *Science
Museum*

The seventh, but least known, preserved 'Deltic' is incarcerated on the second floor of the Science Museum, a position that has so far thwarted tentative attempts to see it relocated at a more acceptable railway location. The locomotive is in excellent fettle apart from the power units, which are missing pistons and crankshafts. Worse, the failure to acquire replacement power units from the production Class 55s being broken up at Doncaster Works in 1982/83 makes its future as a runner extremely bleak.

'Deltic's' garish pale blue livery with cream 'go-faster' stripes created a stir when it took to the rails at the Vulcan Foundry, Newton-le-Willows, early in 1955, and after a quarter of a century is still an acquired taste. 'Deltic' was never formally part of the BR fleet. It had been constructed by English Electric to demonstrate the rail potential for the high-powered 18-cylinder opposed piston power unit which had already been proved in marine use. (The word 'Deltic' is derived from the Greek letter delta, and refers to the shape of the engine.)

Allocated to Speke Junction and Edge Hill,

'Deltic' ran extensive trials over the Settle & Carlisle line and on Liverpool-Euston and London-Carlisle rosters, and switched to the East Coast Main Line in January 1959, where its out-of-gauge body collided with more than a few platform edges. Allocated to Hornsey, York, St Margaret's (Edinburgh) and finally Finsbury Park, its success led to an order for 22 of the now well-documented production Class 55 'Deltics'.

After 450,000 miles in traffic, and maintenance in the less-than-ideal surroundings of steam sheds, 'Deltic' suffered a major failure in March 1961. Even so it had conclusively proved that diesel-electric transmission was the only way ahead. A Canadian sales trip fortunately fell through, and the decision was taken by English Electric to present the locomotive instead to the Department of Education and Science, rather than dismantle it for spare parts. After a tortuous road journey through south London streets, it was formally handed over to the Science Museum in a ceremony on 28 April 1963.

Unclassed 4w No ED10

Built: Ruston & Hornsby,
February 1958
Numbers carried: (1) ED10,
(2) E9
First allocation: Beeston Sleeper
Depot
Final allocation: Beeston Sleeper
Depot
Withdrawn: February 1965
Preserved: Irchester, Northants

In its second career, No ED10 at
the Trackbed Hovercraft site,
Earith, on 17 March 1973.
R.N. Pritchard

A total of 217 48hp 48DS diesel shunters were constructed by the Lincoln firm of Ruston & Hornsby between 1941-67, to a total of seven different gauges to satisfy the needs of industrial users. Two of these four-wheel diesel-mechanicals became BR property, including this one now preserved in Northamptonshire. After an uninspiring start as shunter at the 3-foot gauge system at the Beeston sleeper creosoting works near Nottingham, it went on to play a role in two major construction projects.

No ED10, whose identity followed the ED (Engineering Department) series originated by the LMS, was fitted with a Ruston 4YC engine, and weighed 7½ tons. It worked at Beeston until February 1965 when it was withdrawn and sold to Sheffield dealer Thomas Ward, who in turn sold it on to the Cleveland Bridge & Engineering Co, Darlington, a construction firm engaged on bridge contracts all over the UK, which included the motorway viaduct at Tinsley, within a stone's throw of the BR marshalling yard. In November 1969 ED10 moved on to the firm of Shepherd Hill & Co, and then followed perhaps its most significant role as a test locomotive on the abortive Hovertrack through the Cambridgeshire Fens at Earith, near Huntingdon.

It was equipped with rubber tyres to enable it to work on the raised concrete structure through the Fens, but the project eventually ran short of finance and failed to attract Government support. ED10 was bought at the closing-down sale by a farmer based at Fenstanton, near St Ives, Cambs, and was stored in an agricultural building for almost 15 years until a preservation deal was organised. He might not have realised its value but for a continual weekend procession of enthusiasts keen to confirm its continued existence.

Unclassed 4w No ZM32

Built: Ruston & Hornsby, 1957
Number carried: ZM32
First allocation: Horwich Works
Withdrawn: March 1964
Preserved: Narrow Gauge
   Railway Centre of North
   Wales, Gloddfa Ganol, Blaenau
   Ffestiniog

Narrow gauge No ZM32 at
Horwich Works, 13 October
1963. *T.J. Edgington*

This locomotive actually went missing for five years, having been presumed exported to British Honduras! However, the failure of the export deal and its subsequent discovery fortunately led to its preservation.

ZM32 was built by Ruston & Hornsby of Lincoln, at the time a prolific builder of industrial locomotives of all gauges, for shunting at the once extensive narrow gauge system of the former Lancashire & Yorkshire Railway's Horwich Works. Withdrawn in 1964 and sold two years later to Furnace Equipment of Manchester for re-use abroad, the deal eventually fell through and the loco was forgotten and 'lost'. It was rediscovered in November 1971 in the Bootle, Lancashire, warehouse of Howwitt Brothers, and acquired for display.

Converted to 2-foot gauge, it was at first stored at Pen-yr-Orsedd slate quarry at Nantlle, Gwynedd, and moved to its present home at Gloddfa Ganol in May 1978, where it rests in the company of over 85 other machines, reputed to be the largest collection of locomotives in the UK aside from the Channel Tunnel construction fleet!

PRESERVATION CHRONOLOGY

As will be seen from the accompanying table, it is only in recent years that interest in preserving ex-BR locomotives has mushroomed. There is a clear pattern to the type saved, with occasions of large numbers of one type being preserved over a short space of time as they were withdrawn by BR, most often in operational order.

More locomotives, particularly English Electric Class 40s, might have been rescued during the mid-1980s but for a short-term ban on the private sale of any machine suspected of containing poisonous asbestos insulation. This was later resolved. In addition, the withdrawal of rail facilities to (and often total closure of) many private industrial locations, especially those related to coal and steel, resulted in the rescue of many ex-BR shunters sold out of service in the late 1960s and early 1970s.

It is worth noting that at least one locomotive has been saved every year since 1968; that the first main-line locomotive bought from capital stock was Class 42 'Warship' No D821 Greyhound; that the first mass sale was of the Class 52 'Westerns' in 1977; and that in two years (1987 and 1990) ten locos of one type have been bought in one year (Class 25s and 50s respectively).

1961 (1)	:	7051
1963 (2)	:	BEL2, 'Deltic'
1964 (1)	:	26500
1966 (1)	:	D0226
1968 (2)	:	D2578, 75S
1970 (2)	:	D2192, D2860
1971 (1)	:	ZM32
1972 (3)	:	D2117, D2271, D5032

1973 (2)	:	D821, D2381
1974 (1)	:	D2207
1975 (5)	:	D7017/8/29, 18000, 41001
1976 (2)	:	D2090, E5001
1977 (9)	:	D1010/3/5/23/41/8/62, D2511, D5500
1978 (4)	:	D2245, D2994, 12077, 26020
1979 (5)	:	D832, D2203, D4067, E3036, 7050
1980 (3)	:	D5081, D5705, D9526
1981 (11)	:	D2041/72, D2279, D8000, D9002, D9516/20/3/4/9/51
1982 (16)	:	D4/8, D306, D2062, D2298, D3002/3, D5054, D8568, D9009/19, D9537/9/53, 12131, 15224
1983 (10)	:	D2022/3/4, D2205, D2587/95, D2767, D3022, D7076, D9000
1984 (11)	:	D345, D2178, D2554, D3101/80, D3358, D3420/9, D8233, D9015/6
1985 (9)	:	D2138, D2284, D2953/6, D3079, D3190, D3336, D5217, D5353
1986 (16)	:	D100, D2120/52/82/4, D2774, D3059, D3265/90, D3462, D3586/91, D7535, 27000/1/3
1987 (39)	:	D2119/48/99, D2325, D2420, D2866, D3000/29, D3559, D3605, D5209, D5347/51/86/94, D5401/10, D7523/41/94, D7615/28/9/33/63/71, D9500/2/4/13/8/21/5/31/55, 12061/98, 7069, ED10
1988 (31)	:	D99, D200/12/3, D318/35, D1842, D2059/63/78/89, D2112, D2337/71, D2854, D2991, D3014, D3167, D3255/61,

255

D3452/76, D4092, D5185,
D5207/22/33, D7612/59,
12052/93

1989 (8) : D2162, D2334/99, D2985,
D5061, D7622, 12074/88

1990 (11) : D40/67, D2070, D2196, D2229,
D3019, D3308, D5370, D6552,
D7585, 12099

1991 (39) : D22/61, D120/3,

D402/17/9/27/31/5/42/3/4/9,
D2027/66/9/73/94,
D2113/34/80/9/97, D3174,
D7672,
D8001/20/31/48/56/69/98,
D8107/10/66, D8327, E3003,
PWM650

1992 (3) : D2084, D2158, 12082